D0820932

RENEWALS 458-4574

Altering Party Systems

Interests, Identities, and Institutions in Comparative Politics

Series Editor:
Mark I. Lichbach, University of California, Riverside

Editorial Advisory Board:
Barbara Geddes, University of California, Los Angeles
James C. Scott, Yale University
Sven Steinmo, University of Colorado
Kathleen Thelen, Northwestern University
Alan Zuckerman, Brown University

The post–Cold War world faces a series of defining global challenges: virulent forms of conflict, the resurgence of the market as the basis for economic organization, and the construction of democratic institutions.

The books in this series take advantage of the rich development of different approaches to comparative politics in order to offer new perspectives on these problems. The books explore the emerging theoretical and methodological synergisms and controversies about social conflict, political economy, and institutional development.

Democracy without Associations: Transformation of the Party System and Social Cleavages in India, by Pradeep K. Chhibber

Gendering Politics: Women in Israel, by Hanna Herzog

Origins of Liberal Dominance: State, Church, and Party in Nineteenth-Century Europe, by Andrew C. Gould

The Deadlock of Democracy in Brazil, by Barry Ames

Political Science as Puzzle Solving, edited by Bernard Grofman

Institutions and Innovation: Voters, Parties, and Interest Groups in the Consolidation of Democracy—France and Germany, 1870–1939, by Marcus Kreuzer

Altering Party Systems: Strategic Behavior and the Emergence of New Political Parties in Western Democracies, by Simon Hug

Altering Party Systems

Strategic Behavior and the Emergence of New Political Parties in Western Democracies

SIMON HUG

Ann Arbor

THE UNIVERSITY OF MICHIGAN PRESS

Library
University of Texas
at San Antonio

Copyright © by the University of Michigan 2001
All rights reserved
Published in the United States of America by
The University of Michigan Press
Manufactured in the United States of America
Printed on acid-free paper

2004 2003 2002 2001 4 3 2 1

No part of this publication may be reproduced, stored in a retrieval system, or transmitted in any form or by any means, electronic, mechanical, or otherwise, without the written permission of the publisher.

A CIP catalog record for this book is available from the British Library.

Library of Congress Cataloging-in-Publication Data

Hug, Simon.
Altering party systems : strategic behavior and the emergence of new political parties in Western democracies / Simon Hug.
p. cm. — (Interests, identities, and institutions in comparative politics)
Includes bibliographical references and index.
ISBN 0-472-11184-1 (cloth : alk. paper)
1. Political parties—Mathematical models. 2. Democracy—Mathematical models. I. Title. II. Series.

JF2051 .H83 2001
324.2'09171'3—dc21 2001018111

Contents

Acknowledgments

This book is based on my dissertation "Time to Party? Strategic Behavior and the Emergence of New Political Parties" (University of Michigan 1994). On the long journey from a vague idea to a dissertation and finally to a book I accumulated debts to many people. Enumerating them all would be tedious and would almost certainly lead to embarrassing omissions. To avoid both pitfalls I will refrain from using any names in these acknowledgements. All persons who have helped me and given me support on this journey will recognize themselves in the following lines.

To start without the help of my family I would have not been able to undertake my studies and pursue them to the present stage. Their constant support facilitated my intellectual progress at all times. Professors in the Department of Political Science of the University of Geneva have given me, first, as teachers, then as colleagues, the craving for research in this fascinating field. Thanks to grants from the Fulbright Commission and the Fondation Schmidheiny, I was able to pursue my studies at the University of Michigan. With extreme luck, I found teachers, colleagues and friends who helped enormously in giving shape to my ideas and in rendering them concrete. Back at the University of Geneva, I returned to colleagues and friends who encouraged me in my ideas and helped me complete this dissertation. The final version of the manuscript was completed while I was visiting the Department of Political Science at the University of California, San Diego. The intellectual (and physical) environment made this tedious task almost a pleasure. During these last revisions I was able to draw on the excellent comments by two reviewers and, to make an exception to my rule of not employing names, by Chuck Myers from the University of Michigan Press. The second exception I wish to make is in thanking John Brehm for letting me use his LaTeX styles to typeset this book. Thanks is due to all of them, since without them I would still be stuck with a vague idea.

CHAPTER 1

Introduction

Scholarly interest in new political parties has followed strong attention-cycles, largely defined by the changing success of several classes of new actors on the electoral scene. Green parties stimulated the study of new parties with their early successes in the late seventies. Their waning, especially of the German Greens (Poguntke 1990; Frankland 1995a, 1995b) at the end of the eighties, has heavily reduced the attention paid to their fate. Shortly before the end of this decade, several right-wing parties have emerged and provided further stimulus for research on the reasons for their existence (Husbands 1992a, 1992b; Ignazi 1992). Should these parties have a fate similar to that of the German Greens, the study of new parties would most likely experience another setback.[1]

Understanding the formation of new parties is important for at least three reasons. First, some new parties, even when starting small, are here to replace established parties.[2] Consequently, they significantly modify the party systems in which they appear. Second, even when new parties are not successful in becoming central actors, e.g., in government policies, they have, by their sheer presence, an impact on the electoral competition. Good examples for this tendency are changes in positions taken by several conservative parties on the immigration issue after the surge of right-wing parties in Europe. Similarly, Green parties have had a long-lasting impact on environmental policies in most developed countries (Schmitt 1987; von Oppeln 1989; Rohrschneider, 1990). To a certain degree, they blackmail established parties (Downs 1957, 128). Third, groups that consider forming a new party sometimes threaten existing parties. They force the latter to adopt policies that they would have preferred not to address. Here it becomes crucial to understand why new parties do not form. Beyond these three substantive reasons, the numerical importance of new political parties, even when taken on its own, gives reason enough to

1. These trends also clearly appear in systematic studies of the literature on parties and party systems in Western Europe (Bartolini, Caramani and Hug 1998; Caramani and Hug 1998).

2. Janda (1980) in his sample of new parties finds several which have replaced existing parties. Similarly, Downs (1957, 128f) illustrates his theoretical framework by using the replacement of the Liberals by the Labour party in Great Britain.

Fig. 1.1. Number of new parties per election year

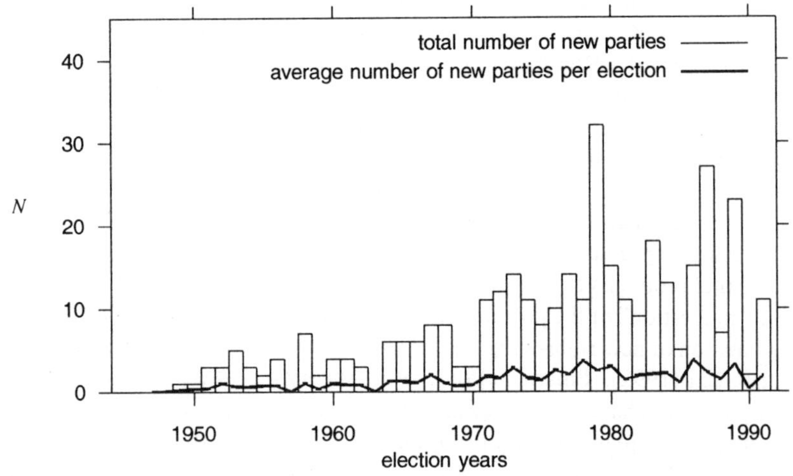

study them. Figure 1.1 shows for 22 democracies[3] the number of new parties per year and the average per election. On average one new party participates at each election in these democracies.

Thus, the goal of this study is to provide an explanation for the formation of new political parties. This research objective presupposes the existence of a common underlying logic to the formation of new parties. I will argue that this logic is present in all party formation processes, whether the new party addresses immigration issues or is concerned about environmental degradation. Institutional constraints, which are present in the environment where new parties emerge, forge this logic to a considerable extent. Pre-existing parties also intervene in this environment, which might be described as the party system of a given country. Consequently, I envision the emergence of a new political party as a possible outcome of an interaction between existing parties and groups that consider to form a new party. This interaction takes place in a structured environment, where constraints appear through the presence of electoral laws, ballot access restrictions, the structure of government, etc.

3. The countries under consideration are Austria, Belgium, Denmark, Finland, France, Germany, Greece, Iceland, Ireland, Italy, Luxembourg, Netherlands, Norway, Portugal, Spain, Sweden, Switzerland, Great Britain, Canada, the United States, Australia, and New Zealand. More details on the dataset figure in chapter five and in the appendix.

This idea is not entirely new in the literature on new political parties. Several authors insist on the importance of the behavior of existing parties in the explanation of new parties (Hauss and Rayside 1978; Rosenstone, Behr, and Lazarus 1984; Kitschelt 1988, 1989; Harmel, Svasand, and Gibson 1992; Ignazi 1992; Müller-Rommel 1993; Inglehart and Andeweg 1993). But these authors do not embed this interaction in its strategic context, and focus mostly on particular classes of new parties. Kitschelt (1988) shows that the presence of a social-democratic party in government has favored the emergence of left-libertarian parties. Similarly, Müller-Rommel (1993) illustrates the same effect for the formation of Green parties. Inglehart and Andeweg (1993), on the other hand, argue that existing parties in the Netherlands have addressed environmental problems from early on, preventing the formation of a Green party. The "congestion" of the political center appears as an important element in the explanation of new right-wing parties by Harmel, Svasand, and Gibson (1992) and Ignazi (1992). Pinard's (1967, 1975) theory on third parties also relates new parties to characteristics of the party system. According to him, new parties in Canada are more likely to appear in districts where one party dominates. Hauss and Rayside (1978) and Rosenstone, Behr, and Lazarus (1984) look at different classes of new parties and find support for the importance of existing parties and their behavior in explaining new party formation. Their theoretical framework, however, does not set this element in the broader context of a strategic interaction.

The literature on new political parties provides other insights, which are again partially shared across different classes of new parties. Neglected or new issues are often at the heart of the emergence of new parties. Immigration problems seem to increase the likelihood of new right-wing parties and enhance their success (Mayer and Perrineau 1989; Husbands 1992a, 1992b; Ignazi 1992; Harmel, Svasand, and Gibson 1992; Betz and Immerfall 1998). The importance of the controversy over nuclear energy appears to have favored the emergence of left-libertarian and Green parties (Kitschelt 1988; Müller-Rommel 1993). Similarly, post-materialist values appear to increase the vote for Green parties (Müller-Rommel 1993, 164f). Harmel and Robertson (1985), however, find that neither the number of new parties nor the number of new ecology parties relates to post-materialist values. Regional issues are at the source of most regionalist parties (Urwin 1983; Levi and Hechter 1985; De Winter 1995; Müller-Rommel 1995; Seiler 1995; De Winter and Türsan 1998). More cross-nationally oriented studies by Harmel and Robertson (1985) argue that the size of the population is related to the number of new issues and stimulate the formation of new parties. The same authors find that the characteristics of a society influence the emergence of new parties. Pluralist, heterogeneous, and sectional societies give rise to more new parties than their counterparts.

Another shared aspect in the formation of new parties appears to be economic problems. Rosenstone, Behr, and Lazarus (1984, 204f) show that positive changes in agricultural prices decrease the likelihood of third party candidates in the United States. Harmel and Robertson (1985) hypothesize that countries with high income inequality should see more new parties. Their empirical evidence, however, goes against this hypothesis. For Green and left-libertarian parties Kitschelt (1988) finds a positive relation with per capita GNP, while Müller-Rommel (1993, 107ff) reports negative relationships between the vote for Green parties and inflation, unemployment and economic growth. Insecurity, linked to rising unemployment, also often appears in explanations for the rise of right-wing parties (Mayer and Perrineau 1989; Ignazi 1992).

Finally, institutional constraints appear to play an important role in the formation of new parties. Rosenstone, Behr, and Lazarus (1984) show convincingly that formal requirements for third parties heavily influence the emergence of new competitors. Similar arguments concern the role of the electoral system. Most authors agree that proportional representation should enhance the formation and success of new parties. Plurality systems, on the other hand, should decrease the chances of the latter. Harmel and Robertson (1985) find, however, that this relation only holds for the explanation of the success of new parties. The emergence of new competitors appears to be more likely in majority systems. Müller-Rommel (1993, 116f) reports, however, a negative relationship between the vote for Green parties and the proportionality of the electoral system. Since the proportionality is consistently higher in proportional representation than under plurality rule, this contradicts Harmel and Robertson's (1985) finding. Finally, Kitschelt (1988, 324f) argues that the electoral system probably explains little in the formation of new parties.

These institutional factors are also at the heart of most game-theoretic models, which allow some deductions as to the likelihood of new candidates.[4] Several models of spatial competition[5] address the question of entry, but their results do not often allow any direct deductions for an empirical study. While Downs (1957, 127ff) discusses informally the "origin of new parties," Palfrey (1984) proposes one of the first spatial models, where entry is formally addressed. In his model, entry always occurs, although the new party will never win a majority under plurality rule. Hence, the model does not provide any insights into the circumstances under which new parties emerge.[6] Quite simi-

4. Shepsle and Cohen (1990) and Shepsle (1991) review in detail these different models.

5. Useful reviews of spatial models are also Austen-Smith (1983), Krehbiel (1988), and Osborne (1995), where some information on candidate entry appears.

6. In addition, Osborne (1993) shows that if parties also have to make a decision on whether to run in an election, three-way competitions do rarely exist.

lar is the conclusion for a model proposed by Greenberg and Shepsle (1987). They show that when more than two seats are to be won, equilibria with a fixed number of candidates are unlikely to exist. They take this as an indication that entry becomes more likely. But, again, their results do not give us clues to the formation process of new parties. More interesting are the insights stemming from the model by Feddersen, Sened, and Wright (1990), which shows that, in plurality elections, the number of parties competing varies with the ratio between benefits of holding office and the cost of running in an election. As the ratio increases, the number of parties increases. This result, however, only holds under plurality rule, and the equilibrium is, in and of itself, quite counterintuitive (Shepsle 1991, 76f). Most other game-theoretic models on candidate-entry, while providing interesting insights, are hard to relate to the empirical world.

This brief review of the most central insights on new party formation shows that several explanatory factors appear across very different objects of study. Whether an author focuses on Green, third, or right-wing parties, the general explanatory variables differ little. Most often, factors describe the problem "push" and the opportunity "pull" (Rüdig 1990), or in other words "new strains" and "facilitators" (Hauss and Rayside 1978). But, by focusing on different classes of new parties, certain factors are emphasized and others neglected. And the changing fortunes of these different classes of new parties have resulted in varying attention paid to certain sets of explanatory factors. Consequently, the literature on new political parties has suffered from strong cyclical tendencies. These tendencies are unfortunate for at least two reasons. First, they lead to a very uneven development of the theoretical work on new parties.[7] Second, the interest in new parties is tightly linked to particular classes of new actors on the electoral scene. While this is not too problematic on a purely empirical level, important problems appear on the theoretical level. A consequence is the existence of theories of new Green parties, of new extreme right-wing parties, of new centrist parties, of new "new politics" parties, of new left-libertarian parties, etc.

All of these different theories, while stressing specific aspects of certain classes of new parties, rely also on common factors contributing to the explanation of new competitors. I argue in this study that this is a very problematic situation. The formation process of new political parties follows, because it is embedded in a very specific institutional arena – the electoral arena –, an underlying logic, defined by constraints, strategic aspects, and interactions, which are common to all classes of new parties. To neglect that these elements are shared is not problematic in itself. But most theoretical frameworks

7. Lowe and Rüdig (1986) criticize very strongly the state of both empirical and theoretical work in the field of Green politics in general and Green parties in particular.

on specific new parties are developed inductively, so that the empirical world determines, for example, which institutional and political factors are theoretically deemed significant. Consequently, there is rarely a complete overlap in the institutional or political factors considered in these different theories. On the empirical level this leads, almost by definition, to biases.

This study will, therefore, attempt to develop a general theoretical model, explaining the formation of new political parties. Before discussing the outline of the present study, I have to stress some limitations. First, the theoretical framework addresses only the emergence of new political parties in stable democratic systems. The research question does not address the formation of party systems in new democracies (LaPalombara and Weiner 1966; Lipset and Rokkan 1967; Kitschelt 1991, 1995; Aldrich 1995), but wishes to focus on the circumstances under which new competitors appear on a well-established electoral scene. While these two questions seem very similar, the logic of party formation in the two cases is fundamentally different. In the former case, parties appear in a setting where the nonexisting party system has no influence on the formation process. Established parties do not, by definition, exist. The bargaining over issues between new organizations is definitely different from an interaction between an established party and a possible newcomer in a stable democracy.[8] Similarly, the institutional framework is still in the process of formation in new democracies, and its specific impact is very uncertain. In stable democracies both party system and institutional framework have a serious impact on strategic and competitive considerations. By this very fact these two research questions differ noticeably.

Second, my theoretical model does not address directly the success of new political parties. It allows, however, for some insights on the initial strength and electoral success of newcomers. This stems from the fact that new parties are likely to anticipate in their formation decision the likely electoral success they will have. If this expected electoral success is an accurate estimate then my model should predict quite well the new party's initial success. This, because the expected success is playing a crucial role in my theoretical model to explain the formation of a new party.

Nevertheless, these preliminary insights into the initial success of new parties have to be taken with some caution. I will argue below that this aspect of party development is distinct from the formation process and requires a very detailed and specific theoretical model. Beyond addressing the formation process, a complete model would have to include the electoral competition, which

8. Aldrich (1995) demonstrates in his fascinating book that solving coordination and collective action problems played a crucial role in the formation of parties in the United States. A similarly fascinating study by Kalyvas (1996) deals with the formation of Christian-democratic parties in Europe.

is likely to change after the entry of a new competitor. Also, the success of new parties can often only be measured after several elections. Hence, the model would have to consider the electoral competition over several elections. For this sequence of elections I would have to provide a model which explains the behavior of both parties and voters. Given that many new parties appear in multiparty systems, the model should be able to explain the electoral competition in such systems. These models are, however, much less developed (Shepsle 1991; Cox 1990) than corresponding models for two-party systems. Consequently, such a model, including both an explanation for the formation of new parties and their success, is beyond the scope of this study. Nevertheless, given that my model provides some insights into the expected initial strength of new parties, this aspect of party development also appears in the present study.

By providing a general theoretical framework my study attempts to improve on some shortcomings in the literature on new political parties. As already mentioned, a large part of the literature is concerned with a specific class of new parties. Here, the line that divides what is specific to this particular class and what is a more general relation often becomes blurred and difficult to distinguish. Besides, as I already argued, the emergence of new parties takes place in a very structured environment, which is the same for all classes of new parties. The latter distinguish themselves by important aspects, like the issues they address and their organizational structure. But, as I will argue and illustrate, the emergence of a new party seems to follow a very particular process. And this common process is precisely what is neglected in most studies on a given class of new parties.

Existing general frameworks on new political parties have other shortcomings, which fall into two categories. First, the theoretical arguments are founded mostly in empirical observations; important links and interactions between several aspects of the model are neglected. Often, authors propose a series of variables or characteristics of party systems which should induce or discourage new political parties to form. In this undertaking, authors often rely on previous research, which mainly attempts to explain particular classes of parties (Harmel and Robertson 1985). The bias discussed above also finds its way into theoretical and empirical work. While there is usually a certain truth to these hypotheses, the fact is often neglected that the relationships do not hold in all contexts. For instance, a new issue might be very important in a given country, but no new party appears, because an existing party has quickly picked up the new demands. Similarly, it might be very easy to gain access to the ballot, but high electoral thresholds could discourage groups from forming a new party. Only a consistent theoretical framework can help us to understand these interactions.

The second category of shortcomings that general theories of new political parties present, concern some puzzles that they fail to explain. The first puzzle comes from situations where all conditions appear to be present and no new party emerges. There exist several cases where this occurs, although all authors agree that the conditions were very favorable to the formation of a new party. For instance, the extended wait that Dutch voters had to endure until they could vote for a genuine Green party goes squarely against most theoretical work in the field.[9]

Another puzzle concerns the relationship between the electoral system and the emergence and initial success of new political parties. Most authors agree that plurality rule works heavily against newcomers on the electoral scene. It first discourages them to emerge and, once they have formed, it discourages voters to vote for them. These relationships find strong theoretical support in the literature on electoral systems (e.g., Rae 1967; Taagepera and Shugart 1989; Lijphart 1994; Cox 1997). Lijphart (1994) shows convincingly that the electoral system has an important impact on the effective number of parties.[10] When one concentrates, however, on the number of new parties and their success, these relationships somehow fail to materialize. Authors omit the variable because of missing variation (Kitschelt 1988), or report conflicting results. Harmel and Robertson (1985) find fewer new parties in proportional representation than plurality systems. But their success appears more likely under the former electoral rule. Quite to the contrary, Müller-Rommel (1993) finds that the vote for Green parties decreases as an electoral system becomes more proportional.

These shortcomings in the literature seem to relate to two major aspects of the study of new political parties. First, as already argued, existing theoretical frameworks somewhat neglect the interactions between different factors influencing the formation and success of new parties. By stressing the internal coherence of the theoretical model, implications should become more precise and uncover possible interactions. Second, on the empirical level, the question of the appropriate research design is often neglected. I will argue that the study of new political parties poses some problems in this respect. More precisely, the question of research design is hard-pressing for solving the second puzzle I discussed above. Studying the success of new parties is, as I will show in this study, a far more complex endeavor than is commonly assumed.

---

9. We shall discuss this case in more detail in chapter 2.

10. While giving some indication on the question at hand, the use of the effective number of parties is problematic. Since this number is a transformation of a fragmentation index, it measures both the number of new parties and their shares of the vote. Hence, the impact of the electoral system on the effective number of parties simultaneously measures the impact on the founders of new parties and the voters.

Consequently, the present study has two major aims. First, it attempts to develop a careful theoretical model, attempting to explain the formation of new political parties. Second, in applying and testing the model, it will emphasize the importance of adequate research designs in the study of new parties. In doing this, the study contributes to the explanation of the emergence of new political parties. The empirical tests show under what conditions the emergence becomes more likely and what factors contribute to the initial success of the newcomers on the electoral scene.

The study proceeds in the following way: chapter 2 presents what I consider to be the underlying process in the emergence of new political parties. I briefly tell three tales on new and old parties. Through these tales it will become apparent that the interaction between established parties and groups advocating new issues, is very similar across different situations. The way this process evolves and how the different actors involved behave also seem to give some explanatory leverage for the absence of new parties. The presentation of these three tales allows me, in addition, to illustrate the main theoretical arguments in the literature on new political parties. As will become apparent, some find support in these tales, while others fail to do so. But here I must underscore that these tales do not intend to disprove or support particular stances in the literature. They serve more as preparation of the reader for what will follow.

The third chapter will take up the main elements of the three tales and discuss them in the light of the literature on new parties and party systems. Here, as well, considerable support is found for my argument that the process highlighted in the second chapter is a general one. On that basis, I will develop a theoretical model which attempts to explain the formation of new parties. Since the process discussed above involves strategic interactions between actors, I will employ a game-theoretic framework. Such a framework provides useful tools for developing a theoretical model, which stresses the importance of interdependent choices. The model allows me to derive several implications that relate the likelihood of seeing new parties with variables employed in the game-theoretic model. In addition, some of these implications also give limited information on the initial strength of the new competitors.

The theoretical model also highlights a central problem for the empirical study of new parties. Because of this, chapter 4 discusses questions of research design. I propose a twofold research design. With the help of the first design, it should be possible to study the formation of new political parties in a meaningful way. It focuses on elections and looks at the number of new parties appearing at each election. This number should vary according to the implications that I derive from my theoretical model. The second design, which has links to the previous one, will allow me to explore the initial success of new political parties. Its focus is on each individual new party, the success of which will depend on characteristics of its environment. I compare this twofold research design to those employed in the literature. As I will argue, the design adopted in the present study has several advantages over competing designs.

This twofold research design finds application in chapters 5 and 6. Employing it allows me to test the implications of my theoretical model. While the empirical data provide far from perfect measures for the theoretical variables, quite consistent support for my model appears throughout the analyses. The emergence of new political parties appears to vary along the lines predicted by my model, as I show in chapter 5. New issues and institutional factors like the electoral system appear as powerful predictors of party formation. Similarly, chapter 6 shows empirical support for the limited insights the model provides for the explanation of the initial success of new political parties. Again, new issues play a significant role in explaining the initial success of new parties.

Some implications, however, run into opposing evidence. I will discuss the consequences of this in the conclusion of this study. There, I will first emphasize the contribution that my study makes to the study of new political parties. Theoretical, empirical, and methodological insights will figure prominently in this last chapter. The discussion of the shortcomings, both on the empirical and theoretical level, will be the next focus. This will naturally lead to a critical discussion of the achievements and possible avenues for future research.

CHAPTER 2

Tales of New and Old Political Parties

There are times when the formation of a new political party comes as a surprise to both politicians and scholars alike. At other times the surprise comes from the fact that no new party has appeared despite an urgent problem prevalent in a given society. In this chapter I present three tales of new and old parties. All three tales illustrate peculiarities of the formation process of new parties. In two of the three tales a new party appeared very quickly, while in the third its emergence was late. This lateness surprised most scholars, since by conventional wisdom a new party should have already been in existence for a long time.

The selection of the tales is arbitrary. They do not intend to prove a certain statement or proposition. Instead, they aim at preparing the reader for the chapters that follow. The three tales illustrate what I consider to being the basic underlying process that is crucial to the formation of new parties. The outcome of this process is sometimes the emergence of a new party, but may often result in policy changes adopted by the established parties. These changes may discourage or prevent the emergence of a new party.

I chose these three cases because they differ according to several criteria. They all come from different countries, one taking place in the first half of the twentieth century, the other two in the second half. In the first tale, which concerns a late-coming Green party, the existence of a new policy issue seemed to be important. In addition, the institutional constraints, for instance, electoral thresholds, are considered to be very low in the country in question, the Netherlands. Despite these favorable conditions, the new party's appearance was late. In the tale about Germany, the institutional constraints were also very low. Several authors argue that the extreme proportionalism allowed for the rise of the Nazi party and the demise of the Weimar Republic (e.g., Hermens 1972).[1] Similarly, the issues that the group addressed were of increasing importance. In contrast to the first tale, a new party appeared quite quickly and rose to an important success, which had very serious consequences for the

1. Kershaw (1999) presents a dissenting view by arguing that a wide spectrum of the political elites of Weimar Germany was hardly supportive of the parliamentarian democracy.

whole world. Finally, the tale from Great Britain illustrates a new party that formed despite important institutional constraints and new issues that at the outset appeared of relatively little importance.

While differing according to these criteria, the three cases discussed below seem to suggest that, despite the differences separating them, their formation process follows a very similar path. I refrain from claiming that by presenting these tales and relying on historical and political science accounts a clear case for this common path is made. Lustick's (1996) warnings about problems of selection bias in historical sociology are only too persuasive. My claim is more modest, namely that support for a common formation path for these three cases can be found in the historical and political science literature.

Furthermore, these three tales allow me to present the theoretical arguments of the literature on new political parties. Some of these arguments will reappear in later chapters, where I develop my theoretical model and proceed to test it empirically. As for others, I will try to show that, on the empirical level, they do not account for the tales that I present below. Proceeding in this way should give the reader both an overview of the literature on new parties, as well as some empirical cases toward which this literature is geared. Before doing this, however, it is necessary to define more clearly my object of study: namely, new political parties. Since new parties form a subgroup of a larger entity of actors, which is the overall set of political parties, I will first define this wider term.

Defining political parties has provoked extensive discussions in the literature.[2] These discussions sometimes seem to miss the point that a definition must provide a clear criterion for selecting the objects that belong to a certain class; it does not have to completely characterize every aspect of the object under consideration. In keeping with this I adopt one of the most concise definitions of what a political party is:

> Party is defined simply as an organization that appoints candidates at general elections to the system's representative assembly. (Sjöblom 1968, 21)[3]

This very simple definition has the virtue of relying on a single criterion: namely, that an organization presents candidates at general elections. This criterion is what distinguishes political parties from all other organizations.

2. See, e.g., Duverger (1951 [1976]), Wright (1971); Sartori (1976, ch.1-4), Eldersveld (1982), and Schlesinger (1991, 5ff).

3. Sjöblom (1968, 21) continues his definition with "... and other political positions." But this addition introduces a considerable vagueness into the definition without any gain in scope. Definitions similar to the one I have used can be found in Sartori (1976) and Schlesinger (1991).

Quite similar is Downs' (1957, 25) definition that "[A] political party is a team of men seeking to control the governing apparatus by gaining office in a duly constituted election." But compared to Sjöblom's (1968) definition, the emphasis on "seeking to control the governing apparatus" seems unduly restrictive.[4] Consequently, Sjöblom's (1968) definition serves in this study as a guiding principle to determine what is a party.

Having defined political parties, I will move on to the definition of my object of study: new political parties. At first sight, this term should not cause more problems than the previous one. It should, in essence, cover political parties that have recently been formed. But the term "new parties" covers a range of political organizations that have quite distinct origins. Mair (1990), for example, distinguishes between new parties that result from a fusion of two or more parties, or those that are the outcome, conversely, of a fission. In the former category one finds parties that are composed of several entities, which were separate parties before the fusion occurred. A prominent example is the Christian Democratic Appeal (CDA) in the Netherlands, which resulted from a fusion of several religious parties (Kriesi 1993). Fissions occur when members of an existing party decide to form a new and separate party. Such new parties are more numerous than those represented in the previous category and include the British Social Democratic Party (SDP), a split-away of the Labour Party (King and Crewe 1991), for example. To these two categories, one can add genuinely new parties, which emerge without any help from members of existing parties. Probably the purest example is the Danish Progress Party, founded by Mogens Glistrup in 1972, a party which has attempted to abolish taxes (Harmel, Svasand, and Gibson 1992). And, finally, a last category includes organizations which are electoral alliances. These are very similar to the first category, but do not result in the formation of a new party. Often, electoral alliances are the first steps on the way to a fusion, as happened, for example, with the British Alliance (King and Crewe 1991; Stevenson 1993).

These four categories cover all new "organization[s] that appoint[s] candidates at general elections," as stipulated in the definition. But new parties in two of the four categories are basically just established parties that have reorganized. Such reorganizations have often been necessary for the survival of existing parties. Sometimes combining forces might increase the likelihood of winning elections and gaining power (Mair 1990). The formation of electoral alliances and fusions follows a different pattern than the emergence of genuinely new parties and fissions. This becomes evident when one considers the role of existing parties during new party emergence. For established

4. Downs (1957, 127), in his later discussion of new parties, suggests that the latter may either wish to win elections or only influence established parties. Obviously, adopting Downs' (1957, 25) definition of a political party would automatically exclude the latter type of new parties.

parties, genuinely new parties and fissions represent new competitors on the electoral scene. While this is also the case for electoral alliances and fusions, their emergence simultaneously implies the disappearance of other competitors. Seen from this perspective, established parties might even welcome electoral alliances and fusions, though they certainly prefer not to see any new challengers on the electoral scene.[5]

Electoral alliances and fusions, however, most often form outside the sphere of influence of the established parties. The latter can rarely hinder such new parties from emerging, since the necessary components already exist. In contrast, genuinely new parties and fissions are very sensitive to what the established parties do. Such new parties emerge in protest against the existing parties, which they would like to influence or even displace.[6] Additionally, new parties often represent complete unknowns to the established actors on the electoral scene. For these reasons, I have chosen to restrict the term "new political parties" to encompass only genuinely new parties and fissions and, consequently, I have adopted the following definition:

> A new political party is a genuinely new organization that appoints, for the first time, candidates at a general election to the system's representative assembly.

This definition rules out all parties that rely on organizations that already exist to appoint candidates to elections. Consequently, my definition excludes electoral alliances and fusions, but includes genuinely new parties and fissions. The new parties that I will study all impose a new challenge on the existing parties. They try, for the first time, to compete for votes that have gone exclusively to established parties. By default, the latter include all the parties that do not qualify for the status of new political party. This implies, according to my terms, that a party becomes established at its second participation in a general election.

This definition also lays the ground for another important notion in this study, namely the notion of a potential new political party. The emergence and formation of a new political party are the outcome of a process in which a group, an organization, or a political entrepreneur comes to the conclusion to present candidates at a general election. Before presenting candidates the group, organization, or political entrepreneur is not a new party yet, but a po-

5. This is not always true, since a new party might hurt one established party more than another. The French Socialist Party (PS), e.g., was happy to change the electoral rules for the 1986 elections, allowing important gains for Le Pen's *Front National*.

6. Downs (1957, 127) distinguishes between two types of new parties: Parties that form to win elections and parties that attempt to influence existing parties.

tential new political party. Not all potential new parties will take the step to become new political parties. Hence, a potential new party is a group, organization, or political entrepreneur that contemplates presenting candidates at a general election. Obviously, this definition makes it hard to determine at any given time whether a given group is a potential new party. The only thing we can be sure about is that the formation of a new political party is preceded by the existence of a potential new party. Sometimes the potential new party corresponds to a social movement or a part of it, as it seems to have been the case for numerous Green parties. In others, such as Anders Lange's Party (Anders Langes Parti) (Harmel and Svasand 1997; Mackie and Rose 1991, 358f; Kitschelt 1995, 121-158) an individual almost singlehandedly takes the step from a potential new party to presenting candidates at a national election. Given this wide spectrum of potential new parties, these are largely an unobservable quantity, but play a significant role in any formation of a new party.

With these definitions at hand I will proceed to the illustrations announced above. The next three sections present tales on new parties and potential new parties that considered forming one. These tales highlight aspects of the formation process, which prove to be important. They also illustrate the empirical content of the definitions adopted in this study.

The Late-Coming Green Party in the Netherlands

In the late 1970s, and in the beginning of the eighties, a whole wave of new parties swept over Europe, bringing environmental issues to the forefront. So-called Green parties emerged in practically all Western Democracies.[7] However, the country where most scholars would have predicted the emergence of a new party, remained without a challenging Green party:

> One of the most intriguing questions about recent developments in Dutch politics concerns the possible consequences for the party system of the existence of a substantial number of voters favoring 'New Politics'. Because of the extremely low threshold at 1/150 of the valid votes, it is easy for new political movements to enter Parliament. However, no Green party has yet succeeded gaining a seat in parliament. . . . How to explain the seeming paradox that the country with the highest number of people favoring 'New Politics' has not seen the rise of a powerful party propagating those views is a perplexing question. (Thomassen and van Deth 1989, 74)

The Netherlands had to wait quite some time to see the formation of an

7. Parkin (1989) and Müller-Rommel (1989, 1993) give detailed descriptions of these new parties.

environmental party, despite a series of factors that should have, according to most authors, favored its formation.[8] It was only in 1983 that a new party appeared – "De Groenen" – with the declared goal of defending environmental issues.[9] Its first participation at national elections occurred, however, only in 1986.[10]

Facilitating Factors for a New Party in the Netherlands

Green parties most often find their origins in environmental movements (Brand 1982; Bürklin 1984; Kitschelt 1988; Poguntke 1993, 36ff; Müller-Rommel 1993, 147ff). These movements play a crucial role in mobilizing people for the new issues, which concern the protection of the environment. The rise of environmental consciousness in the Netherlands was not much different from those in most other European countries. Jamison, Eyerman, Cramer, and Laessoe (1990, 121f)[11] note, however, the special relationship the Dutch people have with nature. This relationship has its roots in the fact that a considerable part of the Netherlands is below sea level and is only inhabitable thanks to numerous levees. Consequently, nature is, on the one hand, largely affected by human intervention. On the other hand, there is also an implicit agreement that some places have to be left untouched. This, together with the very high population density, might explain why the traditional environmental organizations quite early addressed the problem of pollution.

While up to the beginning of the 1970s traditional environmental organizations were dominating the scene (Tellegen 1981; van der Heijden 1992), the beginning of this decade heralded the appearance of a series of new movements. These movements brought other problems to the forefront and, initially, acted at the local level. In parallel, during the 1970s, other new social move-

---

8. In the cross-national literature the Dutch parties often have to endure quite interesting classification decisions. Kitschelt (1988) considers both Pacifistic Socialist Party (PSP) and the Political Party of the Radicals (PPR) as left-libertarian parties, despite the fact that the origins of these parties hardly were in this tradition (Lucardie 1980, 94ff, 169ff). Similarly, Müller-Rommel (1993) considers the "Gren Progressive Accord" (GPA), formed as a temporary electoral alliance between the PSP, the PPR and the Communist Party of the Netherlands (CPN) in 1984, as Green party. That this alliance fell apart before 1986 and only reformed in 1989 escapes the attention of this author. In 1990 these three parties formed a new party ("Green Left") and disbanded their individual party organizations in 1991 (Lucardie, van der Knoop, von Schuur, and Voerman 1991). Thus, according to my definition "Green Left" does not qualify as a genuinely new party.

9. Lucardie, Voerman, and van Schuur (1993, 44ff) report the early history of "De Groenen." See also Parkin (1989, 180-183).

10. In the 1986 election "De Groenen" presented themselves as "Federatieve Groenen" (Lucardie, Voerman, and van Schuur 1993, 46).

11. This book serves as a major source for what follows on the environmental movement in the Netherlands.

ments, especially the anti-nuclear and the peace movement, started to gain steam (van Praag 1991). This is important for the environmental movement, because there is often a strong overlap between the participants in these movements (Kriesi and van Praag 1987; Kriesi 1988, 1993). The peace movement, in particular, proved to be of considerable strength. A petition that it circulated, protesting against the stationing of cruise missiles, was signed by more than three million people. This shows clearly the importance of the new social movement sector in the Netherlands. According to most authors (Kitschelt 1988; Rüdig 1990; Müller-Rommel 1993, 147; Poguntke 1993), strong environmental movements should increase the chances of seeing a new Green party appearing on the electoral scene. This stands in parallel to more general theories on new parties (Hauss and Rayside 1978; Harmel and Robertson 1985; Rüdig 1990), which emphasize the importance of new issues, here reflected by the importance of the movement. But, despite the importance of new issues and the new social movements to which they gave rise, no new party appeared. In this respect, the Netherlands is again a deviant case.

Apart from an extensive environmental movement sector, the Netherlands also displayed a high attraction for "New Politics." This includes not only environmental concerns, but also demands for more citizen involvement and emphasis on the quality of life. But, here as well, the:

> problem is that whoever wants to argue that the 'New Politics' has affected the party system will have to explain a seeming paradox. The Dutch electoral system of proportional representation places an extremely low barrier to new political movements attempting to enter Parliament. It is a popular understanding that new political movements found fertile soil in the process of deconfessionalisation and depillarisation that accelerated in the 1960s. Some of the new parties (D'66 [Democrats '66], PPR) entered the political arena with a platform that could easily be interpreted as an expression of the 'New Politics'. However, the basis of the traditional parties has not been further eroded since 1971. (Thomassen and van Deth 1989, 63)[12]

"New Politics" is closely associated with Inglehart's (1977, 1990) theory of value change and his concept of post-materialism. He predicts that after periods of economic affluence new generations will demonstrate different values by putting more emphasis on non-economic problems. Questions of life-quality, participation, and so on become increasingly important. Inglehart (1990, 262ff), like numerous other authors (Harmel and Robertson

12. This statement by Thomassen and van Deth (1989) contradicts Lucardie's (1980, 187) finding that the PPR was hardly a "New Left" party in the beginning.

Fig. 2.1. Difference between percentage post-materialists and percentage materialist

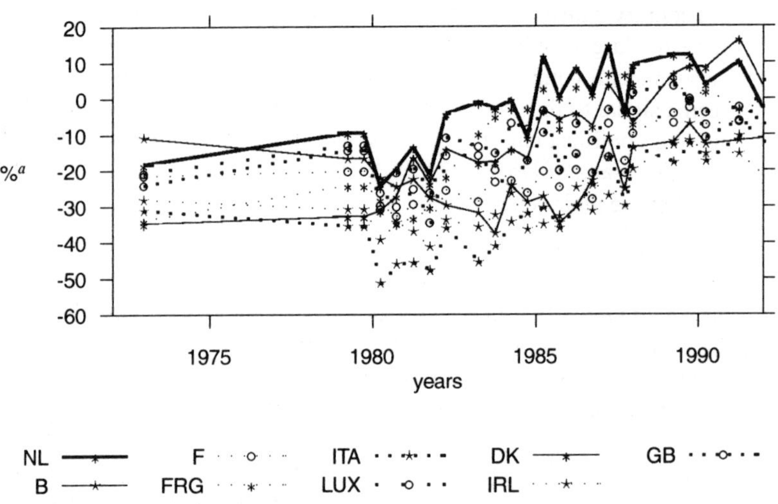

a. *Source:* European Community Studies, 1973; Eurobarometers 6-35

1985; Kitschelt 1988; Müller-Rommel 1993; Poguntke 1993), argues that post-materialism increases the likelihood of seeing a Green party emerging. Interestingly enough, the Netherlands has headed, for a number of years, the score-list of the most post-materialist European nations in the Eurobarometer survey (Figure 2.1).[13]

Figure 2.1 shows that the Netherlands has the highest difference between the percentage of post-materialists and materialists in three-fourths of the 21 time points considered.[14] While Germany has displayed similarly high levels of post-materialism throughout the 1980s, it has also enjoyed the rise of a successful Green party. The Netherlands remained without one. Inglehart and Andeweg (1993), replying to the critical remarks of Thomassen and van Deth

13. Individuals are classified as post-materialists if they mention as most important societal goals the participation of citizens in government decisions and protecting freedom of speech. These two items figure on a list of four, from which the person interviewed has to choose two items (Inglehart 1977, 1990).

14. Inglehart and Andeweg (1993, 348, 350) document with additional data this high level of post-materialism in the Netherlands.

(1989) on New Politics, give some hints as to what might be the cause of this difference:

> In a country with a low electoral threshold, successes of small parties often make the larger parties pay attention to the issues or interests advocated by such small competitors. The emergence of 'New Politics' parties has been a signal to the established parties that they need to take the changes in Dutch political culture seriously, and they have tried to take the wind out of the sails of D66, PPR, PSP, and EVP [Evangelical Peoples Party] by adopting their key policies.
>
> Sometimes such adaptations are successful, and thus we can explain the absence of a vintage Green Party in the Netherlands (as we have shown the history of Green Left distinguishes it from ecological groups elsewhere): the established parties adopted Green policies in their manifestoes long before Green parties broke through much higher electoral thresholds in other countries. (Inglehart and Andeweg 1993, 358)

This hint, which links the openness of established parties toward new demands with the extremely low electoral threshold in the Netherlands, brings us to the last facilitating factor. Most authors argue, quite in opposition to Inglehart and Andeweg (1993), that low thresholds should facilitate the entrance of new parties, and render the latter more numerous and successful (Kitschelt 1988; Hauss and Rayside 1978; Harmel and Robertson 1985; Müller-Rommel 1990, 1993). When a party reaches 1/150 of the total vote in a Dutch election, it cannot be excluded from parliament and obtains at least one seat. The threshold of exclusion, as Lijphart and Gibberd (1977) call this value, is in consequence equal to 0.67 percent of the total vote. By law the threshold of representation has the same value.[15]

Conventional theories would argue that such low thresholds should heavily favor the emergence of a Green party (e.g., Harmel and Robertson 1985; Müller-Rommel 1990). Despite these low thresholds, the Dutch had to wait until 1986 to finally see a Green party on their ballot. Clearly, Inglehart and Andeweg (1993) provide an interesting lead for the solution of the Dutch puzzle. But a question arises as to whether the increased openness of parties is a general feature in systems with low electoral thresholds, or if it depends on other factors. Given the mixed results on the relationship between the electoral system and the formation of new parties, it is likely that the relation is more complex.

---

15. These thresholds will appear in the empirical part of this study. Detailed descriptions of them are in the appendix.

Established Parties and the Environmental Issue

A series of factors should have made the emergence of a Green party in the Netherlands quite simple. Environmentalism was active and demanded better protection against pollution. The peace movement, as well as the anti-nuclear movement, organized several events in order to give voice to their demands. Post-materialists were already, for some time, more numerous than pure materialists (Inglehart and Andeweg 1993, 348). In addition, the hurdle to cross to be elected into the parliament is extremely low in the Netherlands.

All of these elements figure prominently as explanatory factors in the literature on new parties in general and Green parties in particular. But, for all of them, the Dutch case represents a puzzle. One possible answer, suggested by Inglehart and Andeweg (1993) might lie in the responsiveness of the established party: The parties in parliament would adopt positions on environmental questions from the outset. Jamison, Eyerman, Cramer, and Laessoe (1990) argue that, as early as the sixties, environmental concerns were voiced and gained attention from existing parties. Van der Heijden (1992) shows that the traditional environmental organizations dominated the scene up to the 1970s. They were, however, much more open to new types of environmental problems due to the special relationship of the Dutch with nature. From early on these organizations, along with concerned scientists, voiced demands. Jamison, Eyerman, Cramer, and Laessoe (1990, 125) cite the example of pesticide control. Government submitted in the early sixties to demands for stricter control and passed a law in 1962. Similarly, the traditional environmental organizations were already participating in several governmental commissions during that period. According to van der Heijden (1992, 150), this was demonstrating their apolitical character. Probably also thanks to these efforts, the beginning of the 1970s witnessed some changes at the governmental level. A department for Health and Environmental Hygiene was created, and several environmental laws were passed (Tellegen 1981, 27; Jamison, Eyerman, Cramer, and Laessoe 1990, 138). All of these activities may be regarded as reaction to the demands voiced by organizations concerned with the environment. Interestingly enough, these activities all happened at the governmental level and did not find their way into the programs of the political parties:

> In this first phase [(1962-1968)], no political party included environmental issues as an important item in their political programme, except for the 'Pacifistisch Socialistische Partij' (the Pacifistic Socialistic Party, or PSP), a small radical left party. In most other political parties environmental problems were acknowledged only by individual party members. (Jamison, Eyerman, Cramer, and Laessoe 1990, 126)

In the case of the PSP, founded in 1957, first attempts to consider environmental issues date to the early sixties. But only in the electoral programme of 1967 did these problems appear in a "lengthy paragraph" (Jamison, Eyerman, Cramer, and Laessoe 1990, 180). In the 1970s the PSP's environmental policy lost its originality as other parties started picking up environmental issues. This seemed to go together with international events, like the publication of *The Limits to Growth* (Meadows and Club of Rome 1974) and the United Nations Conference on environmental pollution in Stockholm. In addition, the early 1970s also saw environmental movements of a newer type appearing (van der Heijden 1992, 150f). These groups started to voice more serious demands. Together, these elements stimulated more active responses from the established parties:

> While in the 1960s only the PSP (Pacifistic Socialistic Party) paid any real attention to pollution problems, most political parties began openly to recognise the seriousness of the environmental crisis in the 1970s, . . .
>
> Among the left-wing politicians the breakthrough of environmental concern was largely stimulated by the Dutch report of the 'Committee of Six', which was issued right after publication of *The Limits to Growth*. . . . This 'Committee of Six' consisted of six prominent representatives of three major left-wing political parties: the Partij van de Arbeid (Social Democratic Labour Party, PvdA); D'66 (Democrats '66); and the PPR (Political Radical Party). . . .
>
> For all three parties, however, this was one of the first times that they gave voice explicitly to their environmental concern and the need to take steps as quickly as possible. This concern was also reflected in their common political programme for the Second Chamber elections in 1972. . . . In the course of the 1970s all political parties, both of the left and the right, integrated environmental concerns into their programmes. (Jamison, Eyerman, Cramer, and Laessoe 1990, 137f)

Apparently, after initial pressure from traditional environmental organizations and the subsequent demands of newer movements, parties, first of the left, then also of the right, adopted positions on ecological problems. Compared to other countries, these reactions were much quicker and profound. Van Praag (1991) relates this to the openness of the Dutch political system. Also, concerning other movements and their demands, there appears to have always been at least one political party ready to listen. For instance, Schennink (1988, 256) notes the strong involvement of the churches in the peace movement and the presence of the PSP and the PPR, especially in the activists' core.

An even stronger case in point is the debate over nuclear energy. While the Netherlands, thanks to the presence of natural gas, was less dependent on other energy sources, two nuclear plants existed in 1973 (van der Heijden, 1992, 152). In 1974, the government presented plans to construct three new plants. This announcement led to serious reactions of the environmental movements and several demonstrations took place. One group demanded a five-year moratorium in the decision making on the development nuclear energy (Jamison, Eyerman, Cramer, and Laessoe 1990, 157). The government reacted in a conciliatory way, backed down from its plan (van der Heijden 1992, 152), and created a forum where energy problems were discussed. This

> took away much of the direct confrontation between the anti-nuclear activists and the government, and clearly stimulated a more co-operative attitude on the part of the environmentalists towards the established political system. (Jamison, Eyerman, Cramer, and Laessoe 1990, 158)

This shows again that throughout the 1970s and eighties the demands of the environmental movement were either met by the government, or found considerable support in existing political parties.[16] Apparently, since either government or established parties were so responsive, no need was felt for forming a new party:

> The complex and delicate network of relations between the environmentalists and the established political culture is also among the reasons why a Green Party has failed to gain much support in the Netherlands, compared with other Western European countries. (Jamison, Eyerman, Cramer, and Laessoe 1990, 169)

While Green parties emerged in most other Western democracies, the early reactions of the established parties seem to have prevented the formation of a Green party in the Netherlands. The reasons for these reactions might lie, as Inglehart and Andeweg (1993) argue, in the vulnerability of established parties, due to the low electoral thresholds.

Conclusion: Better Late than Never?

Only in 1986 did a Green party finally appear on the ballot of a national election. It polled a mere 0.2 percent of the votes, which, despite the extremely

---

16. Van der Heijden (1992, 151) shows that starting in 1974 the environmental movements became more politicized. Some organizations privileged their relations with political parties, such as the PSP, the D'66, and PPR.

TABLE 2.1. Potential Vote for Ecologist Parties

Countries	Potential Vote[a]
Ireland	57
France	56
Germany	55
Luxembourg	53
Italy	52
Belgium	49
Netherlands	**43**
Northern Ireland	36
Denmark	36
Britain	31
Greece	27
European Community	47

a. Source: Inglehart and Rabier 1986, 466, $N = 9{,}745$

low electoral thresholds, was not sufficient to gain a seat in parliament. Only in its second election participation did this new party finally achieve to win seats. This late emergence and limited success questions several theoretical explanations of new political parties in general, and Green parties in particular. The considerable importance of post-materialists among the Dutch electorate should have prompted the early creation of a strong Green party according to most theories on "New Politics." Even more generally, the widespread and deep-rooted concern of Dutch citizens for environmental problems and the strong new social movement sector are supposed to be ideal grounds for the formation of a new party. Similarly, the low electoral threshold a party has to cross before winning a seat should have led to a quick formation of a successful new party.

The question then arises as to whether it is too late for a Green party or whether these are just the starting problems of a newcomer on the electoral scene. Some very limited insights might be gained from table 2.1, which shows the percentage of voters which might vote for a Green party. For the Netherlands, the figure shows that even shortly after the formation of the new party in 1984, its potential electorate was slightly below the European average. Among the electorate less than half even considered giving their vote to a Green party. This is much lower than the corresponding figures, for instance, for Germany, which has a similar level of post-materialists.

These figures seem to suggest that the reactions of the established parties to the demands of the environmental movements were adequate. For a majority of voters there appears to be no sufficient reason for voting for a Green party to emphasize environmental problems. The Dutch puzzle in this case challenges us to determine why the established parties reacted so promptly to new demands. While Inglehart and Andeweg (1993) provide an informed guess,

I will try to provide answers based on a theoretical model in the subsequent chapters.

The Deutsche Arbeiterpartei and Its Fearsome Successor

The second case under scrutiny is quite similar to the previous one with respect to some elements. The electoral system of the Weimar Republic was of an extreme proportionality (Hermens 1972, 214). Consequently, the necessary number of votes to gain a seat in the Reichstag was very low. The inter-war period in Germany was a time of great of turmoil, economic crises, unsolved foreign policy issues, etc. Thus, our second tale starts one evening in September of 1919, when a *Gefreiter* of the German Army attended a meeting of a group of people in Munich, who called themselves "Deutsche Arbeiterpartei (DAP)" (German Workers' Party). His mission was to explore this supposedly socialist organization and report to the German Army's political department (Shirer 1960, 60f; Kershaw 1999, 126ff). The encounter between this group of people around Anton Drexler and the Gefreiter Adolf Hitler is at the very root of a new party, which has attracted an enormous amount of scholarly interest. A series of academic works tried to illustrate and understand the emergence of this new party. But, in the light of the horror that was to come after its emergence and successful seizure of power, the question of emergence paled.[17]

As Shirer (1960, 61f) documents, Hitler's presence at this meeting in 1919 might have gone by without any consequences. Hitler seemed little impressed by this organization, and only the intervention of one attendant sparked off a verbal outburst by him (Franz-Willing 1962, 66). This made such a positive impression on the members of the DAP that they offered him immediate membership. After some time of reflection Hitler decided to join this group. From then on, Hitler's influence over the group only increased, until it became completely his tool.

In this section I will try to give a very limited overview of the emergence of the "National-sozialistische Deutsche Arbeiterpartei (NSDAP)."[18] Numerous books (for example Franz-Willing 1962; Horn 1972; Orlow 1973; Maser 1981; Fischer 1995) discuss in detail the first years of what was to become the most successful, as well as the most fearsome, new party. My aim is not to summarize these historical works, but to set the emergence in a particular framework. First, I will show how the national-socialistic movement devel-

17. Maser (1967, 7) also notes this less studied aspect of the Nazi period. A very detailed bibliography on this period figures in Stachura (1983).

18. I argue below that the DAP in itself, even after its renaming into NSDAP, was not actually a party, but more of a debating club. Consequently, the emergence I will consider here is the re-foundation of the NSDAP after the failed "Hitler Putsch," when a genuine party emerged.

oped in its early years. The emphasis will be on the period before the "Hitler Putsch" of 1923, as a consequence of which the NSDAP was banned. During this period the movement attempted to organize support and voice demands. Second, I will attempt to illustrate the behavior of the established parties with respect to the Nazi movement. The emphasis will be on the period following the "Putsch," since this event made the Bavarian Nazi movement known in the whole Weimar Republic. In conclusion, I will try to put these elements together and attempt to illustrate what theories on new parties have to say about this case.

Movement or Party? The DAP and the Early NSDAP

The DAP was essentially the brainchild of Anton Drexler, a toolmaker, and Karl Harrer, a journalist. Its creation in 1919 was the product of the "Politischer Arbeitszirkel" (Workers' Political Society), which was a discussion group founded in 1918 by the same two persons. Harrer would have preferred to keep the format of a debating club but Drexler insisted on forming a political party " . . . to publicize the group's political views, and win members for its cause." (Orlow 1973, 12). But even Drexler did not consider the DAP, which had become the NSDAP in 1920, as a genuine political party. Concerning the "Völkischen Beobachter," the newspaper of the group, he wrote:

> Intentionally, I do not use the term party newspaper, because we are no party and we should not become one. We want the revolution of the honest workers against the domestic and foreign exploitation. (cited in Franz-Willing 1962, 82, my translation)

When Hitler decided to join this group, he quickly acceded to an important position, becoming responsible for the propaganda. He emphatically insisted on calling the movement a party, if only for its publicizing effect. Here, he entered into conflict with one of the founding fathers, namely Harrer, as Franz-Willing (1962, 68) notes. This shows quite clearly the ambiguity, even inside this movement, of what its precise status was. It registered in 1920 as a club under the name of "National-sozialistischer Deutscher Arbeiterverein, eingetragener Verein (NSDAV)." In addition, the club or party did not have the intention to participate at elections:

> Hitler at one point considered participating in the Bavarian elections, but by the beginning of 1923 he had rejected electoral activity for the NSDAP and fully accepted the necessity of a cooperative armed uprising. (Orlow 1973, 40)

By most modern theories on political parties, the NSDAP did not at this time qualify for political party status. Instead, it was what I call a potential new party. It was only a group that considered forming a new party, so as to participate in elections. It had a set of demands, but decided for the time being not to participate at elections. The demands of the NSDAP were at first quite vague, but became more specific in the program that was adopted at the founding meeting of the NSDAP in 1920. This program sketched out in 25 points the ideas of the Nazi movement.[19] Later these demands became even more specific and Hitler publicized them in the party's newspaper:[20]

> Already on September 18, 1922, shortly after Luedecke met with Mussolini on Hitler's request, Hitler, according to a report in the Völkischen Beobachter, formulated the following demands, which proved to be decisive for his policies: Punishing of the November-criminals, death penalty for profiteers and informers, informing the population about the peace treaty and the question of guilt, expulsion of Jews, remedy of housing needs, ending of the national dishonor and naming of streets and places after German heroes. (Maser 1981, 355, my translation)

These demands are of a serious nature and, in fact, almost imply the abolishment of the Weimar Republic. Neumann (1965, 73) therefore characterizes the NSDAP as a protest group. During this period the NSDAP was actively collaborating with other conspiracy groups against the Weimar Republic. With the help of the Bavarian government serious preparations were made to overthrow the Weimar Republic in a march to Berlin. But, in November of 1923, the head of the Bavarian government informed the paramilitary units that there was to be no Putsch (Orlow 1973, 44). Hitler, who had become the leader of these paramilitary units, decided to go against the government's will and went ahead with "his" Putsch. It failed miserably since, counter to Hitler's hope, the army did not intervene on his side. The police overcame the putschists easily and arrested Hitler. He was imprisoned in 1924 with a very lenient sentence. In addition, the government decided to dissolve the NSDAP.

Weimar Parties and the Formation of the NSDAP

Up until the Hitler Putsch in 1923, the NSDAP had enjoyed mostly regional fame. It was barely known to the wider public of the Weimar Republic. It was definitely the most prominent of the right-wing groups in Munich, and it was

---

19. Franz-Willing (1962, 80f) gives a short overview over all these demands.

20. Fischer (1995, 144-147) reports the full programme in the appendix of his book.

growing. But at the time, the NSDAP remained of limited size. In 1919 Hitler judged it to be:

> a new organization like so many others. This was a time in which anyone, who was not satisfied with developments . . . felt called upon to form a new party. Everywhere these organizations sprang out of the ground, only to vanish after a time. I judged the German Workers' Party no differently. (quoted in Shirer 1960, 61)

It is hardly surprising then that reactions from the established parties were almost nonexistent. In the turbulence of the after-war period, so many groups appeared and formulated demands, most of them extreme, that it was almost impossible to keep track (e.g., Kershaw 1999, 137). In addition, the NSDAP, even though it had a very capable propaganda chief, was, and remained, quite small. It proved able to stage important meetings, but as Hitler argued, he counted more on the support of the Army than of the masses to reach power. Unfortunately for him, this reliance proved disastrous in the Putsch attempt of 1923. The army did not join his effort to seize power. The NSDAP won, however, a sympathetic ear in the right-wing circles of Bavaria, which were also part of the government.

After the Hitler Putsch, the Weimar parties saw no reason to consider the demands of this extremist group in Bavaria. Some of the most serious economic problems started to fade away in 1924. Inflation came down quite considerably, and the political elites felt confident about the stability of the new Republic (Broszat 1984, 79ff). By late 1924 the support for the *völkisch* right fell to around 3 percent (Kershaw 1999, 258). Consequently, the Weimar parties felt little compelled to deal with the Bavarian nuisance. This lack of reaction also finds its cause in a considerable underestimation of the Nazi movement. Even later, the established parties exaggerated their proper strength, and minimized the danger of the emerging new party. Hebel-Kunze (1977, 58ff) illustrates nicely how leading figures of the Socialists belittled the NSDAP. Kershaw (1999, 25) reports that

> [a] confidential report by the Reich Minister of the Interior in 1927, pointing out that the NSDAP 'was not advancing,' realistically described the party as 'a numerically insignificant . . . radical-revolutionary splinter group incapable of exerting any noticeable influence on the great mass of the population and the course of political events.

Similarly, when Hitler was named chancellor, the conservatives still hoped to contain him. Kershaw (1999, chapter 10) precedes his discussion of these events by quotes of two conservative politicians: "We've hired him." (Franz von Papen), "We're boxing Hitler in" (Alfred Hugenberg). These politicians, as numerous others, heavily underestimated Hitler's and his movement's strength (Kershaw 1999, 424).

But to get to this stage, Hitler employed a more peaceful strategy than his failed Putsch attempt. During his imprisonment in 1924, Hitler had ample time to reconsider his demands and developed a detailed plan. In *Mein Kampf* he spelled out most of his aims and goals in accurate detail (Shirer 1960, 122). After finishing his prison term he returned to Munich to find the banned NSDAP split into two opposing factions. He resisted intervening in the conflict and instead appealed to the Bavarian government to revoke the ban on the NSDAP:

> In a talk with the new Bavarian Minister-president Held, taking place as early as the beginning of January 1925, he declared his legal intentions, and took distance from the anti-Christian völkischen positions, which Ludendorff, under the influence of his wife Mathilde, had increasingly adopted.
>
> As a result of this talk and the decreasing strength of the Völkischen at the elections in December 1924, the Bavarian government lifts the prohibition of the NSDAP and the 'Völkischen Beobachter.' (Broszat 1984, 85, my translation)

In February, Hitler called upon his old comrades to re-found the NSDAP at the very place where the Hitler Putsch had started a little more than a year earlier. At this meeting, he proved adept at overcoming oppositions between the two groups that had formed during the ban of the NSDAP. This time, the open aim of the party was to participate in elections, as Hitler affirmed in a conversation during his prison term:

> When I resume active work it will be necessary to pursue a new policy. Instead of working to achieve power by an armed *coup*, we shall have to hold our noses and enter the Reichstag against the Catholic and Marxist Deputies. If outvoting them takes longer than outshooting them, at least the result will be guaranteed by their own Constitution. Any lawful process is slow. . . . Sooner or later we shall have a majority – and after that Germany. (cited in Bullock 1964, 130, emphasis in original)

Conclusion

The explanations for the emergence of the NSDAP and its subsequent success are abundant. In this conclusion I will not delve into this formidable amount of explanations, but focus on two elements that are recurrent in contemporary theories on the formation of new parties. First, these theories, as well as many historical accounts, emphasize the importance of the electoral system of the Weimar Republic. It was one of extreme proportionality, and this was achieved by allowing combined lists over several districts (Nohlen 1978, 211ff). This encouraged a considerable number of organizations to propose candidates. Vogel and Schultze (1969, 258) report that 24 party lists competed at the 1920 election. This number increased to 29 in 1924, 35 in 1928, and finally reached 42 in the first election of 1932. Consequently, the low electoral barriers might have rendered the formation of a new party easier and more beneficial.

Some authors (e.g., Hermens 1972) further argue that the electoral system also increased the fractionalization in the parliament and led to numerous difficulties in forming governmental coalitions. Vogel and Schultze (1969, 258) note, however, that the number of parties represented in the Reichstag hardly followed the trend of party lists competing in the elections. It increased from ten parties (in 1920) to twelve (in 1924) and finally fifteen both in 1928 and the first election of 1932. They conclude that attributing the rise of the NSDAP primarily to the electoral system, as Hermens (1972, 231) unequivocally does, is exaggerated. Kershaw (1999) supports this claim by emphasizing various elements that pushed toward the demise of the Weimar Republic, chief among them the thinly spread support for democracy among considerable parts of the political elites.

Another explanation focuses more on the issues that the NSDAP brought to the forefront. Some of them, according to the chief prosecutor of the Nüremberg trial, might even appear to a normal citizen as legitimate (Franz-Willing 1962, 83). Some others, especially concerning the Jews, could hardly be conceived of as legitimate. But, among the former, the recurring theme of the unjust peace played an important role. Versailles and the reparation-payments placed a considerable burden on the German economy and people. Attacking this peace treaty was from early on a major element of Hitler's and the NSDAP's program. This tactic proved to be powerful, since it was widely felt in the population that the treaty was not fair. In addition, after having signed the treaty, the Weimar parties had a difficult time justifying this decision. Specifically, they feared an invasion of the allies, in the case that the treaty was not signed. But this fear was no longer felt by the general public.

Together, these elements recur in both the historical and political science literature as explanations for the emergence of the NSDAP. It is likely that it was this mixture of several important issues, unresponsive parties, extreme demands, and low electoral barriers that allowed the emergence of the NSDAP.

A Party at the Center: The British Social Democratic Party

A new party[21] (or a so-called third party) in a country with plurality rule goes against what is often considered as the only "law" (Palfrey 1989, 69) in political science. Duverger (1951 [1976]), in his famous book on political parties, argued that plurality rule inevitably favored the emergence and maintenance of two-party systems. Consequently, third parties should be rare in such systems.

The present tale concerns a party which emerged despite this forceful law working against it. The British Social Democratic Party (SDP) formed as a breakaway from the Labour Party in 1981.[22] The potential new party was formed by several prominent members of the Labour Party, and their actions lead to a fission. While the preceding two tales concerned two movements which were either extreme or brought an altogether new issue to the forefront, the SDP characterized itself as moderate. In addition, both preceding tales took place in political systems characterized by an electoral system of proportional representation. One might therefore conclude that new parties appear predominantly in countries that know proportional representation. The present tale tries to show that a new party can also appear under plurality rule, and this despite being a non-extremist movement.

In this section, I will first show the context in which the SDP emerged. The British political system had undergone changes in the 1970s; these changes provide important background for the present tale. I will then show how opposition within the Labour Party was raised against certain policies. Third, I will turn to the reactions that these demands stimulated in the ranks of the Labour Party, which eventually led to the formation of a new competitor. I will conclude by summarizing the main elements of this last tale.

Britain in the 1970s

Pure two-party systems are hard to come by. Only when using definitions based on Sartori's (1976, 121ff) counting rule or the number of effective parties (Taagepera and Shugart 1989, 77ff), does one encounter political systems with a bipolar electoral competition. In these approaches, Great Britain belongs certainly to two-party systems:

> Anyone asked to describe the main characteristics of the British party sys-

21. The title of this section is inspired from the title of Roy Jenkins' (1991) autobiography.

22. It is not the goal of the present section to present a complete history of the SDP. The interested reader can find such a history in Crewe and King's (1995) book on the SDP.

> tem in the period 1945 to 1970 would almost certainly begin by stating that it was essentially a two-party system. (Denver 1983, 75)

In elections, all third parties together garnered rarely more than a tenth of the total vote. Given the plurality electoral rule, this translated, at most, as a handful of seats. On average, third parties gained almost 9 percent of the vote between 1945 and 1970. This corresponded, however, to barely more than 2 percent of the seats in parliament (Denver 1983, 76). As most other European democracies Great Britain underwent important changes in the 1970s. Social-structural transformation was important and had a considerable impact on the British political system:

> [In the United Kingdom] . . . almost all of the common causes of structural change are present and have existed long enough to be considered a trend: electoral volatility (certainly), party organizational fragmentation (yes, recently), the existence of an ideological void (yes, both parties and especially Labour moved away from a "catchall" electoral approach), demographic or social-structural change (yes, with the decline of the traditional occupations and class cohesion), the occurrence of traumatic political events (in Northern Ireland, though not really elsewhere), and above all the politically corrosive effects of economic crisis. (Pridham 1988, 233)

These important transformations did not occur without seriously affecting the two-party system. Both Denver (1983, 76f) and Pridham (1988, 233) document the important decline in the vote for Labour and Tory: 64.8 percent of the electorate in 1970, 60.7 and 56.1 in the two elections of 1974, and 62.9 in 1979. In parallel to this decline in votes, the two-party system also came under attack from other parties, which succeeded in replacing established parties in by-elections. Both the Liberals and the Scottish National Party scored some successes, but these were merely temporary ones.

All of these changes occurred under the leadership of Labour governments, elected in 1974. With varying success, the governments of Harold Wilson and James Callaghan tried to cope with the problems and transformations (Koelble 1991, 70f; Crewe and King 1995, 3-26). But the 1979 election ended the presence of Labour in government. The Tories inflicted a serious defeat on the Labour party. In this humiliating election, even a majority "of manual workers who voted, voted against the Labour party" (Drucker 1986, 112).

Quarrels inside Labour

While this election defeat brought the inner divisions within this party to the forefront, it must be mentioned that these divisions were already present well before. David Owen (1991, 426), for instance, mentions the defection of 69 Labour members of parliament in a vote to support entry into the European Community. He, who later became one of the driving forces in the emergence of the SDP, sees here an important milestone in the formation process. The European question continued to occupy this party throughout the 1970s:

> One issue divided the social democrats from the Party most painfully: British membership of the European Communities. . . . When (in 1975) the division in the Labour leadership could not be contained and a referendum was agreed, Roy Jenkins resigned as Deputy Leader. (Drucker 1986, 112)

Jenkins, another driving force behind the new party, subsequently resigned as Home Secretary in the government to become President of the European Commission. After that, as he notes (Jenkins 1991, 509), he "was quiet on any issue of British politics which did not touch directly upon Europe" Only in 1979, when invited to give the Dimbleby lecture, did he address such issues again. In this lecture he launched the idea of a "radical center" (Jenkins 1991, 519), as a way to bring new people and ideas into politics. Some consider the Dimbleby lecture as the first milestone on the way to the new party (Denver 1983, 79; Pridham 1988, 236), while others disagree (Jenkins 1991, 522; Owen 1991, 426; Crewe and King 1995, 58).

This early call for a new party was resented by some members of Labour, who still believed in the party's capacity to cause change for the better. But, more and more throughout 1979 and 1980, other conflictual issues appeared. An important one concerned organizational questions in the party and the links with the trade unions. The serious election defeat in 1979 cruelly brought the divisions inside the party to the daylight. Several moderate members of parliament, and groups around them, felt that the left was taking over the leadership of the party:

> Extreme left-wingers were alleged to be infiltrating the party, 'moderate' MPs were said to be threatened with dismissal by left-wing activists, left-wing policies were adopted by the party conference and the National Executive Committee came to be controlled by the Left. Left-Right conflict was particularly acute over three constitutional questions – control of the party election manifestoes, the method of electing the party leader, and the mandatory re-selection of incumbent MPs as parliamentary candidates. (Denver 1983, 79)

Inside the party, prominent members like David Owen, Shirley Williams, and Bill Rodgers developed stronger ties in trying to oppose these policies (Crewe and King 1995, 27-51). Owen (1991, 435), for instance, reports his speech at a Special Labour Conference, where he defended, with little success, some of his policy proposals:

> For the social democrats, outmanoeuvred in a party which ignored their ideas, while moving further and further from electoral popularity, the final blows came in the aftermath of the election. So far from reforming itself, the Party gave way to a spasm of witch-hunting directed at the MPs. Election of the Leader and Deputy Leader by the Parliamentary Labour Party was replaced by a complicated system which gave weight to MPs (30 per cent), constituency parties (30 per cent), and trade unions (40 per cent). MPs were also to be (relatively) easily removed by their local parties from renomination. (Drucker 1986, 113)

While throughout this period most prominent moderate members of Labour were ready to stay on in the party and fight from within, in 1980 this willingness diminished more and more. In the middle of this year a party committee statement announced that ". . . Labour Party policies and the demands of European Community membership were irreconcilable . . . " (Owen 1991, 438). This sparked off a meeting between David Owen, Shirley Williams, and Bill Rodgers, and led to the publication of a declaration criticizing this party statement. According to Owen (1991, 439) "[t]he Gang of Three was born."

Rejection and Formation

These three prominent members of Labour, later joined by Roy Jenkins, were at the root of the new party. After their first declaration, they intended to work on a policy statement. At the beginning of 1981, they wrote a statement, the so-called Limehouse declaration, which can be considered as the launching pad of the new party. A first step was to set up a Council for Social Democracy inside Labour to give more weight to their ideas. While still not actually considering forming a new party, this formation became practically inevitable, since Labour reacted so little to the demands of the social democrats. After this declaration:

> [i]t was only a matter of time before a new party was formed. On 5 February an advertisement (signed by 100 prominent persons) appeared in the *Guardian* supporting the Council. This prompted a remarkable response. Around 80,000 letters of support were received and opinion polls indicated

> substantial public enthusiasm. Gradually those who had allied themselves with the Council broke their ties with the Labour Party and finally on 26 March, the new SDP was formally launched amid much publicity. (Denver 1983, 80)

This evolution clearly shows how little reaction the Labour Party showed in response to the demands of the moderate members. Both in organizational and policy questions, the moderates' position was quickly eliminated and more left-wing policies were adopted. Koelble (1991) illustrates nicely how the left wing of the Labour Party was able to impose its views on the whole party. He argues that this success is mostly due to the special relationship Labour had with the trade unions. Crewe and King (1995, 3-26) discuss this and other explanations of the leftward drift of Labour.

Left unanswered, however, is why these dissidents did not join an already existing party at the center, namely the Liberals. Jenkins (1991, 514) thought that simply joining the Liberals would not have the same effect on the political system that the creation of a new party would have. Such an endeavor appeared much more useful for the media and, consequently, was more powerful. Owen (1991, 466), on the other hand, had more doubts concerning the policies of the Liberals. Similarly, the other members of the "Gang of Four" could not conceive of moving from Labour to the Liberals.[23] They preferred to stay on inside Labour.

Conclusion

Contrary to the preceding two tales, this one shows the possibility of a new party appearing as a breakaway. Most of its initial prominent members felt that the two major parties had become too extreme. Labour moved heavily to the left after the election defeat in 1979. The Conservatives, on the other hand, took a strong turn to the right under Margaret Thatcher. A considerable number of deceived Labour members decided to leave their party and create a new political formation. Strikingly, the process leading up to this breakaway is very similar to the ones appearing in the other two tales. A potential new party formulates demands which in the case of the SDP faced almost outright rejection by an established party, namely the Labour Party. After this rejection a set of prominent members of this established party decided to break away and create a new party.

This tale shows also that new parties can successfully appear in party systems that are characterized by plurality rule. Despite important electoral hur-

---

23. Stevenson (1993, 76-82) describes the relationship between the SDP and Liberals from the latter's perspective.

dles, it succeeded in forming and drawing a lot of attention.[24] Its initial success was quite astonishing. It succeeded in several by-elections, and a survey in 1981 credited the party, together with the Liberals, with more than a third of the vote (Bogdanor 1981, 287). This alliance would have had a majority of the vote, though not of the parliamentary seats. Despite these important early successes, the party quickly ran into serious problems. King and Crewe (1991), for instance, enumerating possible causes for these problems, draw a depressing picture of the former SDP. The party only participated in two general elections, namely in 1983 and 1987. In both elections it formed an electoral alliance with the Liberal party.[25] It has disappeared meanwhile through a merger with the Liberals (Crewe and King 1995).

Conclusion

The three tales in this chapter hardly cover all possible situations in which a new party might appear or refrain from forming. In two of the chosen cases (Germany in the twenties and Great Britain in the eighties) a new party appeared quite quickly on the electoral scene. One of them, namely the NSDAP, started a crusade through the institutions of a democracy to undermine it and eventually destroy it from the inside. The other (the SDP) seemed able, at first, to fundamentally change the party system in which it emerged. The two new parties also distinguish themselves under another aspect. The first one had almost no personal ties to another party, while the second one clearly formed as a breakaway from an existing party, namely the Labour Party. In the remaining case (the Netherlands), a new party seemed, for a long time, hardly necessary and, therefore, failed to form rapidly.

The groups that stood behind the three new parties or potential new parties also distinguish themselves considerably. In two of the cases, the demands the groups voiced were either extreme or quite new. In the last one, the demands were much more moderate and can be placed at the center of an ideological scale.

The three tales differ also by the institutional environment in which they took place. In two cases, the electoral rules seemed to work very much in

---

24. Bogdanor (1981) discusses the barriers the SDP had to overcome in detail.

25. Given the exclusion of electoral alliances from my definition of new political parties under consideration, the question arises why I consider the SDP at all. My exclusion of electoral alliances as new parties only concerns the alliances themselves. The SDP, while participating in an electoral alliance, presented in 1983 for the first time candidates in a general election. In addition, the SDP was not an electoral alliance, but was part of one both for the 1983 and 1987 elections. For both elections it is possible to determine the SDP's electoral success, despite it having been achieved in an electoral alliance.

favor of the emergence of a new party. But only in one case (the NSDAP) did a new party appear rapidly. In the third tale, the electoral rules worked against new competitors. Despite these adverse conditions, the new challenger scored some surprising initial successes, only to fade and finally merge with an existing party.

Despite the many differences among the three tales, there exists a common thread. The formation of a new party, or its failure to form, appears to follow a similar process, which I attempted to highlight in this chapter. At the outset in all three tales a group of people is unhappy about some political issues. These may cover quite different problems in society. The questioning of democratic institutions, environmental problems, questions of European integration, or organizational problems in an existing party might all figure prominently on a list of neglected demands.

In all three tales, a potential new party attempts to voice its demands in one way or another. Quite precise demands appear in the public debate and are addressed to governments and existing political parties. In some cases these demands encounter favorable treatment from the political establishment, while in other cases the demands face outright rejection. In two of my tales (the German NSDAP and the British SDP), this rejection actually occurred, since the concerns of the groups were not sufficiently addressed by existing parties. As a result, NSDAP and SDP emerged quite quickly. In the Dutch case, both established parties and the government proved through their actions that they took the issues seriously, and consequently a Green party was very slow to emerge in the Netherlands.

While the process described in the previous paragraph gives a heavily stylized picture on new party formation, it appears to be shared by the three tales. This process seems to unravel largely independent of context, whether the resulting new party is genuinely new as in the first two tales or a fission as in the last tale. In the next chapter, I attempt to show that this picture finds considerable support in the literature on changes in party systems. Consequently, I will try to formalize this process in a theoretical model, which should allow me to gain additional and more focused insights into the emergence of new political parties.

CHAPTER 3

A Theoretical Model

There is a degree of consensus among students of new political parties that the presence of a neglected demand or a new issue is not on its own a sufficient reason for the emergence of a new actor on the electoral scene. This appears clearly in one of the tales of the previous chapter. Despite the early formation of an environmental consciousness in the Netherlands, a new party failed to emerge for some time. In the words of Rüdig (1990, 8) the "problem push" does not suffice; there also has to be an "opportunity pull" motivating the emergence of a new party. Hauss and Rayside (1978) claim that the crucial elements which influence this "opportunity pull" are political and institutional factors. As already discussed above, the way that these factors influence the formation of new political parties is not explained in most theoretical frameworks. I argue that they are important for understanding the emergence of new political challengers, given that these political and institutional factors are common to the formation process of all new political parties. These new parties must all overcome or take advantage of political and institutional "facilitators" (Hauss and Rayside 1978).

While several authors have explored the importance of these different "facilitators" on the empirical level (e.g., Hauss and Rayside 1978; Rosenstone, Behr, and Lazarus 1984; Harmel and Robertson 1985; Müller-Rommel 1993), they have partially neglected the questions of why the formation process is influenced and how it is influenced. My argument is that these authors, by focusing almost exclusively on new parties, have failed to appreciate the importance of preexisting parties. To understand more clearly the emergence of new parties, it is necessary to include established parties when designing the theoretical framework. Several authors have made attempts in this direction (Kitschelt 1988; Müller-Rommel 1993), but do not place the interaction between established parties and potential new parties in its strategic context. In particular, I will argue that such an inclusion will allow me to explain why the "opportunity pull" is important in the emergence of new parties. Furthermore, it will also enable me to unravel puzzles discussed above, which remain unsolved in the study of new political parties.

In this chapter, I propose a theoretical model for the study of new parties. It emphasizes the interaction between established parties and groups that contemplate forming a new party in a given polity. These potential challengers address neglected demands or new issues.[1] I argue that this interaction contains strategic elements, which are best addressed with the aid of a game-theoretic model.

The argument in favor of using a game-theoretic model for studying the emergence of new parties appears in the first section. The second section presents the theoretical model and discusses the assumptions upon which it is based. Several authors writing about party system change and the formation of new political parties implicitly support arguments which reinforce my assumptions. I will, therefore, use these statements to tie my model more closely to the substantive literature in both fields. The third section presents at an intuitive level the outcomes that may result in equilibrium in this model. Analyzing these possible outcomes and their respective likelihood yields several testable implications. I will present these implications in the fourth section and compare them to existing hypotheses in the literature. In the subsequent conclusion, I will summarize my theoretical findings and discuss criticisms that might be leveled against my model.

Interdependent Choices and Game-Theoretic Models

In the literature on comparative politics, game-theoretic models on the formation of new political parties are rare.[2] Consequently, I will first defend my choice of a game-theoretic model. As briefly mentioned above, I contend that a crucial element in the emergence of new parties is the behavior of the existing parties. Most authors agree on the importance of the way in which established parties in a polity react to a new demand or a new issue. They often assume, however, that this reaction is entirely determined by the internal characteristics of the parties (e.g., Koelble 1992) or by the parties' positions on the electoral scene (e.g., Kitschelt 1988; Müller-Rommel 1993). Koelble (1992) argues, for example, that the British Labour Party reacted differently to challenges than the West German Social Democrats. He explains these differences by the importance of the trade unions in the former party. Müller-Rommel (1993) argues that the composition of the government, at a time when environmental

1. Below, I will often use the term "new issues" to cover both aspects of the "problem push."

2. Levi and Hechter (1985) propose a rational choice model to study the rise of "ethnoregional political parties." Their model relies mostly on elements of the collective action literature, emphasizing the benefits which an ethnoregional party can offer. Kalyvas's (1996) study of the formation of Christian-democratic parties in five West European countries is much closer to my study. But since the emergence of these parties often went together with the formation of the party systems, the explanatory elements between his model and mine differ to some extent.

issues were becoming important, is essential to an explanation of the success of Green parties. In particular, when a social-democratic party was part of the government, he argues, it was less likely to react positively to these new demands.[3]

While agreeing that these are interesting arguments, I contend that they have to be considered more carefully in their strategic context. More precisely, individuals or groups which bring new demands such as environmental issues to the forefront are engaged in a strategic interaction with the established parties. The former would like the established parties to adapt their programs and integrate the new demands; the latter are confronted with the task of integrating these new demands, while simultaneously satisfying their voters and activists.[4] In such strategic situations, individual actions should not be considered in isolation, but understood in a larger context. The actions of a group defending a new issue are dependent on actions taken by the established parties. Consequently, the choices of the established parties and groups advocating new demands are interdependent. These interdependent choices often lead to unexpected outcomes which, by neglecting the strategic context, remain unintelligible or even undetectable by the researcher.[5]

Game-theoretic models, by directly addressing the issue of interdependent choices, allow the researcher to explore the consequences of these strategic interactions. And, in the study of new political parties, these interactions have largely been neglected. But some puzzles that remain in this field may find their answers in these unexpected consequences of interdependent choices. The choice of a game-theoretic model is further warranted by the fact that the interaction between established parties and their potential challengers takes place in a well-structured environment. Questions of access to the electoral process, of the criteria of forming parties, and of the appointment of candidates in elections, are largely determined by institutions. In such environments, game-theoretic models are especially well suited, since the choices available to the actors are relatively well defined.

A Game-Theoretic Model of Party Formation

In this section I will propose a theoretical model based on a game in exten-

---

3. Kitschelt (1988) makes a similar argument, when he relates the success of left-libertarian parties to the duration of social-democratic government participation.

4. In Koelble's (1991) work the most important element is the organizational level. He argues that trade unions have a considerable impact in the British Labour Party, while the unions in other European countries have much less influence on the social-democratic parties.

5. Dixit and Nalebuff (1991) illustrate this with a series of stimulating examples from different fields.

sive form. This model attempts to formalize the process that I have laid out by use of the three tales in the previous chapter. Therefore, I do not follow the tradition of game-theoretic models on candidate entry. These traditional models use almost exclusively models of spatial competition. As I showed above, these models do not easily lead to empirically relevant insights. Choosing an alternative formalization allows me to do precisely this. To present it, I will first outline its general thrust with arguments made in the substantive literature. Then, a more detailed and structured presentation of the model will follow, while its technical details and assumptions appear in the appendix for the interested reader.

The model attempts to capture a situation of strategic interaction in which two actors face each other, namely a group that I call potential new party and an established party.[6] The potential new party can be a social movement, a citizen initiative, a political entrepreneur, or even a group of members of an existing political party. It is characterized and defined by the fact that it has a new demand or a neglected issue that it would like to have addressed by the polity. It expresses these demands and hopes that they will be integrated by an existing party. This demand-making decision process is nicely discussed by a Green member of the European Parliament for France:

> From a political viewpoint, it is true that there were two strategies, which opposed each other for quite a long time until the Presidential Elections. The two suggestions were the following: form a movement and negotiate very quickly with the socialist party for some positions as elected officials or a participation in the Executive; or first form a strong movement and negotiate with several political parties, without priority for the Socialist Party; understood that the Front National was completely excluded. (Briquet, Courty, and Legarve 1990, 9, my translation)

This Green Eurodeputy describes how the ecological movement faced the decision as to whether to make a small demand and work quickly with the Socialist party, or to form a stronger movement and make a bigger demand. Such a decision would have a very important impact on the way the established parties would react to demands. I argue that the established party is faced, at any particular time, with many demands directed toward it. Every demand requires a decision from the established party, to accept it or to reject it. Such a decision is hardly easy. In an interesting contribution Mair (1983) addresses

6. In the conclusion of this chapter we shall discuss two underlying assumptions: Namely, that these two protagonists are unitary actors, and that the interaction between a potential new party and only one established party is sufficient to address the issues that interest us.

> the question of whether certain parties are more 'adaptable' than others, and indeed whether certain issues or conflicts are more capable of being adapted than others. Further, insofar as the notion of adaptation suggests that the response of parties can help determine whether issues or conflicts will be contained within an existing area rather than emerging to affect inter-area competition, it is then a notion that takes us back to the centrality of party per se, as well as to the identification of further parameters. (Mair 1983, 414)

The question of "adaptability" has become increasingly important with respect to recent challenges to the established party systems. Several authors argue that parties sometimes fail (Lawson and Merkl 1988) and do not integrate issues or demands that are important among the public. Mair (1983) frames the question of party failure within a larger context, linking it to the relationship that parties entertain with other non-electoral organizations:

> [P]arties should be seen not as being in complete control of the political agenda, but rather as sharing that control with other, non-electoral, organizations. The key question then becomes the degree of linkage that exists between the parties and the various non-electoral alternatives, and therefore the degree to which the parties indirectly augment their own specific control. . . . This sharing of roles presents no problems for the parties as long as these latter organizations are linked to them in some way. A weakening of these links, however, and/or the emergence of new, non-party associated organizations, and/or a weakening of the agenda-setting role of those associated non-electoral organizations that do exist, could imply a challenge to the hold of party systems on the mass public. (Mair 1983, 420f)

So the task of deciding whether to accept or reject a demand is far from being trivial. I argue that one reason for this is that the judgment of the importance of new demands is quite difficult on the electoral level. In particular, established parties rarely know how much damage they might suffer should they fail to integrate a particular demand into their political program. It is unclear to them how big the electoral losses would be, should a new party form. So they face some uncertainty about the importance of new demands.

Sjöblom (1983), while discussing an inventory of reasons as to why the accountability of parties might weaken, formulates three hypotheses:

- The larger the number of issues, the more unpredictable is the agenda-setting.

- The larger the number of actors who influence the agenda-setting, the more unpredictable will be the result.

- The greater the unpredictability of the agenda-setting, the greater will be the strategic uncertainty of the parties. (Sjöblom 1983, 389f)

Sjöblom argues that the increase of the number of issues is very much linked to the growing importance of the public sector and, consequently, he limits its impact on the more recent history of our societies. But his hypotheses apply much more widely in democratic polities. Political parties always face a series of issues that appear to be important in the electorate. They find themselves almost permanently in a situation of uncertainty, never knowing precisely which of these different issues will become important. A case in point for this comes with the example of the rise of the NSDAP in the Weimar Republic, which I discussed above. Hebel-Kunze (1977, 58ff) documents the position of the social-democratic party toward the NSDAP, by citing Kautsky:

> In order to exert a political influence, the Fascists would have to appear in great number – about half a million in Italy out of a population of 39 million. In Germany, to reach these proportions, they would need to be one million. In an industrialized country it is impossible to find so many scoundrels in their best man years for such a capitalistic goal. In Italy the conditions were especially favorable for Fascism. . . . (cited in Hebel-Kunze 1977, 58, my translation)

This shows that in the Weimar Republic parties were uncertain about the support the NSDAP enjoyed in the population (Kershaw 1999, 25). It also rejoins the argument made above, that established parties underestimated the strength of the future Nazi party. Consequently, I assume that the established party, when making its decision, is always in a situation of uncertainty, while the potential new party has slightly more information on how much success it would have, should it form a new party. The uncertainty faced by the established party is also neatly illustrated by Schoonmaker's (1988) contribution on the formation of the Green party in Germany:

> In the mid-1970s, the leaders of the traditional parties saw their power waning, but most felt, or hoped, that the protest groups would follow the usual surge and decline cycle. (48)

While most authors would agree that the established party has to make decisions in an environment of uncertainty, the question arises about whether the potential new party has more information on its own strength in comparison. It might well be that, through surveys, the established party could obtain accurate information concerning potential challengers. A good example to this effect comes from Pridham (1988, 236):

> There had been poll evidence of strong potential interest in, if not demand for, a "center party" before the SDP was founded, and even before the Dimbleby lecture. As far back as 1972, a poll commissioned by *The Times* indicated that a center force linking Jenkins-led Labour moderates with the Liberals would be likely to cut deeply into the Labour Party's electorate, by 44 percent. In January 1980, the same paper that had been monitoring potential center-party support (and also promoting its cause), published a detailed survey showing continuing strong sympathy for a center party (54 percent would welcome the formation of a center party, combining the interest in differently composed versions of it), although there was also a fragmentation of this passive consensus when it came to the possibility of actually voting for one version over another. (*The Times*, Jan. 17, 1980)

This might very well prove to be a striking counter-example, challenging my game-theoretic assumption. But I would argue that both the established party and the potential new party, in this case the Labour Party and the future SDP, had exactly the same information concerning this poll. This poll was published, and was consequently accessible to everybody. Furthermore, it is very likely that the leaders of what was to become the SDP knew more about how many people would follow their lead out of the Labour Party and how much support they might garner. The same also holds for the case discussed by Schoonmaker (1988). The tight networks that exist in ecological movements allow the leaders to gain considerable information concerning their strength. This type of information, contrary to well-publicized polls, is very likely to be private and accessible only to the movements. Consequently, I assume that the established parties are at a disadvantage with respect to this type of information, in comparison to the potential new parties.

This can have important consequences, as was the case with the German Greens. From the eyes of most authors who wrote about this case, which was also discussed by Schoonmaker (1988), the traditional parties failed to adopt the demands of the protest groups.[7] Interestingly enough, only after the German Green party was actually formed, did they finally realize how important these demands were:

---

7. Von Oppeln (1989) illustrates this very convincingly in her study of the nuclear protest movement in Hessen.

> The massive demonstrations against the building of nuclear facilities began at Whyl in 1975 and continued for the next six years. . . . By the beginning of the 1980s, the Green movement was poised for a national party organization. The citizen initiative movement had galvanized a sizable number of young citizens, recruited disillusioned established party members, and developed the groundwork of an interlocking network of political action groups which felt that the winds of democratization and decentralization were in their sails. The traditional parties were slowly realizing that an increasingly large number of very active citizens were putting the brakes on further industrialization. (Schoonmaker 1988, 49)

By that time the Green party had already been formed, in part because the traditional parties had rejected the demands of the protest groups, or according to my terminology, of a potential new party. This implies that once the established party has decided to reject a demand, the potential new party can decide whether it will go ahead and form a new party.

The main thrust of my game-theoretic model can thus be summarized in the following way: A potential new party makes a demand. The demand can be either a high or a low one. The established party either accepts or rejects the demand, but it has to reach its decision without knowing precisely how strong the potential new party is. If the established party rejects the demand, the potential new party decides whether or not it wants to form a new party. I first represent this simple model in Figure 3.1 on a time line. To represent the uncertainty under which the established party has to decide whether to accept the demand formulated by the potential new party, I depict a move by nature determining the strength of the latter actor.[8] The potential new party can either be a strong or a weak challenger. The established party has some prior knowledge about the probability of facing a weak or a strong challenger, but ignores the exact strength of its opponent.

Assumptions

To give this model more precise meaning, I now turn to a more formal description of its structure and underlying assumptions. Figure 3.2 depicts the model as a game tree, where actors take a sequence of actions (Table 3.1). Since one of my central assumptions is that the established party makes its decision as to whether to integrate a new demand under uncertainty, the model is a game of incomplete information. I model this with the assumption that the potential

8. This is a convention in game theoretic work, which allows for representation of the uncertainty of actors involved in a strategic interaction. It corresponds to the so-called Harsanyi transformation of a game (Fudenberg and Tirole 1991, 209ff).

Fig. 3.1. A model of new party formation

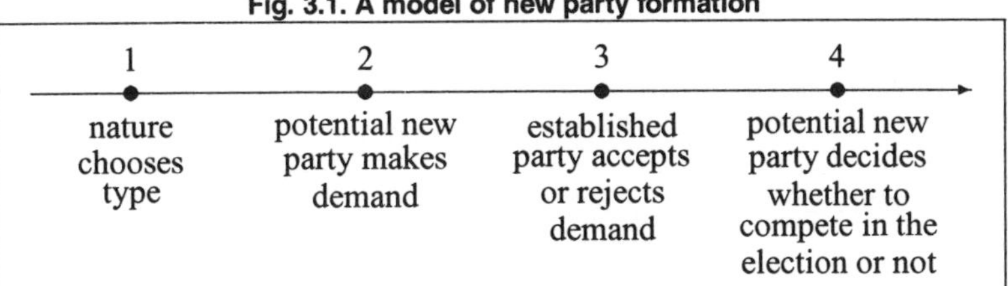

new party can be either strong or weak.[9] Its strength is determined according to how much harm it could cause the established party should it form a party and fight an electoral battle. As noted above, I represent this uncertainty by letting one actor called Nature (N)[10] decide whether the potential new party is a strong or a weak type. Nature chooses a strong type (s) with probability $b(s)$[11] and a weak type (w) with probability $1 - b(s)$. This first action is represented by two lines starting at an open circle in the middle of the game tree (Figure 3.2). The potential new party (P) knows its strength (s or w) and on the basis of this knowledge decides whether to make a high (h) or a low (l) demand.

Without knowing which type it faces, the established party (E) has to decide whether to accept (a) or reject (r) the demand. This uncertainty of the established party is reflected in figure 3.2 by the dashed lines connecting its decision nodes.[12] They imply that the established party does not know whether it takes its action in the upper or lower part of the game tree after a high or low demand has been made. It will have some beliefs about the likelihood of each eventuality, and only under very special circumstances will it know with certainty whether it faces a strong or a weak challenger.

If the established party accepts the demand the game ends and no new party appears on the electoral scene. If, on the contrary, the established party rejects the demand, the potential new party (P) can either challenge the decision or acquiesce. If it challenges the decision of the established party, it will form a new party and compete in the next election. If it acquiesces, it refrains from entering the electoral arena. After this decision, the game ends and payoffs are distributed. Implicitly, since some payoffs depend on the occurrence

9. In another model (Hug 1996) I assume that the types come from a continuous distribution. While some differences appear in the results, the general thrust of the substantive insights are similar to the ones obtained with the model employed in this study.

10. The abbreviations used for the actors and their respective actions appear in table 3.1.

11. I have used $b(s)$ to denote this probability, since it is equivalent to the prior belief the established party holds. Since this prior belief is shared with the potential new party, I do not subscript it. Below I will consistently use $b_{.}(.)$ for beliefs and $p_{.}(.)$ for strategies of the two actors.

12. In game-theoretic terms the dashed lines in figure 3.2 represent information sets.

TABLE 3.1. Actors and actions in the game

Actors and actions		
N	Nature	
	s	chooses strong type
	w	chooses weak type
P	Potential new party	
	h	makes high demand
	l	makes low demand
E	Established party	
	a	accepts demand
	r	rejects demand
P	Potential new party	if E rejects demand
	a	acquiesces
	c	challenges and forms new party

of an electoral bout, an additional stage corresponds to an election. But since this last stage only determines the payoffs, I can drop it without any further consequences.

The general structure of the game has now been described. Important remaining elements of the game are the payoffs associated with the different outcomes. Instead of characterizing the 16 possible outcomes of the game, I will discuss directly the respective payoffs for the two players. I derive these payoffs analytically, by discussing the consequences of each outcome. In figure 3.2 the payoffs of the established party are shown at the top of each terminal node,[13] while the ones of the potential new party figure at the bottom. For both players, the payoffs are normalized to equal zero if a costless demand by the potential new party is rejected and it decides to acquiesce.

The payoffs of the potential new party include both benefits and costs. The benefits stem either from the satisfaction gained by an accepted demand or from the electoral success after the formation of a new party. If the established party accepts a demand the potential new party gets a benefit of b_h or b_l for respectively a high or low demand. If a new party is created, the benefits for the potential new party are either b_s, if it is a strong type, or b_w, if it is a weak type. I assume that these four benefits for the new party are related in the following way:

13. Terminal nodes distinguish themselves from decision nodes by the fact that arrows point toward them.

Fig. 3.2. Extensive form of model of party formation

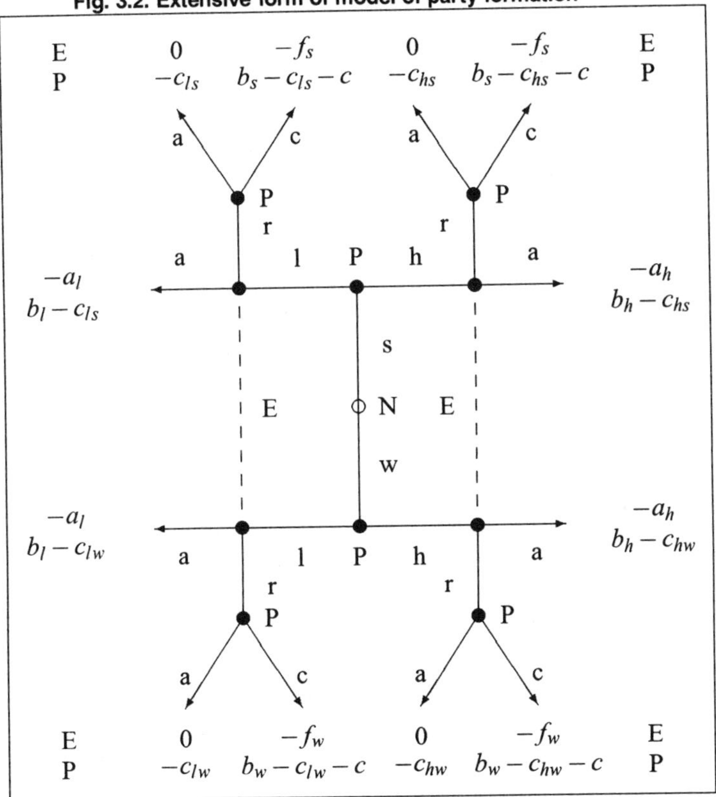

Assumption 1

$$0 < b_w < b_l < b_s < b_h \tag{3.1}$$

Before discussing the implications of this assumption I will discuss another element of the payoffs of the potential new party, namely the costs it has to bear. Among these costs, one of the most important is the cost of forming a new party (c). In almost all countries a new party has to bear some costs when it forms. They include administrative costs, fulfilments of certain administrative requirements, collection of signatures, or even monetary deposits to be able to propose candidates for an election. I assume that these costs are the same for both types. The second type of costs, which a potential new party must bear, are the costs of making demands. I include these costs because I assume that the established party will not listen to demands which do not cause some costs to the potential new party.[14] If it was to pay attention to such demands, even single individuals could make demands and attract as much attention as a demand supported by a huge group. Hence, the potential new party has to somehow show its strength; this will imply costs. On the substantive level these costs reflect such factors as the effort necessary to stage a big demonstration or to file a petition, etc. Such costs clearly vary according to both the demands a potential new party makes and its strength. Making a small demand, involving only minor changes in the platform of an existing party, requires much less effort than an attempt to completely modify such a platform. Signatures for petitions are more easily obtained, and the recruitment of demonstrators causes fewer problems. Similarly, if a potential new party is very strong, staging a big demonstration is not as costly as it would be for a weak type. Then it would only need to mobilize its most active supporters in order to stage a sizable demonstration. Hence, I advance the following assumption concerning the costs of making demands:

Assumption 2

$$0 < c_{ls} < c_{hs} < c_{lw} < c_{hw} \tag{3.2}$$

The cost that a strong type bears when making a low demand (c_{ls}) is the smallest one. If the same type makes a high demand (c_{hs}), the costs are slightly larger. The costs for the weaker type are even larger, as can be seen in assumption 2.[15]

The payoffs of the established party include two types of costs. The first one stems from the acceptance of demands: a_h and a_l represent, respectively, the costs of accepting a high or a low demand. Fighting a challenger in an election makes up the second cost: f_s and f_w represent, respectively, the costs of fighting a strong or a weak challenger. I assume that the four costs interrelate in the following way:

Assumption 3

$$0 < a_l < f_w < a_h < f_s \tag{3.3}$$

---

14. Schoonmaker's (1988) account of the way established parties reacted to the demonstrations of the anti-nuclear movement illustrates and supports this assumption.

15. In the appendix I introduce three additional assumptions which are of a more technical nature. In addition I discuss the consequences of changing these assumptions.

This assumption has several implications. First, both fighting a new party in an election and integrating new demands is costly. The appearance of a new party on the electoral scene most often implies a loss of voters to the established party. Furthermore, the established party will use resources to minimize these losses during the campaign. The integration of new demands is costly because it often alienates voters or activists of the established party. Almost no new issues or demands can be integrated into an existing platform without putting other issues into question, and thus making some members of the party unhappy. Second, if the established party knows for sure how strong the potential new party is, it would accept both high and low demands made by the strong type, but only low demands from the weak type.[16]

Results and Outcomes

The game tree presented above, together with the assumptions 1-3, define a simple signaling model with costly signals.[17] The potential new party, by making costly demands, attempts to signal some information to the established party about its strength. As we will see below, sometimes these signals are informative, and sometimes they are deceptive for the established party.

An important advantage of game theoretic models consists in enabling us to derive equilibrium outcomes and pinpointing the assumptions that lead to them. Based on this it is possible to gain considerable insights into the mechanisms that lead to certain outcomes. In presenting the results of my model I will proceed exactly in this fashion. In this section I will first discuss what would happen in this game under the assumption that the established party is perfectly informed about the strength of the potential new party. Then I will go on to present the equilibrium outcomes under the assumption that the established party is uncertain about the strength of the potential challenger. A comparison between these two sets of outcomes shows the importance of the assumption of uncertainty. In the next section I will then proceed to analyze in detail the crucial variables that affect the likelihood of one of these outcomes, namely the emergence of a new political party. This allows me to derive testable implications about the emergence of new challengers on the electoral scene.

---

16. It would accept high demands made by the weak type if $a_h < f_w$.

17. Banks (1991) discusses " [s]ignaling Games in Political Science" in his very instructive book.

Outcomes under Complete Information

A major conclusion from the complete information version of my model is that new parties should never form.[18] This follows rather directly from the assumptions concerning the payoff structure. If both the weak and strong type can credibly threaten to form a new party, the established party will accept both of their demands. The weak type will make low demands, while the strong type formulates high demands. Consequently, there is no reason to form a new party. If the costs of forming a new party exceed the benefits a weak type can expect, its demand will be rejected. It will make a low demand, but in that situation it cannot credibly threaten to form a new party. Consequently, after its demand is rejected the weak type will back down and not form a new party. This mechanism is behind the credibility of a weak new challenger. I will use this notion throughout this study to describe situations where the benefits a weak challenger expects from forming a new party exceed the costs. If this is the case a weak challenger is said to be credible, while it fails to be so in all other cases. The strong type, on the other hand, is by assumption always credible. In the complete information equilibrium its high demand is accepted by the established party, and thus, it has no incentive to form a new party.

This result reflects in some ways the observation made by Lipset and Rokkan (1967) when they studied European party systems in the late sixties. They observed that most party systems of the sixties largely reflected the cleavage structures of the twenties. But they also noted that the issues these parties addressed have largely changed. The two authors seem to have described a situation where established parties successfully integrated demands that came from the outside. They seem to have done this with such success that the need to form a new party was never felt by potential new parties. This empirical observation led the authors to formulate the widely cited "freezing hypothesis." But some authors have challenged this hypothesis (Maguire 1983; Shamir 1984), and some have even found numerous new parties appearing in these "frozen" party systems (Janda 1980; Harmel and Robertson 1985).[19]

Outcomes under Incomplete Information

Since new parties are an empirical fact, it is obvious that the complete information version of my model fails to accurately reflect reality. Consequently, the assumption that the established party has only partial information on the

18. The following discussion of results is based on proposition 1 appearing in the appendix. There, the interested reader can also find the technical derivations of these results.

19. Bartolini and Mair (1990) provide a longer-term perspective on the electoral volatility in Europe and qualify some of these findings.

strength of potential challengers is likely to play a crucial role.[20] To explore this path I will proceed to an analysis of the incomplete information version of the model. Any difference between the previous results and the insights gained below can be attributed to the presence of uncertainty on the side of the established party. Consequently, the results of the complete information should be kept in mind and serve as a benchmark for what follows. In addition, the crucial distinction between cases where a weak challenger can credibly threaten to form a new party and those cases where it cannot carries partly over to the incomplete information version of my model.

If a weak challenger is credible, the established party will always accept low demands, even under incomplete information.[21] Consequently, if a challenger makes only a low demand, the established party will accept it and no new party will form. It follows immediately that new parties can only appear after a rejected high demand. This implies that the formation of new parties hinges almost completely on the decision of the established party to accept high demands. Obviously, given the established party's uncertainty, the decision to accept a high demand depends on its beliefs about the likelihood of facing a strong challenger. If the established party thinks that it is very likely to face a strong party it will accept all high demands. This obviously has consequences both for weak and strong challengers. Both will always make high demands and happily agree to refrain from forming a new party, since their demands are accepted by the established party.

In situations where the likelihood of facing a strong challenger is smaller, the established party does not accept all high demands. With a certain probability it will reject such demands to deter weak challengers from bluffing and making high demands. This leads the weak challengers to refrain from systematically bluffing and to make high demands only with a certain probability. Consequently, in these situations where strong challengers are not too frequent, both strong and weak new parties emerge after facing the rejection of a high demand.

A similar structure of possible outcomes appears in cases where the weak potential new party would never form a new party because the costs for doing

---

20. It might also be the case that either the structure of the model or the payoffs are inappropriate. The three tales of chapter 2 and the theoretical support discussed in this chapter seem to contradict the claim that the structure of the game is misspecified. Concerning the payoff structure it might be that I assumed inaccurate orderings. However, in the appendix I show that under complete information new parties appear only if the payoff structure presents very counterintuitive characteristics. For instance, if the costs of making a low demand exceed those of a high demand, new parties become possible in equilibrium, but such a payoff structure is difficult to justify from a substantive viewpoint.

21. See proposition 2 in the appendix.

so are excessively high.[22] But in these cases the established party rejects all low demands and, obviously, weak new parties never form. Consequently, the formation of a new party depends again on whether the established party accepts high demands. Again the acceptance of such demands depends on the likelihood that the established party is facing a strong challenger. If this likelihood is high, the established party accepts all high demands and no new parties will form. Obviously, the assured acceptance of high demands leads the weak challengers to always bluff and make such demands. If the likelihood of facing a strong challenger is lower, the established party will again accept high demands only probabilistically. This leads strong potential new parties to always make high demands and weak challengers to make such demands only probabilistically. But after a rejection of a high demand, only strong new parties will decide to form, since the costs outweigh the benefits for weak challengers.

Summary

I summarize these outcomes in figure 3.3. In equilibrium, my model can yield three different sets of outcomes, which appear in the three boxes to the right. No new parties will ever appear if the established party is perfectly informed about the strength of a challenger, or if the likelihood of a strong challenger is very high. These two necessary conditions for the event of no new parties appear in the two boxes in the upper left corner of figure 3.3. An immediate consequence of a high probability of strong challengers is that the established party accepts all high demands (middle column in figure 3.3). The end effect of this is that no new parties appear.

A second set of outcomes consists of the emergence of only strong new parties. Necessary conditions for this outcome comprise the uncertainty of the established party, the lower probability of facing a strong challenger, and the lack of credibility of the weak challenger (leftmost boxes in the middle row of figure 3.3). The first two conditions lead the established party to reject high demands with a certain probability. If the high demand of a strong challenger faces rejection, the result is the emergence of a strong new party. Weak challengers, given their lack of credibility, will refrain from forming a new party. This leads the established party to reject all low demands (central boxes in the middle row of figure 3.3).

A final set of outcomes consists of the emergence of both weak and strong new parties. This can only occur if the established party is uncertain, strong challengers are not too likely, and weak challengers can credibly threaten to

---

22. See proposition 3 in the appendix.

form a new party (boxes in the lower section of figure 3.3). The uncertainty and the smaller probability of facing a strong challenger lead the established party to reject high demands with a certain probability. The weak challenger's credibility, however, motivates the established party to accept all low demands (boxes at the bottom of the middle column of figure 3.3). The rejection of some strong demands leads to the formation of both weak and strong new parties.

Fig. 3.3. Necessary conditions for the formation of new political parties

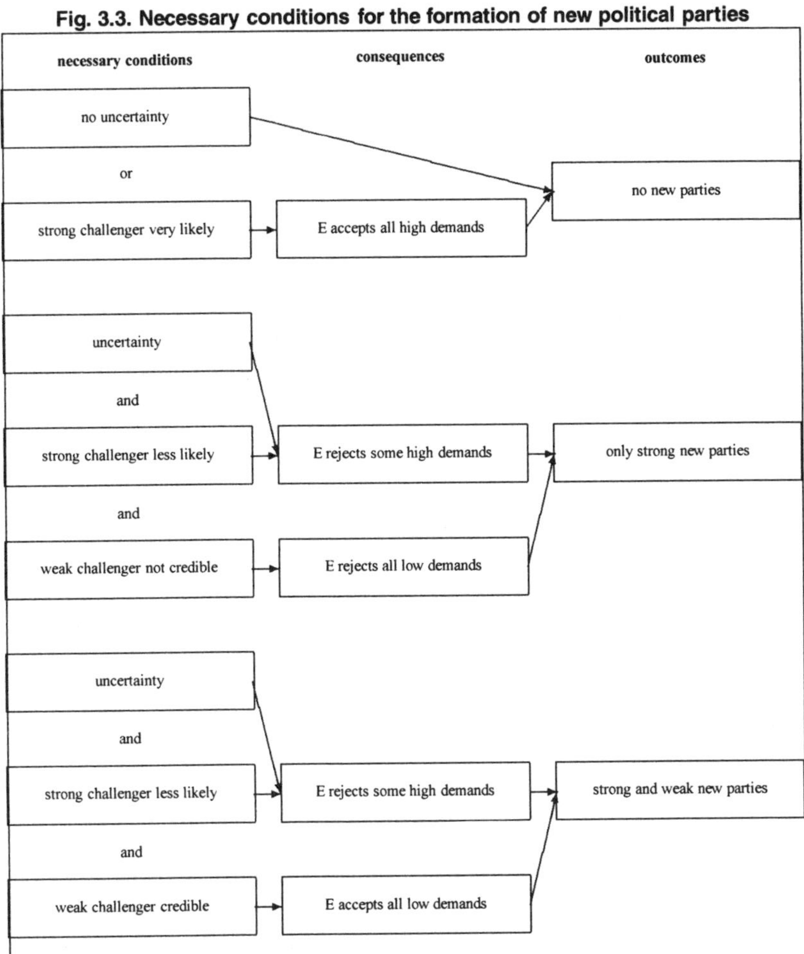

Based on this analysis of the necessary conditions, the formation of new political parties can be traced back to the interaction among three elements. (1) *the prior belief of facing a strong challenger*. This belief cannot be too high for new parties to emerge. (2) *the credibility of weak new challengers.* If the formation costs exceed the benefits weak challengers can expect, the latter will never form new parties. (3) *the likelihood that the established party will reject a high demand.* These three elements interact and determine the emergence of new parties. They also depend on theoretical variables that I discussed when presenting the payoff structure of the game. Consequently, the likelihood of new parties can be traced back to these theoretical variables.

Implications

Since these three central elements determining the emergence of new political parties interact strongly in my game theoretical model it is of little use to look at them directly. It is more interesting to study the effect of the theoretical variables on the likelihood of new parties emerging. These effects work through the three central elements discussed at the end of the last section, but interact with each other. Consequently, I will discuss here a series of implications which link the likelihood of the emergence of new parties with theoretical variables. These implications stem from comparative statics analyses of my model.[23] In such analyses researchers check how changes in particular variables, e.g. the costs of forming a new party, affect the likelihood of a particular outcome, e.g. the formation of a new party.

Some of the implications that derive from my model clearly rejoin familiar arguments in the literature on new political parties, some render more precise such insights, while still others are in stark contrast to existing theories. I will present only the most important insights here. These most often allow for easy links with the existing literature on new political parties. They all revolve around five theoretical variables, which explicitly or implicitly appear in the literature on new political parties. Before presenting these variables and their link to the emergence of new parties in more detail, I will briefly enumerate them.

First, it appears that the importance of new issues plays a crucial role in the formation of new political parties. Countries with a series of unresolved political problems should see more new parties, all else being equal. Second, the costs a new party has to bear when emerging considerably diminish the number of new challengers on the electoral scene. Third, if important demands that are accepted by the established party yield substantial benefits to the potential new party, the emergence of challengers increases. Fourth, new parties appear more frequently when the costs of fighting a challenger are high. Fifth, the benefits that a weak new party can expect from its participation in an election

23. The technical details of these analyses appear in the appendix

relate positively to the probability of party formation.

Some of these relationships between theoretical variables and the emergence of new parties appear to be trivial or simply rephrasing well-established hypotheses in the literature. By focusing on the strategic nature of the interaction between potential new party and established party, however, my theoretical framework enriches these relationships. First, my model shows precisely the mechanisms which link the theoretical variables with the emergence of new parties. As I showed above these mechanisms are rarely specified in the existing literature on new political parties. Second, some of the relationships presented briefly above undergo changes under certain circumstances due to the strategic nature of the interaction. More precisely, some relationships should fail to materialize if a weak potential new party cannot credibly threaten to form a new party. The credibility of a potential new party depends on the formation costs and the benefits it can expect from participating at an election, as discussed above. Since the established party observes both these elements according to my theoretical model, it knows whether a weak new party is credible, that is whether the benefits exceed the costs. Consequently, the established party can condition its decisions on the credibility of the weak new parties. Then my model highlights an interaction between the credibility of new parties and some theoretical explanatory variables. Below I will present in more detail this interaction and the mechanisms underlying the implications of my model.

New Issues Favor New Parties

Among the implications that find support in arguments in the literature appears the relationship between the importance of new issues and the emergence of new parties. The increasing importance of new issues has two main consequences according to my theoretical model. First, the established party anticipates that its opponent is more likely to be a strong challenger. Consequently, it will tend to accept demands more frequently, which makes new parties less likely. Second, and more importantly, this increased willingness on the parts of the established parties to accept important demands encourages even weak groups to make such demands. To diminish the risk of being exploited, established parties must reject at least some demands. These two consequences, taken together, render it more likely that new parties will emerge.

Implication 1 *When new issues become more important, the likelihood of new parties emerging increases. In addition, new parties are more often of the stronger type, provided that the weak potential new parties pose no credible threat.*

The first part of the implication, while being a central insight, is hardly exciting and finds its counterpart in most accounts of new political parties.[24] As new issues become more important, most authors argue, new parties are more likely to appear.[25] My framework adds, however, the insight that this relationship does not depend on the credibility of weak challengers. Whether weak potential new parties are credible or not, the increasing importance of new issues should favor the emergence of new parties.

Of more interest in this respect is the second part of the implication, which relates the importance of new issues to the initial strength of new parties. While most authors argue that the success of new parties is a simple function of the importance of new issues (e.g., Kitschelt 1988; Harmel and Robertson 1985; Müller-Rommel 1993), my model allows for a more precise implication. In fact, if weak potential new parties are not credible threats to the established party, the average strength of new parties should decrease with more important new issues. This goes squarely against stances on new political parties in the literature.

The reason for this counterintuitive result stems from the fact that weak potential new parties are tempted to make big demands if new issues become more prominent. This tendency to ask for bigger policy changes leads to more rejections by the established party. And among the groups whose demands were rejected one finds increasingly weak challengers. If they emerge on the electoral scene, they automatically decrease the average strength of new political parties.

Formation Costs Hinder New Parties

Apart from determining the credibility of weak new parties, the formation costs have a distinct and direct effect on the likelihood of new challengers appearing on the electoral scene. If such costs increase, a logical consequence is that the emergence of new parties becomes less likely. The argument behind this assertion is simply that bluffing becomes much more risky. While some weak potential new parties might still ask for considerable policy changes, this course of action can have rather negative results. Some weak groups might have to back down if their bluff is called. In addition, as formation costs increase, the likelihood that an established party accepts a high demand becomes higher. This is because it anticipates that high demands are increasingly made by the strong challengers. Consequently, this increased acceptance also dimin-

24. The encouraging part of this implication, is that my theoretical model probably rejoins the most important stance in the literature on new political parties.

25. A discussion of the relevant literature appears in chapters 1 and 2.

ishes the likelihood of party formation. But for this relationship the credibility of weak potential new parties exercises a secondary effect. If, from the start, some weak groups could under no circumstances form beneficially a new party, increasing the formation costs does not alter the likelihood of a challenger appearing on the electoral scene.

Implication 2 *If the weak potential new party is a credible challenger, higher costs of forming a party decrease the likelihood of new parties emerging. If the weak type is not a credible challenger, changes in the costs of forming a new party do not alter the likelihood of new parties emerging.*

Again, the first part of the implication finds parallels in the literature on new parties. Costs of ballot access figure prominently among explanatory variables for the formation of new parties (e.g., Hauss and Rayside 1978; Rosenstone, Behr, and Lazarus 1984).[26] My implication predicts, however, that this only holds if weak potential new parties are credible challengers. If they fail to be credible, changing costs do not influence the emergence of new parties. In addition, these costs do not have a direct impact on the strength of new parties. These additional insights gained from my theoretical model render well-established hypotheses much more precise.

Benefits from Important Demands Stimulate Party Formation

Up to now our attention has focused on the decision of a group to form a new party. This decision, according to my theoretical model, occurs only after established parties have rejected a demand. But in the case of an accepted demand, a group that makes policy demands also experiences benefits. The policies it cares about become part of a party manifesto and might even be enacted and lead to policy changes. The importance of these benefits also influences the likelihood that new parties form. More precisely, if these benefits increase, which would stem from policy changes adopted by established parties, it becomes more likely that new parties will appear. This counterintuitive result is again based in the uncertainty the established party faces, and which induces rival groups to bluff. In the case of higher benefits, these groups are tempted to make more important demands. But the changes in the benefits have no incidence on the likelihood that an established party accepts a demand. Hence, bluffs would be called more frequently, which would increase the expected number of new parties. While the first effect results in the emergence of fewer

26. Interestingly, Harmel and Robertson (1985, 506) hypothesize that countries with easy ballot access should favor the success of new parties, but not influence the emergence of new parties.

strong new parties, the second leads to an increase in the number of weaker ones.

Implication 3 *If the satisfaction derived from integrated high demands increases, new parties become more frequent and tend to be increasingly of the weaker type, provided the latter can form a new party. If they are not a credible threat, new parties tend to be stronger on average.*

Given that this result is strongly counterintuitive, it is no surprise that no parallel exists in the literature on new political parties. Only claims relating federalism with the emergence of new parties come close to the present implication. Chandler and Chandler (1987) argue that in federal systems new parties can count on higher benefits, since the access to power is quicker. In chapter 5 I will come back to this claim, when I will propose empirical tests of my theoretical model.

Fighting Costs Make Parties More Likely

Following the theoretical arguments presented above, an important factor is whether established parties face important costs, when a new party appears on the electoral scene. If these costs increase, it is clear that established parties will more often accept demands, and, consequently, they will frequently modify their programs. This might reflect what happened in the Dutch case discussed in chapter 2. Since the established parties are so vulnerable, due to the low electoral thresholds, they are under much more intense pressure to integrate new issues into their programs. But this higher propensity to accept demands leads weak groups to bluff and to formulate important demands. And again, the established party cannot accept all of them, so that on average new parties become more likely.

An important qualification of this expected relationship concerns the credibility of weak potential new parties. It might be that demands of weaker groups are more likely to face rejection. But if for these weaker groups the formation costs exceed the expected benefits of forming a new party, they will refrain from entering the electoral scene. Hence, if the established parties become more vulnerable, the formation of new parties becomes more frequent only if formation costs are relatively low or benefits for weak new parties high.

Implication 4 *As the established party becomes more vulnerable on the electoral scene, the likelihood of new weak parties appearing increases, as long as they are credible, while there is no impact on the likelihood of strong parties emerging.*

The vulnerability of existing parties is related in part to the electoral system. If electoral thresholds are low, established parties have to fight much harder to keep new challengers at bay. Consequently, the implication predicts that new parties are more numerous if electoral thresholds diminish. This is again a claim that is omnipresent in the literature on new parties. Concerning the strength of new parties it predicts, however, that lower thresholds lead on average to weaker new parties. That claim is hard to find in the literature and contradicts most other theoretical frameworks used for the study of new political parties. One has to note, however, that this claim only holds for the initial strength of the new party. In addition, since my model does not address the issue of strategic voting, the effect of electoral systems on voting behavior is not included. I will discuss these problems in more detail later in chapter 6.

Electoral Benefits for Weak New Parties Favor their Emergence

Another reason for "entry" can lie in the benefits that a potential new party expects from participating at an election. My theoretical model suggests that increasing the benefits of an electoral participation would lead to the formation of more new parties. As these benefits increase, it would become more likely that, for a given group, the benefits of forming a new party will exceed the costs of such an endeavor. Additionally, as these benefits increase, the established party accepts less often high demands. It does so in order to deter more effectively the weak potential new parties from bluffing and making high demands. But again, if the formation costs are already quite high and discourage an important number of potential challengers from making demands, an increase in the benefits does not affect the likelihood that new parties will be formed. Consequently, the relationship only holds if weak potential new challengers are credible.

Implication 5 *If the benefits for a weak new party increase, new parties become more frequent, provided the latter can form a new party.*

Since the benefits of weak new parties are very much related to the costs established parties have to bear when fighting a new challenger in the electoral arena, the last two implications are very close. Again, the benefits of a weak challenger are likely to be higher in countries with low electoral thresholds. Hence, new parties should become more frequent in countries with low thresholds.

Fig. 3.4. Explaining the formation of new political parties

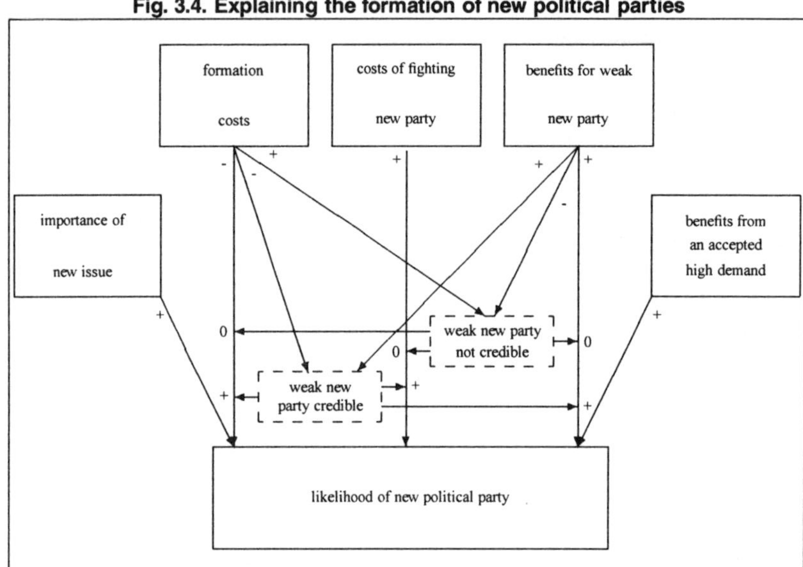

Summary of Empirical Implications

I summarize the implications discussed above in figure 3.4. All explanatory factors are linked to the likelihood of new political parties. But these links are not always simple and direct. Some relationships depend on a crucial factor, namely whether weak challengers can credibly threaten to form a new party. This is only the case if the formation costs do not exceed the benefits a weak new party can expect from competing in an election. Hence, as shown in figure 3.4 increasing the formation costs diminishes the credibility of weak potential new parties. Conversely, increasing the benefits for weak new parties increases the credibility of weak new challengers. On its turn, the credibility of weak potential new parties, or the absence thereof, influences relationships between explanatory factors and the likelihood of new parties. Since this credibility is only an intervening variable, it appears in a dashed box in figure 3.4. All explanatory variables appear in the upper half of the figure in simple boxes. Arrows link these variables with the intervening variable or the likelihood of a new political party. The signs of the predicted relationships appear next to the respective arrows. Some of these relationships change due to the credibility of the weak potential new party. If this credibility lacks, three relationships should fail to materialize. I depict this by a 0 appearing next to arrows leading from the intervening variable to arrows representing relationships. A plus sign

(+) on the other hand shows that the underlying relationship is unaltered by the credibility of the weak potential new party.

My theoretical framework, based on some simple assumptions, stresses the importance of several crucial explanatory factors for the emergence of new political parties. But it also shows that it is not sufficient to look at these factors separately, which is almost standard procedure in the literature on new political parties. Several elements that contribute to the explanation of new political parties are tightly intertwined. Looking at them separately, like for instance the numerous instances where the electoral system is correlated with the frequency and the success of new political parties, often leads to doubtful insights. Hence, my theoretical framework provides guiding lines for more interesting empirical explorations into the reasons for the emergence of new political parties.

Conclusion

I conclude this chapter with a brief summary of my theoretical model. I will highlight its crucial assumptions and discuss two important criticisms that can be leveled against it. They concern, on the one hand, the structure of the game, and, on the other, the definition of the actors in the game.

My theoretical model tries to explain why, and under what circumstances, new political parties emerge in existing party systems. To find an answer, one has to look at the strategic interactions in which established parties find themselves with respect to potential new parties. This chapter proposed a game-theoretic model with two actors to understand these strategic interactions. A potential new party addresses a demand for policy change to an established party. This demand can either be a high or a low one. The second actor, without knowing how much support this potential new party enjoys in the electorate, has to decide whether to accept or reject the demand. After this decision of the established party, the potential new party can either acquiesce or challenge it with the formation of a new party. Then, in the next election, the payoffs are distributed as a function of the decisions reached in the game.

I have imposed several assumptions on the payoffs of the two actors, which lead to equilibria under complete information, where new parties never appear. The established party accepts all reasonable demands because it knows exactly how strong a potential challenger is. In this context they prove to be very adaptable. Under incomplete information, the very same game with the same payoffs leads to situations where new parties appear on the electoral scene. This results from the fact that the weak potential new parties sometimes have an incentive to pretend to be strong. Then, the established party occasionally accepts even unreasonable demands, namely, important demands from weak challengers. But established parties will also often reject some demands, in order to deter weak challengers from making important demands.

Consequently, the strategic interaction between the potential new party and the established party results sometimes in the emergence of a new competitor, but sometimes such an emergence is deterred. The theoretical model hightlights the crucial theoretical variables explaining these two possible outcomes. Based on comparative statics results I was able to derive a series of implications that relate explanatory factors with both the formation and the initial success of new political parties. Some of these insights rejoin well-known hypotheses discussed in the literature, while others differ considerably. Their foundations reside in the game-theoretic model, which relies on two crucial assumptions that can be the object of important criticisms. The first concerns the structure of the game, or more precisely, the decision to limit my model to the interaction between only two actors. I will defend my modeling choice with two arguments. The first operates on the substantive level, while the second is of a more technical nature.

It is quite clear that demands potential new parties make usually are addressed to all existing parties. Such is the case with environmental movements, which would have liked very much to change the platform of all existing parties, and have them adopt ecologically sympathetic policies. But usually the behavior of a single established party counts for the potential new party. Taking again as an example environmental movements, it was clear to these movements that the crucial response to their demands would come from leftist parties (e.g., von Oppeln 1989; Briquet, Courty, and Legarve 1990; Müller-Rommel 1993).[27] This was so because the environmental issue seemed to be much more closely allied to the preoccupations of the leftist parties than to the parties on the right. Furthermore, it was evident that a new party addressing environmental problems was more likely to hurt left-wing parties than right-wing parties. Similarly, integrating such demands into the platform of the latter would have been much more costly for right-wing parties than for left-wing parties. Consequently, if demands were rejected by left-wing parties, they were likely to experience the same fate at the hands of right-wing parties.[28] This implies that there is usually only one established party whose reaction to a given demand has a vital impact on whether a new party does or does not emerge. My assumption relies, therefore, on the argument that, with respect to the potential new party, only the response of one established party is important in the

27. See especially von Oppeln's (1989) careful study of anti-nuclear movements in the Land of Hessen in Germany and in two *départements* in France.

28. Implicitly both Kitschelt (1988) and Müller-Rommel (1993) subscribe to this argument, since they argue that the presence of a socialist party in government influenced the emergence and success of Green parties.

decision as to whether to form a new party or not.

The second argument which I put forward in defense of the structure of the game is more technical. In an alternative model, I could have had a series of established parties; these would all have to decide whether or not to integrate a demand in their electoral platform. Here, I must distinguish between two situations. First, if all of these established parties had the same payoff structure, i.e. the same costs, the results would not vary at all, except if I made the structure of the game more complicated. If all established parties had the same information and one party decided to reject a demand, all other parties would also have rejected the demand. Similarly, if one party accepted a demand, all others would have done the same, since their payoffs would be identical.[29] Consequently, the model would yield the same outcomes and predictions as the model I discussed above.

Second, if the established parties all had different payoff structures, then this would describe a classical situation in signaling games, namely the Spence-model (Fudenberg and Tirole 1991, 456ff). Here, a whole set of potential employers want to hire a person, without knowing her capabilities. The job candidate signals her abilities by acquiring education. But the presence of many potential employers results in the fact that the candidate is hired by the employer who can offer the best contract (Banks 1991, 9ff). Hence, the model only looks at the interaction between this employer and the job candidate, without changing the basic insights. In my model this simply implies that the reaction of the established party, which has the lowest costs for integrating a demand, compared to fighting the challenger, is the most important.[30] Consequently, from a purely technical perspective, the assumption that the reaction of only one established party is important can be justified.

The second important criticism concerns my implicit assumption that both the established and the potential new party to be unitary actors. Evidently, this criticism is well justified, since most parties comprise several factions, each of them formed by individuals. The question as to whether the aggregate, namely the political party, acts in strategic situations as a single individual would act is very important. To defend my model against this criticism, I will discuss the unitary actor assumption in some detail.

In most game-theoretic models on political parties, authors assume that the latter are unitary actors. But even in other theoretical frameworks, especially

---

29. This relies on the assumption that once an established party has accepted a demand, the payoffs of the other parties do not change. Such an assumption is evidently implausible but any change in it would be quite arbitrary and imply an extension of the model to include electoral competition between the established parties.

30. Again, this assumes that the established parties have perfect knowledge of the other established parties' payoffs.

in theories on the formation of government coalitions, researchers implicitly argue that political parties act like single individuals. They assume that in coalition negotiations the party leadership decides for the whole party. Hence, most authors concede that in such instances the party behaves like a unitary actor (Laver and Schofield 1990, 217ff).

A similar defense might be marshalled in support of the unitary actor assumption in my model. Given the setup of my model, however, a simpler, though technical justification is adequate. In the theoretical model the established party only chooses between two options, namely whether to accept or reject a given demand by a potential new party. The binary character of the set of actions renders my justification for the unitary actor assumption much easier. For instance a simple majority vote among party members in favor or against accepting a particular demand will look like a decision of an individual with a consistent preference schedule. A complication appears with the fact that in the equilibria discussed above, the established party sometimes adopts a mixed strategy, implying a probabilistic acceptance of a particular demand. Consequently, my technical justification for the unitary actor assumption only holds, if either all relevant party members have similar risk attitudes, or the aggregation of the individual risk attitudes leads to a well-behaved aggregate. Along similar lines the unitary actor assumption for the potential new party can be defended. For this composite actor the defense is less difficult, since in equilibrium it always adopts a pure strategy. This pure strategy describes whether the potential new party should make a high or a low demand. Again, this set of actions is binary, which allows for a representation of a whole group as an individual actor.

CHAPTER 4

Studying New Parties

My theoretical framework mainly yields predictions on the formation of new political parties. It suggests a series of relationships between theoretical variables and the likelihood of party formation. Some implications also address the relative strength of these new competitors. Together these two sets of predictions offer insights into the two central questions in the study of new political parties: Why do new parties emerge and what determines their subsequent success?[1] These two questions are obviously related, since the success of a new party is dependent on its prior emergence. My theoretical framework renders this link even more explicit, since both sets of predictions stem from a common model. In addition, this model suggests that the success potential new parties expect is part of the explanation of their emergence. Provided that this expected success is related with the realized success of new parties, my framework suggests a close link between the explanation of the success of a new party and its emergence. This link is also the reason why my theoretical model, which focuses on the emergence of new parties, allows for some limited insights into the initial success of newcomers on the electoral scene. These insights are obviously on stronger footing, if the relationship between expected and realized initial success is strong.

This close link between explanations of success and emergence, while derived from my theoretical framework, is also implicit in most contending models attempting to explain the success of new parties.[2] While this link only partly affects the appropriate research design to study the emergence of new political parties, it raises considerable problems for studies focusing on the

1. Here I neglect studies of a more exploratory character. These focus mostly on organizational forms (e.g., Poguntke 1987; Lepzy 1989) or the electorate of new parties (e.g., Boy 1981; Mayer and Perrineau 1989, 1992).

2. This is most obvious in Rosenstone, Behr, and Lazarus's (1984) study on third parties in America. These authors directly address this link, and the problem it gives up for the appropriate research design, in their empirical work. The link is much more implicit in other work, where similar or identical variables are used to explain formation and success of new parties (e.g., Harmel and Robertson 1985), or where no distinction between formation and success is made (e.g., Kitschelt 1989; Müller-Rommel 1990). In these latter studies the problem raised by this link for the appropriate research design is hardly discussed.

latter's subsequent success. Given that the link is implicitly acknowledged in most studies on new political parties, it must surprise that the ensuing problems for the appropriate research design are seldomly addressed. For this reason, this chapter discusses in some detail the research design employed in this study. In the next section I first discuss the research design proposed for the empirical study of the emergence of new parties. As argued above and reiterated in this section, this research question can be dealt with separately from the appropriate design for the study of the success of new political parties. I deal with this second research question in the second section. The close link between the two research questions suggests a particular approach, taking into account problems of selection bias. More precisely, the new parties that we can observe empirically form a self-selected sample from all potential new parties that ever considered competing in a national election. As I will demonstrate both conceptually in this chapter and empirically in chapter 6, failing to take into account this selection problem may lead to erroneous results.

Given that both research designs employed in this study are considerably different from the ones prominent in the literature, I discuss competing designs in the third section. While some of them have considerable advantages, they often achieve these at the price of serious drawbacks. Provided that my arguments in support of the research designs employed in this study are correct, empirical results obtained with competing designs have to be taken with considerable caution. It is likely that faulty research designs largely explain puzzling empirical findings. Similarly, differences in research design may also explain some empirical results which are at odds with the existing literature (chapters 5 and 6). I will address these likely differences in the conclusion to this chapter.

Studying the Formation of New Parties

Proposing a research design for the emergence of new political parties is the easier part of the task which lies before me. Since the emergence of a new party precedes its possible success, the research design for this first question can neglect the issues that the second one has to deal with. In addition, my theoretical framework suggests a series of testable relationships between theoretical variables and the likelihood of party formation. These relationships are independent of the future electoral success of new parties, except for the latter's link with the expected success that potential new parties anticipate. While the theoretical model focuses on a single interaction between one established party and a potential new party, it is likely that over time a series of such interactions takes place. Some of these interactions will result in the formation of a new electoral competitor, while some others lead to no changes in the party system. Given my definition of new political parties, we observe the outcome of these interactions at the time of a national election, when newcomers present themselves for the first time. Since we do not observe the individual interactions between established parties and potential new ones, a natural unit of observation is the time of a national election in a particular country. At that time we can determine which parties compete for the first time at the national level, and are thus considered as new parties.

Given this unit of observation an obvious way to define the dependent variable is to count the number of new parties that appear on the ballot for the first time at a particular national election. Since we cannot directly observe the processes that lead to the formation of new parties and those that failed to produce newcomers, counting the number of successful outcomes is an appropriate aggregate measure. Obviously, for a series of elections this dependent variable will take as value zero (no new party), while in all others it will be strictly positive. This property of the dependent variable questions the use of traditional statistical models, since a series of assumptions are violated.[3] Nevertheless, the properties of this dependent variable nicely fit the increasingly used event-count models, which rely on Poisson or related distributions. These allow the researcher to correctly model the way in which the data are generated (King 1988, 1989a, 121ff, 1989b).

In the present case the theoretical model presented in chapter 2 nicely matches the assumptions of such event-counts. The model relates a series of variables with the probability of party formation. This probability finds as natural equivalent the probability of an event occurring in the framework of an event-count. In both cases we do not directly observe the process that leads to the event (or non-event), but only the number of events taking place. Consequently, I will employ in my empirical tests an event-count model to estimate the various relationships suggested by my theoretical model.

Having determined the unit of observation and the dependent variable, we still have to determine the universe of observations. Since my theoretical model specifies relationships which should not be context dependent, a comparison between different countries is of particular advantage. A series of theoretical variables discussed in chapter 3 are likely to vary only from country to country. Consequently, only a cross-national design may capture the effects of such variables. But at the same time some of these theoretical variables are also likely to vary across time in a particular country. For instance, changes in the electoral system or the requirements to access the ballot undergo changes over

3. The standard solution is to take the logarithm of the count variable to which one half is added. Adding a constant is necessary, since the logarithm of zero is not defined. The transformed variable follows approximately a normal distribution. See King (1988) for a critique of this standard solution.

time. Aggregating these time-varying measures into single indices is likely to depreciate their effects compared to variables that do not change over time. Consequently, I keep as basic unit of analysis a national election in a particular country. Given the already defined comparative dimension, this suggests a cross-national cross-time design of the dataset. For the period of observation and the countries considered the number of new parties at each national election have to be counted. These counts of new parties then are related to the various explanatory factors derived in chapter 3. Estimating the different effects has to rely on an event-count model, given the particular nature of the data.

This research design comes very close to what Campbell and Ross (1970) call an "interrupted time-series design."[4] Changes in independent variables from one election to the other are the background against which the frequency of new party formation can be checked. This research design also permits the integration of theoretical propositions from other authors as a check for the validity of the model we are using. By using such a procedure I can control whether the choice of my research design leads to substantively different conclusions than the ones other researchers found in their studies.

Studying the Success of New Parties

While the study of the formation of new parties requires a rather straightforward research design, the same does not hold true for exploring the success of new parties. As noted above, choosing a research design for this second important question in the study of new parties cannot be decoupled from the previous one. More precisely, given the intimate link between the emergence and success of new parties, the latter cannot be studied without taking into consideration the factors explaining the formation of a new party.

In addition to this first difficulty, the study of the success of new parties also requires a different unit of observation. Since in most western democracies often more than one new party may emerge at a given point in time, the national election can no longer serve as unit of analysis.[5] Consequently, I employ the newly formed political party as unit of analysis. Given that my theoretical framework suggests several relationships between theoretical variables and the expected success of a newcomer, I employ the initial success of a new party as a proxy for its expected success. I determine this initial success by taking the national vote share in percentages obtained by the newcomer.

4. See also the respective discussion on time series designs in Campbell and Stanley (1963).

5. Rosenstone, Behr, and Lazarus (1984) in their study of third parties in America resort to the solution of using elections as units of analysis. They aggregate, as a consequence, the electoral fortunes of several third-party challengers, if more than one appeared at a given election.

While this strategy solves the problem of the unit of observation, it highlights even more strongly the problem of selection bias. Obviously the set of new parties for which the initial success can be determined is a self-selected sample of all potential new parties that ever thought about competing in a national election (Hug 2000). The process of self-selection, according to my model, is largely dependent on the success a potential new party expects from participating at a national election. If it were the only factor influencing the self-selection, we would face a classical problem of selection on the dependent variable. Scholars in comparative politics have recently been reminded of the dangers of this problem (e.g., Geddes 1991; King, Keohane, and Verba 1994). While in comparative case studies the solution often lies in a more careful selection of the cases,[6] to induce more variation in the dependent variable, this is not possible in the present case. Quite simply, for all potential new parties that judged an electoral bout too adventurous, we fail to have any information. If information on such potential new parties were available, statistical models discussed in detail by Achen (1986) and Brehm (1993) could be employed.

Ideally, we would have a sample of groups or political entrepreneurs which are considering creating a new political party. Some of them would have formed a new party, while others would have refrained from doing so. Then, the task of the researcher would consist of explaining this variation. But this type of research design is not feasible, almost by definition. It is difficult to determine the universe of groups that have considered creating a new party, and some rule of thumb would have to be adopted in order to do so. For example, in the study of Green parties, a researcher could take all social movements and groups that address environmental questions. But, already, this task becomes difficult to carry out. In addition, it might be that some of these groups never considered forming a new party. Perhaps their only aim was to lobby for a new issue. Then the researcher must decide whether all groups should be included or only those that had the intention to form a new party at a given point in time. Probably because of these difficulties no student of new political parties has, to my knowledge, used such a research design.

Given this impossibility to gather information for all potential new political parties, it is important to note that the emergence of a newcomer on the electoral scene is the result of a conscious decision. But exactly this decision whether or not to form a new party constitutes the *explanadum* in the first research design. Consequently, the research design for the second research question should allow for a study of the relationships explaining the success of new parties, conditional on them having appeared. The conditional part of this research design would obviously draw on similar independent variables

6. Dion (1998) argues, however, that for tests of necessary conditions, selection on the dependent variable is the appropriate strategy.

as those employed to explain the formation of new parties, or equivalently, the selection into the sample. The only remaining question is how this can be included into a research design which explores the success of new parties.

The solution comes from the observation that the sample of self-selected new parties is a truncated dataset. The truncating mechanism in this case is the decision to form a new party. This mechanism can be captured by assuming that an unobserved variable and an accompanying threshold exist, below which new parties do not form. The level of the threshold is fixed, while the value of the unobserved variable is a random variable, whose mean depends on the variables that determine the decision to form a new party. The dependent variable measuring success is explained by a series of independent variables, conditional on the fact that the unobserved variable exceeds the specified threshold. Adopting such a framework allows the researcher to correct for the problems of selection bias (Muthen and Jöreskog 1983; Bloom and Killingsworth 1985; King 1989a, ch.9; Little and Rubin 1987; Breen 1996).

Competing Research Designs

Having proposed the twofold research design employed in the present study, I now review the different research designs adopted in the existing literature. This allows me to stress the strength and pinpoint the weaknesses of each design. The most prominent research designs in the study of new parties are either case studies, studies of a class of new parties, or studies of new parties across time or space. The first two designs distinguish themselves by the fact that their unit of analysis is primarily the new political party. On the contrary, the other two designs focus either on temporal or spatial units. Though all four categories have some overlapping characteristics, and some problems concern more than one research design, I will treat them separately in the order in which I have listed them.

Case Studies

Case studies are in all likelihood the most prominent research designs in use for the study of new political parties. The existing literature is replete with monographs and articles in journals on a new party having appeared in a given polity.[7] Some contributions, which I will also consider under this heading, use several case studies to stress differences or similarities. Most case studies have a descriptive focus and attempt to illuminate the particularities of the

7. Müller-Rommel (1991, 205-211) presents an impressive bibliography of studies on small political parties in European countries. Since most new parties start as small parties, most entries concern new parties.

party under consideration. Because of this, they are valuable contributions to our knowledge on new political parties.[8] Consequently, the most important advantage of case studies is their capability to pinpoint important details that are, and, to a certain degree, need to be neglected in more general studies. Rebeaud (1987), Sainteny (1991), Hülsberg (1988), and Poguntke (1993), for example, present very detailed accounts of the formation of three Green parties. Similar accounts of parties on the extreme right figure in the studies by Lepzy (1989), Roth (1990a, 1990b), Betz (1994), and Ignazi (1994) and in the volumes edited by Mayer and Perrineau (1989) and Betz and Immerfall (1998).[9]

Although the main function of case studies is as tools for descriptions and illustrations, some authors attempt to explain the emergence and success of a party by using the case study approach. But these explanations have to rely heavily on counterfactual arguments. This is especially true when one considers the question of why new parties form. It is true by definition that when studying a single new political party, there is no variation in the variable that one tries to explain. As a result of this authors rely on counterfactual statements, arguing that the party would not have formed if certain conditions had not been fulfilled.[10] These arguments are rarely persuasive. Often, the crucial explanatory factors are heavily correlated with other variables, and it is hard to tell why other explanatory factors do not get the same attention. Thus, these kinds of explanations suffer from overdetermination and multicollinearity. In addition, the generalizability of these insights can legitimately be questioned on similar grounds.

When addressing the question of success, researchers using case studies often rely on a disaggregation of their unit of analysis. They study the success of the party either across time or across space, by looking at different elections or different spatial units. Adopting these strategies often leads to more interesting results, since variation appears in the dependent variable. While this is a step in the right direction, the problems of selection bias often escape the researcher's attention. Furthermore, the question again arises as to what degree the results are generalizable. Some insights might very well be dependent on the particular national context in which the party under consideration appears.

To address this dependence on the national context, several authors use a small number of case studies to highlight differences between a small number of new parties (for example, Kitschelt 1989; Harmel and Svasand 1997). These studies are of as much help as individual case studies for explaining

---

8. For example, see the informative case studies assembled in Müller-Rommel (1989).

9. In 1992 special issues of the *European Journal of Political Research* 22(1) and *Parliamentary Affairs* 45(3) contained also a series of case studies on right-wing parties.

10. A striking example for this tendency is the account Hülsberg (1988) gives of the German Greens' formation.

the formation of new parties. Again, there is no variation in the dependent variable and authors must rely extensively on counterfactual arguments. When looking at the success of the parties, these studies are at a comparative advantage, since the national context becomes an independent variable. So Kitschelt (1989), for example, explains the varying success of the two Green parties in Belgium and the one in Germany by the difference in the polarization of the environmental conflict.[11] Such an explanation can only be accounted for when different cases are considered. By this feature, such studies can offer more insights than isolated case studies. Their problem lies in the selection of the cases.[12] Geddes (1991), as well as King, Keohane, and Verba (1994), delivers a very powerful warning concerning the importance of this step in each research. Sometimes "the cases you choose affect the answers you get" (Geddes 1991). Consequently, this step must attract the special care of researchers engaging in comparative case studies. An additional problem with such a research design comes with the number of observations. When particularities of the national context appear as independent variables, such as, for example, the polarization of the environmental conflict, problems of collinearity and overdetermination reappear. With only a limited number of cases, each explanatory factor is likely to be highly correlated with other variables. The reader must let herself be convinced by the researcher's argument that some explanatory variables are more important than others. This problem, while prevalent in these studies, becomes even more apparent in studies of a class of new parties. Here, as we will see below, statistical tools find application which render these problems even more visible.

Studying a Class of New Parties

Since parties of certain classes often appear at roughly the same time in different countries, comparative studies are very prominent.[13] Authors study left-libertarian parties (Kitschelt 1988), new politics parties (Poguntke 1989), Green parties (Müller-Rommel 1993; Vialatte 1996), parties of the extreme right (Husbands 1981, 1988, 1992a, 1992b; Harmel, Svasand, and Gibson 1992; Betz 1994), or regionalist parties (Urwin 1983; De Winter 1995; De Winter and Türsan 1998). Since these parties are present in several countries, such studies allow meaningful comparisons of the different national contexts.

---

11. This is a very reductionist account of Kitschelt's (1989) explanation.

12. Beckwith (1990), for example, criticizes the case selection in Kitschelt's (1989) work. He defends his selection very briefly (Kitschelt 1989, 6f), without going into details about the possible problems it might cause.

13. Müller-Rommel (1993, 209f) again provides an important bibliography of cross-national studies on different classes of small parties.

They thereby become extensions of the previous category of research designs, namely the category of case studies.

The focus on a class of new parties again leads to the absence of variation in the formation variable. Since new parties of a given class are the units of analysis, by definition all of them have formed.[14] A way to address the question of formation, when studying a class of new parties, consists of comparing the timing of the emergence. Harmel, Svasand, and Gibson (1992), for example, look at the emergence of parties at the extreme right and tie their explanation to the timing of the formation and the links these parties have to previous extreme-right organizations. A similar idea appears in Müller-Rommel's (1993, 87ff) book, when he compares the different phases of development among Green parties. But this type of approach again comes very close to the next research design, namely the study of new parties across time, so that I will delay its discussion.

Concerning the explanation of the success of new parties of a particular class, this research design is quite advantageous. Since a particular class of parties is under scrutiny, the issues that they address are very similar across countries. Furthermore, there is often a considerable amount of variation in the success of new parties of a given class. But the fact that these parties are part of a self-selected sample causes important problems. This largely seems to explain why institutional factors like the electoral system are often of minor importance in explaining the success of the new parties (for example, Müller-Rommel 1990), despite strong theoretical foundations for such a contention. These findings are not surprising if one considers them in the context of self-selected samples. The impact of the electoral system on the success of new parties can only adequately be assessed when taking into account the fact that the electoral system has an important role in the initial decision to form a new party. Using this approach leads to empirical results much more in line with the theoretical arguments of the literature on electoral systems and the implications of my model. I will illustrate this in more detail in the empirical chapters of this study.

Studying a class of new parties leads to an additional problem, which is the small number of observations. New parties of a given class often emerge in small numbers. Since most studies in this category use statistical analyses, the problem of a small number of cases becomes very visible. Most researchers refrain from controlling relationships for other variables, and frequently focus on bivariate relations. These relationships often suffer from spuriousness,

---

14. Here I exclude studies of a class of new parties that use countries as units of analysis. In that case one would have variation in the formation variable, since some countries might not have a party of a certain class. I will discuss these studies below, when reviewing research designs that look at new parties across space.

since other variables have a much stronger influence on the success of new parties. But, without controlling for these other explanatory factors, these remain hidden from both the researcher and the reader. Furthermore, with a small sample it is very likely that several independent variables covary heavily, making it difficult to distinguish the independent effects. Researchers attempt to bypass the problem by adopting classification schemes (Kitschelt 1988) or using boolean algebra (Müller-Rommel 1993, 191ff) proposed by Ragin (1987). Such attempts serve as only partial solutions to the problems at hand as King, Keohane, and Verba (1994) convincingly argue.

Studying New Parties across Space

Already in the previous research design, a certain tension pushes the researcher to the adoption of another unit of analysis than the new political party. Such a change in the unit of analysis almost inevitably leads to a solution of one of the crucial problems in empirical studies of new parties. By using countries as units of analysis, authors automatically introduce variation in the variable that measures the formation of parties. For example, Kitschelt (1988), in his study of left-libertarian parties, looks at a series of countries and tries to explain why some of them experienced the emergence of successful new parties of this type, while others did not.[15] Such a change in the unit of analysis leads to viable research designs for the study of the emergence of new parties. Hence, Harmel and Robertson (1985) study the formation of new political parties in a series of countries by looking at how many new competitors appeared in each country under observation. This provides interesting insights into the emergence of new parties. A minor problem with this type of research design stems from the type of dependent variable that is used. More precisely, the number of new political parties in a given country is obviously a count. To use such data as dependent variable does not cause any problems, as long as the researcher considers the particular way in which they have been generated.[16] As discussed above, solutions exist to this methodological problem but have not found sufficient attention in the literature so far.

---

15. While such a research design is already a great leap forward, the problem of combining both the formation and success of a new party in a single variable is problematic (Kitschelt 1988). First, the absence of a new party is qualitatively different from the presence of a weak, unsuccessful one. Second, if some variables only influence the success of new parties, while others explain both the formation and the success, the latter will be thought more important under certain circumstances.

16. Harmel and Robertson (1985) do not directly use the number of new parties as an independent variable. Instead they classify each country in one of two classes, according to the number of new parties. Such an approach inevitably leads to a loss of information that is contained in the data at hand.

While a research design that looks at new parties across space solves the first problem, it does nothing to remove the second problem concerning selection bias. In one sense it is even aggravated by the addition of another new problem to the existing one. The question arises as to what one does with countries where no new parties appeared. One solution is simply to discard the countries where no new parties emerged. In this case, the researcher is back in the previous research design, where the unit of analysis is the new political party. Another solution is to assume that the dependent variable, which measures the success of the new party, is equal to zero in countries where no new competitor appeared. Such an assumption implies that there is no difference between a country with no new party and a country where a new party gets almost no votes. But a country without a new party is qualitatively different from a country with an extremely weak new party. This clearly appears in the implications of my theoretical model, where some variables contribute to the explanation of the emergence of a new party, but should be unrelated to its subsequent success. It is also implicit in all contributions to the literature, which employ different variables for explaining the emergence and the success of new parties (e.g., Harmel and Robertson 1985).

Similarly, imposing thresholds for classifying new political parties into successful and unsuccessful ones (Kitschelt 1988) does not solve the problem. Equating a country with a weak new party to a country with no new party is problematic, since the formation and the success involve different actors. Most often, voters are themselves responsible for the little success a new party has; but to attribute the decision to form a new party to the same actors is quite problematic.

The very fact that a research design focusing on new parties across space leads to a sample which also includes observations without new parties allows us to directly address the issue of selection bias. More precisely, a researcher could attempt to simultaneously explain the formation of new parties, and, conditional on the formation, propose a model to explain the success of the new parties that appeared.[17] Since the unit of observation is the country, it is clear that whenever more than one new party appears on the electoral scene this research design is of little help. A researcher might explain the total vote for new parties at a given election, or even aggregate over both parties and elections when focusing on certain time periods. But neither of these solutions is convincing. Probably for this same reason, such a research design, where the researcher simultaneously explains the formation and the success of new parties, has, to my knowledge, never found application. Consequently, while looking at new parties across space is a viable research design with which to

17. Such models can be estimated both in the traditional regression framework (Achen 1986, ch. 5) or in the maximum-likelihood approach (King 1989a, ch. 9).

study the emergence of new parties, explaining the success of these parties in the same framework is more difficult.

Studying New Parties across Time

As is the case with the previous research design, studying new parties across time is a viable solution for the first research design problem. By looking at different time points, a researcher automatically introduces variation into the variable which measures the formation of new parties. Authors often use election-years as natural focus points. Rosenstone, Behr, and Lazarus (1984, ch.7), for example, study the factors that explain whether there are third-party candidates competing in presidential elections in the United States. Such a research question requires that one use presidential elections as units of analysis and determines whether there were "nationally prestigious third-party candidates" running (Rosenstone, Behr, and Lazarus 1984, 193). Other authors adopt similar research strategies to look at challenges from new parties in particular countries (for example, Fisher 1974; Pinard 1967, 1973, 1975; Marsh 1992; Eagles and Erfle 1993). The use of election years as units of analysis evidently solves the first problem of research designs in the study of new parties. A minor problem might appear with the type of dependent variable that one encounters. In some polities, new parties emerge so frequently that several may appear at the same election. The dependent variable is, therefore, a count of new parties instead of a dichotomy as in Rosenstone, Behr, and Lazarus (1984).

Nonetheless, the problem of selection bias is still present and only few authors have addressed it convincingly. Certainly, Rosenstone, Behr, and Lazarus (1984, 152) propose the most elegant solution. When trying to explain the vote for third-party candidates, they argue that an important factor is the percentage of voters that actually could vote for a third-party candidate. But this variable is hardly a completely exogenous variable, and the authors convincingly make the point that "it is likely that the causes of third-party support omitted from the vote equation are associated with the omitted causes of these candidates appearing on the ballot" (Rosenstone, Behr, and Lazarus 1984, 152). Consequently, they propose a model where they explain simultaneously the presence of third-party candidates and their success. The first variable, while being exogenous, also helps to explain the second dependent variable.[18] This is a viable solution, since they want to explain the vote for third-party candi-

18. More precisely, and in technical terms, they propose a two-stage estimation procedure. Initially, the percentage of voters being able to vote for third-party candidates is regressed on several explanatory variables. The predicted values of this first regression then figure as independent variable in the equation that attempts to explain the success of third-party candidates.

dates. In the context of explaining the success of new parties, however, this research design becomes problematic. Often, at a given election in a certain country, not one, but several new parties appear for the first time on the electoral scene. Consequently, explaining the success of individual parties is not possible in a research design that uses elections as units of analysis. The only thing one could do in such a framework is to explain the total vote for new parties combined, but not for particular ones.

Conclusion

The discussion of research designs used in the empirical literature to study the formation and success of new parties allows two general conclusions. First, though the study of these two questions seems quite simple, two problems are important to consider. These two problems concern the adequate unit of analysis with which to study the formation of new parties, and the problems of selection bias in the study of the new parties' success. While the first problem is relatively minor, the second is at the source of some puzzles that persist in the literature on new political parties. These have persisted largely because researchers have somewhat neglected the strategic context in which the emergence of new parties takes place. This neglect also makes it harder to see the importance of the selection bias problem, since its substantive foundation is grounded in the idea that the new party emerges as a result of an intentional decision.

Second, while some research designs address one of these problems, almost none can propose solutions to both problems simultaneously. Only one empirical study comes close to solving both problems, but it achieves this by focusing on the vote for third parties in general. Since the present study has a comparative focus and is interested in the success of particular new political parties, this research design is only of little help. In this chapter, therefore, I proposed a framework composed of two research designs. This combination of two research designs yields a framework that allows the study of both the formation and the success of new political parties. The link between the two research designs consists of variables that influence the decision to form a new party. In the first research design these variables determine the likelihood of new parties appearing. In the second, they influence the same likelihood, but only enter indirectly through the selection mechanism. While it would be preferable to have a single common research design, this is feasible only at the cost of changing the research question. I would have to focus on the electoral success of new parties in general, instead of looking at them individually. Only by adopting research designs with different units of analysis can the two research questions prevalent in the study of new parties be seriously addressed.

This combination of two research designs is certainly not ideal, and can be the subject of critiques. As I argued, however, the designs that would allow us to simultaneously address the two research questions would force me to change part of one question. Consequently, there exists a tradeoff between two possible research strategies. Focusing on the two initial research questions comes at the cost of not having a unified research design. Conversely, the use of a unified research design comes at the cost of altering slightly the question of explaining the success of new parties. Faced with this tradeoff, I opted for the first strategy. Thus, an interesting extension of the work I will present below consists of adopting the second strategy and comparing its results to those reported in chapters 5 and 6.

As the discussion of competing research designs illustrated, these often fall short of several requirements for an adequate design. Some designs have considerable advantages, but at the same time accepting them has serious drawbacks. Research designs, which use the new political party as their unit of analysis, have the advantage of being able to look at the success of the new competitors. However, the manner in which most of these analyses have been carried out is problematic, since the problem of self-selection has not been addressed. In addition, this type of research design is of limited use when a researcher wants to study the formation of new parties. Here the use of the new party as unit of analysis leads to the absence of variation in the dependent variable. The solution to this second problem is the selection of a different unit of analysis. Viable alternatives to this are studies that employ either countries or time points as units of analysis. Then one automatically introduces variation in the dependent variable, which measures the emergence of new parties.

This is the route chosen by my research design. For the study of formation the use of national elections as units of observation automatically introduces variation in the dependent variable, namely the number of new parties. By doing so, and covering elections both across time and space, the design fruitfully combines the advantages of studies of new parties across time and across space. But this design is only useful for the study of the emergence of new parties and has to be supplemented by an additional design allowing a meaningful study of the initial success of new parties. For this part of the research design I draw on the same tradition of studying new parties across time and space, but avoid the pitfalls of focusing only on newcomers and of failing to distinguish between emergence and success. The research design proposed achieves this by modeling directly the selection process that makes out of the set of new parties a self-selected sample. By doing so, the inherent biases when employing traditional statistical tools can be corrected.

CHAPTER 5

The Emergence of New Parties

The model presented in chapter 3 suggests a series of implications that link several theoretical variables with the likelihood of party formation. Provided that we find appropriate measures for these theoretical variables, hypotheses can be derived and empirically tested. The present chapter proposes empirical tests of such hypotheses. In doing so, however, we have to be careful to employ an adequate research design, as the discussion in chapter 4 suggested. The first part of the research design employed in this study focuses on the explanation of variation in party formation from one national election to the other. Consequently, it also suggests a particular type of dataset that is needed to empirically test the various hypotheses.

I first present and discuss in some detail the dataset used in my empirical tests in this chapter and chapter 6, which deals with the initial electoral success of new parties. The dataset covers new political parties that have presented candidates for the first time at national elections in 22 Western democracies over the postwar period. Figure 1.1 in chapter 1 offered a first glimpse at this dataset. After the discussion of this dataset I summarize the implications to be tested in this chapter. A recurrent and, in many regards, difficult notion is the credibility of a weak new challenger, which derives from my theoretical framework. It influences several of the relationships that link theoretical variables to the expected number of new political parties. I propose a way to measure this credibility, which finds application in the empirical tests that follow. These tests first focus on individual implications, before I propose analyses that respect their interdependence. A summary of the results follows in the conclusion.

Data on New Political Parties in Western Democracies

The appropriate research design for testing my various theoretically derived implications on the emergence of new parties suggests the use of a dataset employing as unit of observation the national election. For each such time point we need a count of new parties that present for the first time candidates for a national elected office. Given the nature of the implications I wish to test,

TABLE 5.1. Countries and elections studied

country	first election after World War II	election years considered for new parties	number of elections
Australia	1946	1949-1990	18
Austria	1945	1949-1990	13
Belgium	1946	1949-1991	15
Canada	1945	1949-1988	14
Denmark	1945	1947-1990	19
Finland	1948	1951-1991	12
France	1946	1951-1988	11
Germany	1949	1953-1990	11
Great Britain	1945	1950-1987	12
Greece	1974	1977-1990	6
Iceland	1946	1949-1991	14
Ireland	1948	1951-1989	13
Italy	1948	1953-1987	9
Luxembourg	1945	1948-1989	10
Netherlands	1946	1948-1989	13
New Zealand	1946	1949-1990	15
Norway	1945	1949-1989	11
Portugal	1976	1979-1991	6
Spain	1977	1979-1989	4
Sweden	1948	1952-1991	14
Switzerland	1947	1951-1991	11
United States	1948	1952-1988	10
total			261

the data should comprise both cross-national differences and variations across time.

Harmel and Robertson (1985) employ such a dataset in their study on party formation. Their dataset covers 19 democracies and comprises 233 new parties over a time span of 20 years. Their number includes all four types of new organizations that I discussed in chapter 2. Almost half of their 233 parties have formed naturally and correspond to my category of genuinely new parties. More than a third appeared as the result of a fission, while the remaining parties are either mergers or "reorganizations of former parties." I will exclude these two latter categories from the analyses in the subsequent sections, for the reasons discussed above.

The dataset for the present study is based on the postwar elections in 22 Western democracies.[1] Table 5.1 shows the list of countries and elections considered. The election immediately following the end of World War II (respectively the first democratic national election in the case of new democracies) is excluded for each country. Most party systems have undergone serious reorganizations in the aftermath of World War II. In order to have an identical base for all countries, I chose the second election after July 1945 as the starting point for my empirical analysis. Consequently, new parties are those formations that presented candidates for the first time in a democratic election after

1. Precise definitions of the dataset and the variables figure in the appendix.

the first one of the postwar period. Obviously, even though considerable time has been spent on collecting information on new parties in the countries studied, the collection is far from complete. Attempting to collect information on all new parties ever formed in Western democracies is an almost impossible task. Often even official election reports fail to give exact returns for all parties. The vote tallies of small parties most often appear collapsed into the category "others." Stöss (1975, 255) notes that even in Germany "fissions . . . often are collapsed in electoral statistics and analyses into the 'others' category." (my translation).[2] Consequently, my dataset is based completely on secondary sources. Employing an identical set of sources across time and space I identify for each election the parties that present for the first time candidates.[3] As in Harmel and Robertson's (1985) study, an important number of new political parties appeared in the 261 elections under consideration. To allow comparisons, it is useful to quickly present all types of parties that emerged in elections since the end of World War II.

Genuinely new parties are the most numerous ones; this finds support in Harmel and Robertson's (1985) dataset. Figure 5.1 shows their increasing frequency over the four decades under consideration. While not completely absent in the fifties, their number is small compared to the spur of genuinely new parties in the middle of the sixties (33 for the whole decade) and especially at the end of the seventies (71 for the entire decade). The eighties show another increase, leading to 94 genuinely new parties in 10 years. This trend also finds reflection in the average number of new parties per election depicted in figure 5.1 as a line.

Figure 5.2 shows the number of elections with given numbers of genuinely new parties. In more than half of the 261 elections under consideration, no genuinely new party made its debut on the electoral scene. But in more than a quarter of all elections, one new party appeared, while in more than a tenth of the cases, two parties made their entrance. Elections with more than two genuinely new parties are rare, but it is worth noting that in one election nine new parties competed for votes.[4] This leads to an average of almost one genuinely new party per election.[5]

The second category in my classification of new parties consists of fissions that have split from an existing party. These are, as Harmel and Robertson

2. In his detailed study on Dutch parties, Lucardie (1996, 1) notes that 257 new parties have attempted to win seats in parliament since 1917. His dataset relies, however, on a painstaking data collection, which would not be possible for all countries under consideration given the state of the official elections reports.

3. More details on the data collection procedure appear in the appendix.

4. This election took place in Spain in 1986.

5. The exact average is 0.885 for 231 genuinely new parties in 261 elections.

Fig. 5.1. Number of genuinely new parties per election year

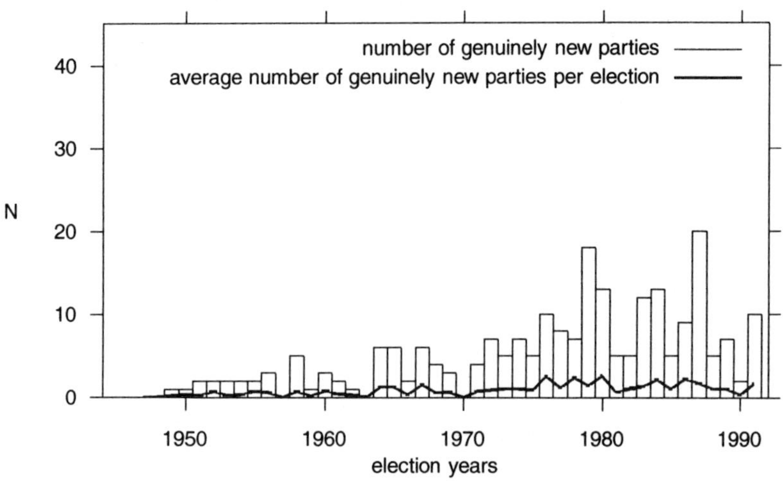

Fig. 5.2. Number of elections with genuinely new parties

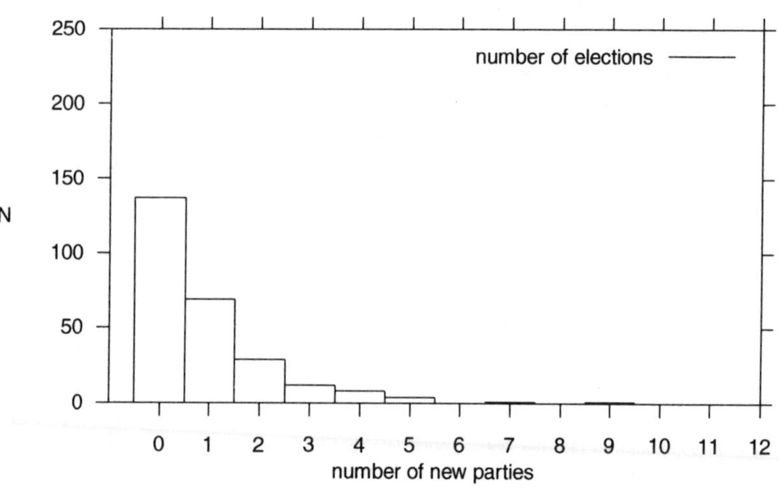

Fig. 5.3. Number of fissions per election year

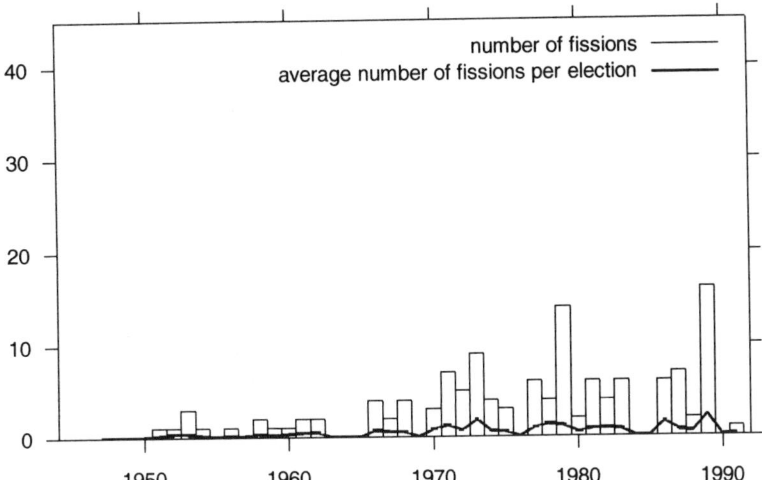

(1985) note, less numerous. Also, as figure 5.3 illustrates, their appearance over time is different from genuinely new parties. While the fifties and the sixties saw very few fissions occurring, the latter became popular in the seventies and slightly less so in the eighties.[6] This different trend also transpires in the average number of fissions per election year.

The smaller number of fissions also becomes apparent in figure 5.4. More than two-thirds of all elections take place without a new party having split from an existing one. In some elections, one, two, or even three fissions compete for the first time. On two occasions eight fissions entered the electoral scene together.[7]

The remaining two categories of new parties, namely mergers and electoral alliances, which are excluded from the subsequent analyses, are less frequent. Mergers occur occasionally over the 40 years of observation. They were most numerous in the seventies, followed by the eighties and the sixties. Con-

---

6. The respective numbers for the four decades are 10 (1950-1959), 15 (1960-1969), 55 (1970-1979), and 50 (1980-1989). I note here that fissions exclude parties that have separated along regional and territorial lines. Consequently, parties that appeared for instance in Belgium through the division of existing parties are not included here. More details on this coding figure in the appendix.

7. The two occasions are the 1979 election in Great Britain and the 1986 election in Spain. On average 0.498 fissions appeared in an election, which corresponds to 130 parties.

Fig. 5.4. Number of elections with fissions

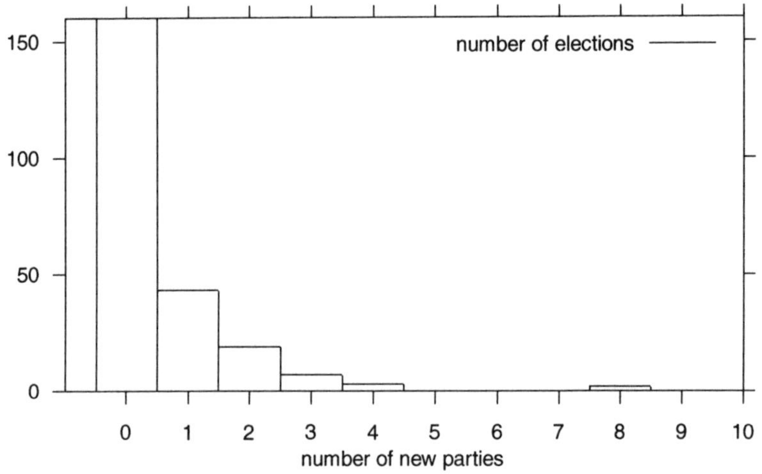

sequently, it is no surprise to note that in most elections no new mergers are present.[8] In less than 30 elections, at least one merger appeared on the electoral scene. The biggest number appeared in the 1979 election in Spain, when four new parties resulting from mergers made their electoral debut. Electoral alliances are even less numerous than mergers. They are also often precursors of the latter, as discussed above. Electoral alliances appear regularly, but in small numbers. A certain increase is observable in the late eighties. But even considering this, most elections take place without new electoral alliances. At most, two such formations appear at the same election, and a large majority of them are just solitary appearances.

After this quick tour through the universe of all forms of new political parties, I will concentrate on genuinely new parties and those that resulted from a fission in an existing party. As I have argued above, only these two types of new parties imply a significant change in the competitive situation faced by established parties. Since I will not distinguish genuinely new parties from fissions in the empirical analyses that follow,[9] it is useful to present the

8. Mair (1990) finds 18 mergers compared to 34 fissions in his sample. However, he excludes France, Greece, Portugal, and Spain when looking at such new parties in the period between 1945 and 1987.

9. I also carried out the empirical analyses presented below for each of the two types

Fig. 5.5. Number of elections with fissions or genuinely new parties

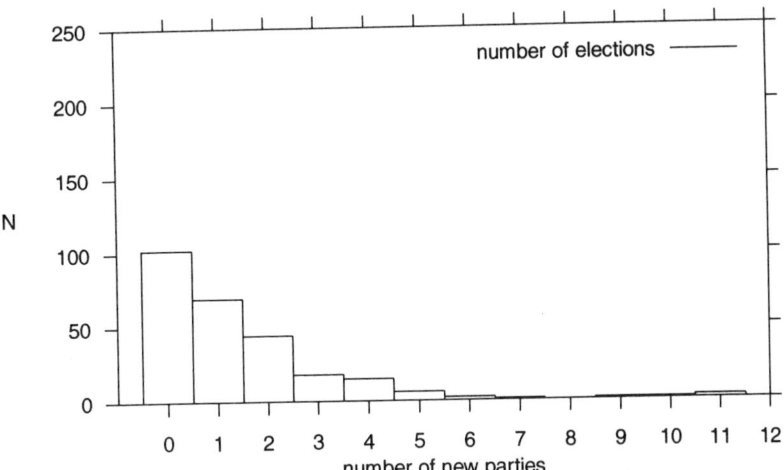

emergence of these two types of new parties together.[10] Figure 1.1 in chapter 1 illustrates the increasing frequency of these new parties. Throughout the fifties and sixties new parties appeared consistently, but the seventies and the eighties saw real bursts of new competitors. In this sense, the electoral year of 1979 is quite exceptional with more than 30 new parties. Overall, however, the eighties witnessed the biggest number of new actors on the electoral scene. This also appears clearly in the average number of new parties per election depicted in figure 1.1. Figure 5.5 shows in addition that in a majority of all elections at least one new party emerged as a new competitor. On several occasions, more than one new party appeared, the maximum number of new appearances being eleven.

While figures 1.1 and 5.5 give us some ideas about the distribution of new political parties across time and any concentration on particular elections, they fail to give us any indication about the cross-national variation. Table 5.2 corrects this by reporting the total number of new parties that have appeared in a given country in the elections under consideration. It also reports the average

---

of party separately. Any differences between the overall results presented below and such additional analyses are duly noted. In addition, these results appear on the author's website: http://uts.cc.utexas.edu/˜simonhug/newparty/.

10. From now on I will use the term "new party" to cover both genuinely new parties and fissions. Only if I specifically refer to a party of particular type will I use the more precise term.

TABLE 5.2. New parties in 22 democracies

country	total number of new parties	mean number of new parties	number of elections
Australia	12	0.67	18
Austria	9	0.69	13
Belgium	16	1.07	15
Canada	16	1.14	14
Denmark	14	0.74	19
Finland	12	1.00	12
France	24	2.18	11
Germany	21	1.91	11
Great Britain	29	2.42	12
Greece	15	2.50	6
Iceland	16	1.14	14
Ireland	16	1.23	13
Italy	20	2.22	9
Luxembourg	11	1.10	10
Netherlands	16	1.23	13
New Zealand	7	0.47	15
Norway	10	0.91	11
Portugal	11	1.83	6
Spain	30	7.50	4
Sweden	7	0.50	14
Switzerland	14	1.27	11
United States	35	3.50	10
total	361	1.38	261

number of new parties per election for each country. This average number varies from a low 0.47 in New Zealand to an extremely high 7.5 in Spain. The theoretically derived implications should account for this variation as well as for the temporal variation of party formation discussed above.

Implications, Hypotheses, and the Notion of Credibility

The implications derived from my theoretical model relate the expected likelihood of new political parties to a set of independent variables. These variables derive directly from the theoretical model. Consequently, a primary task of my empirical research is to operationalize these variables and find adequate measures for them. In most other empirical research in this field, authors start from broad concepts like constraints, the political system, the economic system, etc.,[11] which they measure by a series of indicators. The theoretical underpinnings of these concepts, and how and why they relate to the emergence of new parties, are often neglected or introduced in retrospect.

In my empirical undertaking I will rely heavily on previous research efforts, but will integrate the proposed indicators more closely into my theoretical framework. The idea is to give particular meanings to these indicators,

11. For example, Harmel and Robertson (1985) use the categories of political, social and economic variables, while Müller-Rommel (1993) uses six categories to explain the success of Green parties.

TABLE 5.3. implications

implication	direction of relationship if credible	if non-credible
1 new issues	+	+
2 formation costs	-	0
3 benefits of high demand	+	+
4 costs of electoral fight	+	0
5 benefits of weak challenger	+	0

by linking them to my theoretical variables. By doing so, I can rely on previous research efforts and more easily justify the selection of my indicators. The major problem in this undertaking is that my theoretical model captures the interaction between two actors, namely an established party and a potential new party. The empirical tests, however, rely on data at the level of election years, for reasons discussed in the previous chapter. Several characteristics of a given political system and country influence the theoretical variables of my model. But some of them can only serve as proxy for measures which operate at the level of particular established and potential new parties. Consequently, the empirical tests will focus on those characteristics that describe the general political environment in which new parties form.

I will first study separately the theoretical implications which figure in table 5.3. Doing so allows me to establish links with the substantive literature, which has dealt with similar explanatory factors. Table 5.4 lists for each theoretical variable the explanatory factors I employ. Most of these appear prominently in the literature. Justifications for their use appear in the subsequent sections, where I deal with each implication separately. This table also shows that I collapse the tests of two implications. Table 5.3 suggests that the effects of both the costs of an electoral fight and the benefits of a weak challenger display an identical pattern. In addition, as I argue more thoroughly below, these two theoretical variables are largely two sides of the same coin. Variables that affect the costs of an electoral fight are likely to be the same as those that affect the benefits of a weak new challenger. For instance, a high electoral hurdle like the German 5 percent *Sperrklausel* decreases the costs established parties face in fighting potential newcomers. At the same time such a high threshold is likely to decrease the benefits a weak challenger can expect from competing in an election. Consequently, I will use the same variables to measure these two theoretical concepts and proceed to a joint test.

As mentioned, all the implications to be tested relate the likelihood of new political parties to my theoretical variables. Sometimes, however, the relationships vary according to an additional factor, as shown in table 5.3 and illustrated graphically in figure 3.4. If weak potential new parties encounter serious difficulties in credibly threatening to form a new party, some relationships should, according to the model, either change or fail to materialize at

TABLE 5.4. Theoretical variables and operationalizations

	theoretical variable	empirical variables
1	New issues	degree of pluralism (plural, semiplural)
		linguistic homogeneity
		religious homogeneity
		ethnic fragmentation
		size of population
		economic growth
		unemployment rate
2	Formation costs	public party financing
		ballot access: petition signatures requirement
		ballot access: electoral deposit
3	Benefits from high demands	degree of centralization (taxes)
		government change in previous inter-election period
		majority government
		number of parties in government
		provisions for referendums
4	Cost of electoral fight	threshold of exclusion
5	Benefits for weak challenger	threshold of representation
		federalism
		number of parties in government
		number of governments (per decade)

all. The credibility of a weak new challenger is, however, only a shortcut for a simple criterion deriving from my theoretical model. More precisely, I label a weak new challenger credible provided it is better off forming a new party after its demand was rejected, rather than merely backing down from its demands. In the terminology of the theoretical chapter, this depends on the benefits and costs a weak contender expects from forming a new party. When the former exceed the latter a weak challenger is credible, and if not its challenge fails to be credible.

Consequently, the indicator whether a weak potential new party is credible has to rely on the measures of both the benefits of the weak new party and the formation costs. To measure the formation costs I employ three pieces of information (Table 5.4). The first two measure the difficulty of getting access to the ballot (Harmel and Robertson 1985). Among them, the electoral deposit is the amount a party must pay to place a candidate on the ballot. I express this monetary amount as a fraction of the GDP per capita to allow for meaningful comparisons across time and space.[12] Similarly, in some countries, a certain number of signatures is required to gain access to the ballot. This measure reflects the proportion of the total electorate in a given country that has to provide a signature for a candidate to qualify for the ballot. Again, this standardization permits comparisons across time and space. The third variable indicates whether or not a country finances its political parties from public funds. If that is the case, the formation costs are likely to be smaller.

The benefits of a weak new party depend very much on the electoral sys-

12. A more detailed discussion of this and the other measures appears below.

tem and its thresholds (Table 5.4). I employ the two best-known thresholds, namely the thresholds of representation and of exclusion. They measure, respectively, the minimal vote share with which a party might win a seat and the vote share with which a party is assured of winning a seat. The benefits of a weak party decrease as these thresholds become more important. Weak new parties are also likely to benefit more strongly in federal systems. As Chandler and Chandler (1987) convincingly argue, federal polities increase the points of access for new parties and thus increase the benefits that they may obtain through political offices. In addition, weak new parties are likely to get more benefits when the number of parties in government is important and when governments change before new elections. With an important number of parties in government, the likelihood of participating in a government coalition increases, while frequent government changes result in a similar outcome.

On the basis of these eight measures, I construct a summary indicator.[13] The cutoff point that distinguishes between situations where a weak new party is credible and those where it is not is largely arbitrary. The criterion adopted here is that in one fifth of all elections a weak new party will not be credible. Obviously, the empirical results vary as a function of this cutoff point, but surprisingly only the implications concerning the benefits of the weak new party and the formation costs undergo noticeable changes. I discuss these changes when they are relevant for the findings reported below. In table 5.5, all elections are classified according to whether weak new parties are credible or not, based on the criteria outlined.

Using this admittedly crude measure we can begin testing the different implications of the theoretical model. In order to get sufficient confidence into the dataset used here, I will present for each implication some simple bivariate relationships. These analyses attempt to replicate results discussed in the literature on new political parties. In most cases I am able to reproduce these results with my dataset. This lends some additional credibility to the variables used. After these simple analyses I present tests of the implications, based on the theoretical model. These individual tests of implications give a first hint at the usefulness of the theoretical model. Following the individual tests we shall present analyses which test jointly all the implications for the emergence of new political parties.

New Issues

The first implication of the theoretical model relates the importance of new issues with the emergence of new parties. The general idea of the implication

---

13. This indicator is the sum of the standardized variables, which were adequately signed. I discuss this construction in more detail in the appendix.

TABLE 5.5. Elections with credible and non-credible weak challengers

country	credible	non-credible
Australia	1951-1990	
Austria	1949-1990	
Belgium	1949-1991	
Canada	1962-1965, 1984-1988	1949-1958, 1968-1980
Denmark	1947-1990	
Finland	1951-1966, 1975-1991	1970-1972
France	1951-1958, 1973-1988	1962-1968
Germany	1953-1990	
Great Britain	1974(1)-1987	1950-1970
Greece	1977-1990	
Iceland	1949-1959	1963-1987
Ireland	1951-1961,1977-1989	1965-1973
Italy	1953-1987	
Luxembourg	1951-1989	1948
Netherlands	1948, 1956-1986	1952, 1989
New Zealand		1949-1990
Norway	1949-1989	
Portugal	1979-1991	
Spain	1982-1989	
Sweden	1952-1991	
Switzerland	1951-1991	
United States	1960-1988	1952-1956
total number of elections	209	52

is that new parties should be more frequent when new issues become more important, and this should be independent of whether or not weak new parties are credible. This implication is hardly surprising, and indeed finds support in most of the literature on new political parties (Hauss and Rayside 1978, 36f; Harmel and Robertson 1985; Rosenstone, Behr, and Lazarus 1984, 43f; Kitschelt 1988, 219; Rüdig 1990; Müller-Rommel 1993, 104ff). However, problems arise with regard to finding adequate measures of the importance of new issues. If the focus is on a particular class of parties, for instance Green or right-wing parties, the task is made slightly easier. In the study of Green parties, Kitschelt (1988) uses, for instance, the importance of the conflict over nuclear energy. Müller-Rommel (1993) employs the strength of post-materialism in a given country as indicator. Similarly, studies on new parties on the extreme right often use measurements of immigration problems (Mayer and Perrineau 1989).

Figure 5.6 depicts the relationship between the number of new political parties per election and the level of postmaterialism.[14] Not surprisingly the

14. This analysis uses data presented in Müller-Rommel (1993). Excluded from this analysis are Australia, Canada, Finland, Iceland, New Zealand, Portugal and the United States, due to missing data. In addition one has to note that this indicator only varies across space, and not across time. A comparison across time would be possible for most European countries, but only for the period starting in 1970. At that point in time, Eurobarometer survey series started to ask questions about value preferences.

Fig. 5.6. Post-materialism and the emergence of new political parties

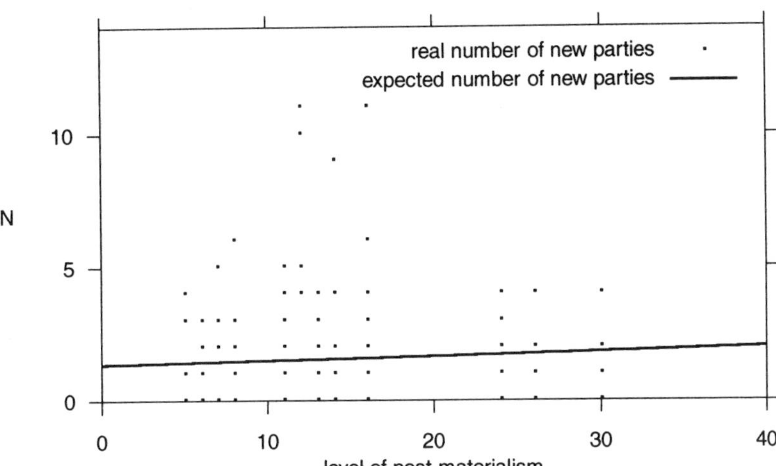

relationship is very weak, though slightly positive.[15] This result confirms the finding of Harmel and Robertson (1985, 516) of no relationship between the formation of new parties and post-materialism. This is hardly surprising, since post-materialism should only favor one type of new party, namely Green parties. But in our dataset a whole set of parties appears, which have nothing to do with post-material values. Nevertheless, the discussion of the Dutch Green party in chapter 2 suggested that even a country with a high level of post-materialism may fail to see a quick emergence of a Green party. Other intervening variables might account for this result. But obviously, univarite analyses cannot account for such a mediating factor. Hence, it fails to surprise that Harmel and Robertson (1985, 516) also do not find a relationship between the level of post-materialism and the emergence of a Green party.

When looking at new parties in a global manner, measuring the importance of new issues becomes more difficult. Harmel and Robertson (1985) provide a series of proxy variables. They use the size of the country, whether the society is plural, heterogeneous, sectionalized, with high income inequality and high

15. A simple bivariate negative binomial event-count model finds the following estimated coefficients (standard errors in parentheses): Intercept 0.29 (0.26), post-materialism 0.01 (0.02) and α 0.84 (0.17) $n = 172$. I used this analysis, as well as the subsequent ones, to calculate the expected number of new parties as a function of the independent variable. This expected number appears as a curved line in each figure.

Fig. 5.7. Growth rate and the emergence of new political parties

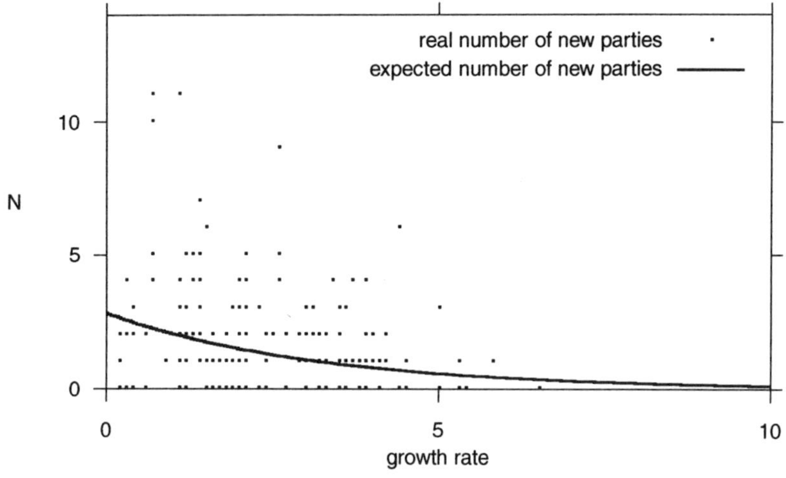

levels of post-materialism. Rosenstone, Behr, and Lazarus (1984, 134-138) add economic measures, as do Kitschelt (1989), Eagles and Erfle (1993), and Müller-Rommel (1993, 107f, 1996).

These general measures taken individually also relate in my dataset with the emergence of new parties. Figure 5.7 shows a rather impressive relationship between the number of new parties in an election and the growth rate of that year. High growth rates considerably diminish the likelihood of party formation.[16] This result rejoins similar findings concerning general economic conditions by Fisher (1974) and Rosenstone, Behr, and Lazarus (1984). Müller-Rommel (1996), however, fails to find any relationship between growth rates and the emergence of successful Green or extreme right parties.

Another economic indicator often related to the emergence of new political parties is unemployment. Müller-Rommel (1996) finds a positive relationship between the unemployment rate and the emergence of successful Green parties, but no relationship between the same rate and the formation of suc-

16. Lane, McKay, and Newton (1991, 60) provide four figures for the growth of real GDP per capita. I have taken their figure for 1960-68 to cover all years before 1968, and their figure for 1979-85 for all elections after 1979. Between these years, I used the two other figures they provide. The relationship depicted in figure 5.7 stems from the results of a negative binomial regression with the following estimated coefficients (standard errors in parentheses): Intercept 1.04 (0.14), growth rate -0.32 (0.06) and α 0.63 (0.12) $n = 261$.

Fig. 5.8. Unemployment and the emergence of new political parties

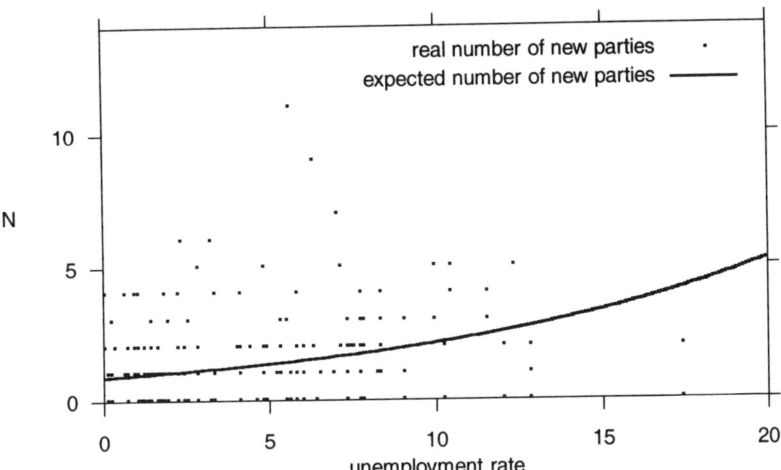

cessful extreme right parties. In my dataset this same relationship is rather strong (Figure 5.8). As the unemployment rate increases, the likelihood of new parties steadily increases.[17]

Harmel and Robertson (1985, 502) argue that countries with a large population are more likely to see new parties appear. The reasoning behind this hypothesis is that in large countries it is more likely that different population groups seek representation through specific political parties. Hence, new parties might be able to mobilize unrepresented groups. In my dataset a rather strong relationship between the size of the population and the emergence of new parties appears (Figure 5.9).[18] This rejoins Harmel and Robertson's (1985,

17. The unemployment data that Lane, McKay, and Newton (1991, 60) present cover five years. I have used their 1960 figure for all elections before 1965, and their 1970 figure for elections between 1965 and 1972. Their 1975 figure covers the years between 1972 and 1977, the 1980 data the period between 1977 and 1982, while their 1985 figure covers the remaining elections. I document interpolations used to complete the data in the appendix. The results from a negative binomial regression are the following estimated coefficients (standard errors in parentheses): Intercept -0.15 (0.11), unemployment rate 0.09 (0.02) and α 0.56 (0.12) $n = 261$.

18. The figures for the population size stem from Lane, McKay, and Newton (1991, 8). In the appendix I give some additional explanations on these figures. The results from a negative binomial regression depicted in figure 5.9 are the following estimated coefficients (standard errors in parentheses): Intercept 0.07 (0.10), population in millions 0.82 (0.24) and α 0.63 (0.13) $n = 261$.

Fig. 5.9. Population size and the emergence of new political parties

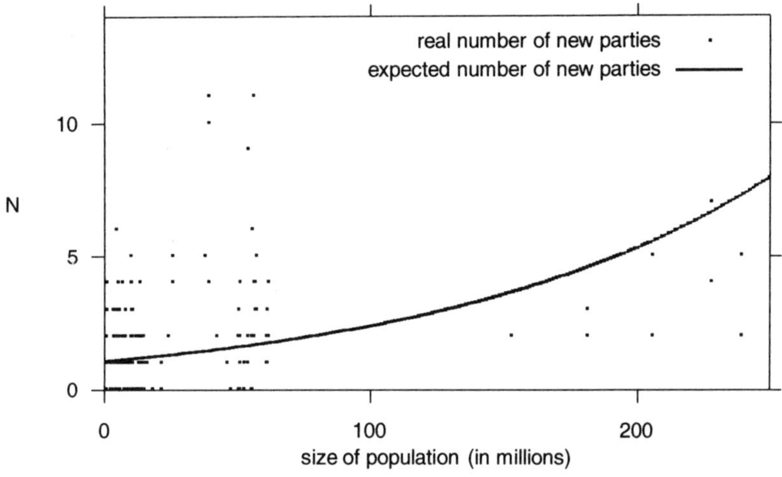

514) finding, who also report a positive relationship between the size of the population and the number of new parties.

Concerning the social characteristics of the country several authors claim that in plural, heterogeneous, and sectionalized societies new parties should be more frequent. Harmel and Robertson (1985, 515) find a positive relationship between party formation and the degree of pluralism when considering all new parties, but a non-significant one when focusing on genuinely new parties. Using their indicator, I find an average of 1.91 new parties per election in semiplural societies, but only 0.26 in plural societies.[19] In non-plural societies one can expect 1.27 new political parties per election.

An important factor is also the homogeneity of the society. Harmel and Robertson (1985, 515) find a positive relationship between the heterogeneity of a given society and the number of new parties. This same relationship also appears in my dataset, but is much weaker.[20] In religious homogeneous coun-

19. These expected numbers of new parties are calculated on the basis of the results of an event-count regression. The estimated coefficients (with standard errors in parentheses) are the following: Intercept 0.12 (0.09), plural society -0.58 (0.26), semiplural society 0.41 (0.20), α 0.76 (0.14). The definition of these variables stems from Harmel and Robertson (1985) and additional details on the coding appear in the appendix.

20. For the linguistic and religiously homogeneity of a country I employed the dataset of Banks and Textor (1968). They provide data for all countries except New Zealand. I have coded

tries the expected number of new parties per election year is 1.34. This number increases to 1.44 for heterogeneous countries.[21] A very similar relationship appears for the linguistic homogeneity of a country. In homogeneous societies one can expect 1.33 new parties per election, while in heterogeneous ones this number increases to 1.57.[22]

The results for these simple bivariate relationships give some additional validity to the dataset used here, since they largely reproduce findings reported in the literature on the emergence of new political parties. Hence, we can use these same indicators with more confidence while integrating them more closely into the theoretical framework.

In the present analysis I will use very similar measures, even though these remain quite problematic. First, I use the set of indicators concerning the homogeneity of a given society. The argument implies that countries that are homogeneous in respect to religion and language give rise to fewer new issues, whereas plural or semiplural countries allow for a multitude of interests to be politicized and consequently increase the potential number of new issues. The same tendency appears in countries with an important population. As its size increases, it is likely that subpopulations have different or opposing interests. This, again, increases the propensity for having more new issues. Finally, economic problems, measured by the unemployment and growth rate, are likely to give rise to new issues, or to render old ones more prominent. Higher levels of unemployment increases problems for certain groups of a society, while high growth rates often diminish these same problems.

By their very generality, these measures for my theoretical variable are bound to be error prone. In spite of this I will proceed to a test of my first implication concerning the role of new issues with the help of these variables. As for all other implications that predict identical relations across the two contexts (elections where weak new parties are credible or not), I will use the following statistical model:

$$E(y_i) = f\left(\beta_0 + \sum_{j=1}^{k} (\beta_{j1} + \beta_{j2} * x_{ci}) x_{ji}\right) \quad (5.1)$$

In this model $E(y_i)$ is the expected number of new parties at a given elec-

---

this country as linguistically homogeneous and religiously heterogeneous, based on information from the CIA World Factbook (1992) and Lane, McKay, and Newton (1991).

21. The estimated coefficients of the underlying event-count regression are the following: Intercept 0.37 (0.12), religious homogeneity -0.07 (0.15), α 0.83 (0.15).

22. The estimated coefficients of the underlying event-count regression are the following: Intercept 0.45 (0.14), linguistic homogeneity -0.17 (0.16), α 0.82 (0.15).

TABLE 5.6. New issues, weak contenders, and new parties

independent variable	base model all elections b (s.e.)	complete model all elections b (s.e.)	complete model only credible b (s.e.)
linguistic homogeneity	-0.47	-0.35	0.12
	(0.31)	(1.28)	(1.29)
religious homogeneity	0.10	0.16	-0.15
	(0.18)	(1.32)	(1.32)
ethno-linguistic fragmentation	-0.87	-1.89	1.82
	(0.69)	(3.10)	(3.03)
plural	-0.06	-0.85	0.57
	(0.23)	(2.73)	(2.74)
semiplural	0.11	0.17	0.08
	(0.20)	(1.90)	(1.91)
growth rate	-0.23	-0.20	-0.04
	(0.07)	(0.15)	(0.16)
unemployment rate	0.04	0.06	-0.02
	(0.02)	(0.15)	(0.15)
population	0.83	0.90	-0.34
	(0.27)	(1.54)	(1.57)
Constant	0.83		0.68
	(0.50)		(0.52)
α	0.34		0.30
	(0.09)		(0.09)
n	261		261
log-likelihood	-386.89		-383.11

tion, x_j are the k variables that measure the importance of new issues, while x_c is a variable that takes only two values. It is equal to one for elections where a weak new party is credible and zero otherwise. Thus, x_c reflects the classification of the elections shown in table 5.3. The assumed functional form f corresponds to a negative binomial distribution, which allows for overdispersion in an event-count model. Overdispersion allows the variance around the expected number of new parties to vary, and accounts for correlated events.[23] If my implication is correct all β_{j2} coefficients should be close to zero. If these coefficients were very different from zero, this would indicate that a given variable measuring the importance of a new issue has a different effect in elections where weak challengers are credible than in all other elections. Systematically, I will report in the tables that follow the results of a restricted base model, where all β_{j2} are set to zero, and a complete specification, where these coefficients are also estimated.[24]

Despite the poor quality of the indicators, the results in table 5.6 confirm to a large degree the implication. The results for the base model suggest a series of significant relationships, which undergo only minor changes when

23. If overdispersion is ruled out the variance parameter is restricted to equal $E(y_i)$, which then results in the familiar Poisson model.

24. More details on the estimation procedures figure in the appendix. There I address, among others, the problems of the distributional properties of the dependent variable, the time dependence as well as possible spatial relations.

compared with the complete specification. The comparison between the base and complete model suggests that they cannot be distinguished statistically. This implies that we cannot reject the hypothesis that the coefficients for the interaction variables are equal to 0.[25] Hence, if a variable is related to the number of new parties in all elections, its impact is most often only slightly different in situations where a weak challenger is credible. For instance, as the population size increases, the effect is not much different in elections where weak new parties are credible, compared to all other elections. Figure 5.10 illustrates that the expected number of new parties increases considerably with the size of the population.[26] While the effect is weaker in elections where weak new challengers fail to be credible, the difference with the effect in all other elections is not significant. In these latter elections increasing population sizes lead to a much higher expected number of new parties.

This strong result can be related to the frequency of new parties reported in table 5.2. All large countries, above all Spain, the United States, France, Germany, Italy, and Great Britain have above average numbers of new parties. In Spain this important number of new parties is strongly related to regionalist movements (Salvador Crespo and Molina Alvarez De Cienfuegos 1996). Presidential elections in the United States also attract a considerable number of new parties addressing a wide range of issues despite the low likelihood of electoral success (Fisher 1974; Sundquist 1983; Rosenstone, Behr, and Lazarus 1984; Mazmanian 1991). Similarly in Great Britain the size of the country appears to be related to the numerous new challengers on the electoral scene. Berrington (1985, 441f) notes that "[t]he British political landscape is indeed littered with the bodies of dead and moribund parties. . . . There has never been any lack of minor parties in Britain."

The results reported in table 5.6 for the economic variables also lend support to the implication. Overall, an increasing unemployment rate leads consistently to more new parties, but in situations where a weak challenger is credible this effect is slightly reduced. The other economic variable, namely the growth rate, also has the anticipated effect on the number of new parties. Increasing growth rates strongly diminish the number of new parties in all elections. The effect in elections where weak challengers are credible is slightly stronger, but this difference can hardly be distinguished from 0. This result resonates with the numerous case studies of new parties that often identify economic conditions as major driving forces. For instance, the Union for the Defence of Traders and Artisans (Union pour la défense des commerçants et artisans), better known under the name of its leader, Poujade, made its appearance when

25. This test is based on the log-likelihood ratio between the two models.

26. The graph represents the predicted number of new parties for the complete model when holding all other variables at their respective means.

Fig. 5.10. Population size and the number of new parties

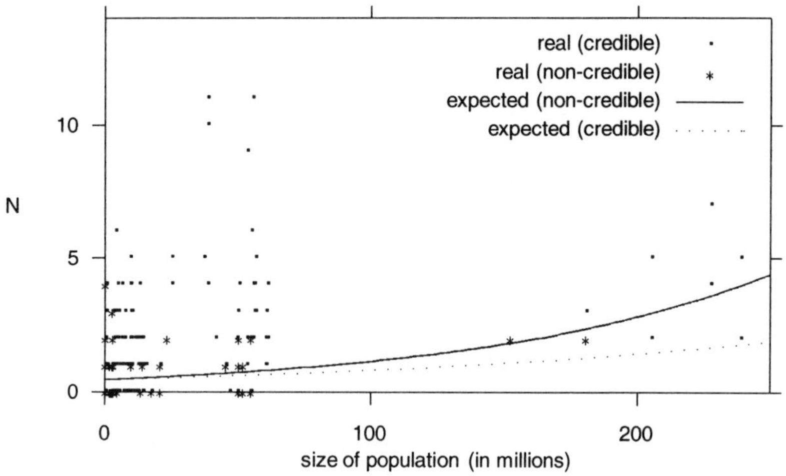

small shopkeepers suffered economically (Hoffmann 1956). Similarly, the rise of right-wing parties is often linked by scholars to economic problems (Mayer and Perrineau 1989; Immerfall 1998, 250f).

The effects of the indicators concerning the characteristics of the society are more mixed. For instance, in a linguistically heterogeneous country the expected number of new parties equals 1.41, while it drops to 1.11 in linguistically homogeneous countries. If the election under consideration allows for credible threats of weak challengers, this effect decreases.[27] This result resonates well with the important number of regional parties in Spain (Salvador Crespo and Molina Alvarez De Cienfuegos 1996). Language issues and regional autonomy are of considerable importance in this case.

Religious homogeneity has a very small effect on the number of new parties. This characteristic of a given society increases the expected number of new parties in all elections, while this effect is weaker when a weak new party is credible. Contrary to my implication, ethno-linguistic fragmentation considerably decreases the number of new parties in elections where weak challengers are not credible. In all other elections the effect of this variable almost

27. Here, as well as in all interpretations of the estimation results, I will present average changes induced by variations in the independent variable. I hold all other variables constant at their means and report changes in respect of this expected average number of new parties.

disappears. The implication predicts, however, that new issues and, thus, new parties, would be more frequent in situations where such fragmentation is important. It is likely, however, that this variable picks up effects that the other variables measuring the characteristics of society, like the two homogeneity measures, fail to pick up. Consequently, this negative effect has to be considered in the larger picture of the empirical results.

These results underpin my implication that the increasing importance of new issues leads to more new parties, independent of the weak challengers' credibility.[28] The substantive literature does not contradict this claim and most authors find similar results. The size of population, the degree of pluralism and heterogeneity consistently relate also in Harmel and Robertson's (1985, 514) dataset with the number of new parties. The important role of economic variables resonates to some degree with two tales in chapter 2. The formation of the NSDAP occurred in the wake of considerable economic turmoil, while economic problems also played a role in the emergence of the SDP in Great Britain. Similarly, in almost all empirical work, the link between new issues and new parties is of considerable importance.

Formation Costs

For the test of my second implication, which concerns the impact of formation costs, I will proceed in a similar way. The formation costs are part of most explanations for the emergence of new political parties. Fisher (1974) mentions this element when discussing minor parties in Germany and the United States. Similarly, Hauss and Rayside (1978) highlight formation costs in their list of facilitators. Among the different types of formation costs, the access to the ballot is of central interest (Harmel and Robertson 1985, 505; Rosenstone, Behr, and Lazarus 1984, 19-25).

In general, two elements can constitute a barrier for new political parties trying to access the ballot in an election. Some countries require a monetary deposit for registering a candidate. Cole (1992), for instance, shows in an interesting way the changes that an increased electoral deposit had on the number of candidates in British elections. Figure 5.11 shows the relationship between the importance of this deposit and the number of new political parties appearing on the electoral scene. I measure the electoral deposit as a proportion of

28. Choosing different cutoff points for the distinction between credible and non-credible elections leads naturally to some changes in the results. If the number of elections where weak new parties are credible increases, the implication finds stronger support. More precisely, the coefficients for situations where the weak challengers are not credible decrease consistently, which gives additional support to my implication. Similarly, when the empirical model is restricted to the explanation of genuinely new parties, no noticeable changes appear.

Fig. 5.11. Electoral deposit and the emergence of new political parties

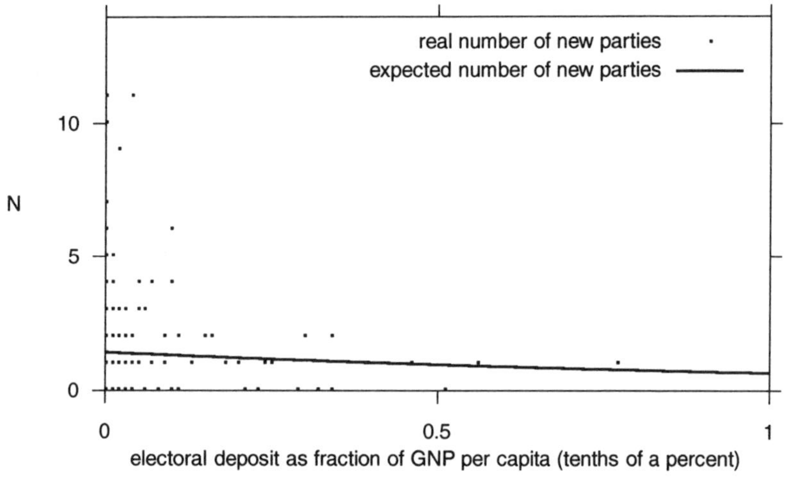

the current GNP per capita, expressed as tenths of a percent. The main sources for this indicator were the Interparliamentary Union (1976) and Sternberger and Vogel (1969).[29]

The relationship is negative, as expected, but surprisingly weak.[30] The expected number of new parties decreases only slightly as the amount of the electoral deposit increases. Ballot access, however, also depends on other barriers. An additional element, apart from the deposit, is the signature requirement. Some countries require that a candidate or a party presents a petition with a specified number of signatures before their name may appear on the ballot. I collected this information for each election drawing on the Interparliamentary Union (1976) and Sternberger and Vogel (1969).[31] The absolute number of signatures necessary to get a candidate on the ballot is weighted by the total electorate. Hence, it reflects the signatures required for each million voters.

Figure 5.12 shows a rather strong negative relationship between the num-

29. Additional information and more up-to-date sources for this indicator appear in the appendix.

30. The results from a negative binomial regression model are the following estimated coefficients (standard errors in parentheses): Intercept 0.35 (0.08), electoral deposit -0.80 (1.66), and α 0.82 (0.14) $n = 261$.

31. Again, I completed these sources with more up-to-date material as discussed in the appendix.

Fig. 5.12. Signature requirement and the emergence of new political parties

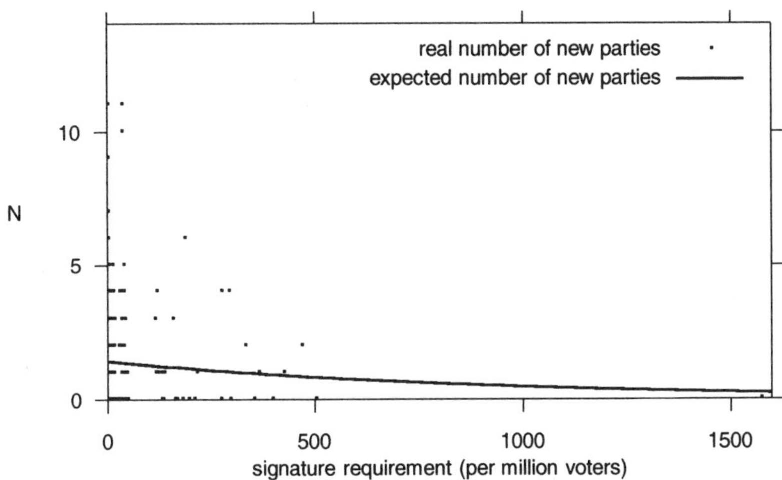

ber of signatures required and the number of new political parties.[32] Comparing these results with the findings of Harmel and Robertson (1985, 516) reveals one of their shortcomings. They rely almost exclusively on categorical indicators, summarizing a large variation in the underlying variables. By using these underlying variables, I am able to show that at least one element of the formation costs has a considerable impact on the likelihood of party formation. The effect is probably stronger still, since some countries use only a signature requirement, while others ask only for an electoral deposit. The joint effect of both variables might be even larger.[33]

Finally, Müller-Rommel (1993, 180f) rightly points out that the presence of public party financing can be an important factor in explaining the success of Green parties. It is likely that the knowledge that some expenses, when launching a new party, are refunded stimulates new party formation. Paltiel (1981) presents similar ideas on the impact of public financing of parties, as do Rosenstone, Behr, and Lazarus (1984).

---

32. The results from a negative binomial regression model are the following estimated coefficients (standard errors in parentheses): Intercept 0.36 (0.08), number of signatures required -0.11 (0.09) and α 0.82 (0.14) $n = 261$.

33. This shows again the usefulness of using several indicators, but also the need for joint, multivariate tests.

In my dataset information on whether public financing of parties is available stems from Paltiel (1981, 164ff), who provides indications for most countries studied here.[34] According to the data used here, on average 1.52 new parties appear in countries with public financing of parties. This number drops to 1.22 in countries where such financing of parties does not exist.[35] This finding rejoins Müller-Rommel's (1993, 181) claim that Green parties are more successful in countries with public party financing.

Having explored the different indicators used to measure the formation costs, I now turn to testing my implication. Its basic argument is that increasing costs of forming a new party should diminish the likelihood of new parties. But this relation should only hold when the threat of the weak potential new party is credible. If it is not, the formation costs should not be related to the frequency of new parties. I will use the following statistical model for all implications predicting that a relationship should only hold if a weak new party is credible:

$$E(y_i) = f\Big(\beta_0 + \sum_{j=1}^{k} (\beta_{j1} * (1 - x_{ci}) + \beta_{j2} * x_{ci}) x_{ji}\Big) \qquad (5.2)$$

Again, x_c is equal to 1 if a weak new party is credible, and equal to 0 in all other cases. x_j are the k independent variables that should help explain the expected number of new political parties $E(y_i)$. The β_{j1} coefficients measure the impact of a given variable (x_j) in elections where a weak new party is credible, while the β_{j2} coefficients measure the same effect in all other elections. If the implication is correct only the β_{j2} coefficients should differ from 0, while the others should approach 0. Again, I report in each table results of a restricted model where all β_{j2} coefficients are set to 0 in addition to the results for the complete specification. The functional form f, again, is assumed to correspond to the negative binomial distribution.

Table 5.7 shows mixed support for my implication. In the base model it appears that party formation is mostly affected by the presence of public party financing. If such public funds are available, new parties form significantly more often in elections where weak new challengers are credible. The effects of the two other measures are small and in addition of the wrong sign. Contrary to my implication as the petition hurdle becomes more important, the expected

34. I have coded all other countries as having no public financing of political parties, except for Portugal and Spain. This was supported by Delury (1987) and checked against the data provided in Katz and Mair (1992).

35. The results from a negative binomial regression are the following estimated coefficients (standard errors in parentheses): Intercept 0.15 (0.12), public financing of parties 0.32 (0.15) and α 0.80 (0.15), $n = 261$.

TABLE 5.7. Formation costs, weak contenders and new parties

	base model	complete model	
	only credible	only credible	only non-credible
independent	b	b	b
variable	(s.e.)	(s.e.)	(s.e.)
electoral deposit	0.80	0.57	-1.37
	(2.31)	(2.31)	(3.14)
signatures for	0.03	-0.00	-0.12
petition	(0.16)	(0.15)	(0.11)
public party	0.39	0.33	0.16
financing	(0.15)	(0.16)	(1.25)
constant	0.11		0.18
	(0.12)		(0.13)
α	0.78		0.76
	(0.15)		(0.14)
n	261		261
log-likelihood	-419.11		-417.56

number of new parties increases. Also contrary to expectancy, increasing the amount of the electoral deposit appears to affect positively the likelihood of party formation. But both of these latter effects are associated with large standard errors, and, in addition, hardly change in the complete model.[36] Interestingly, in the complete model the effects of both the signature requirement and the electoral deposit have the expected sign in elections where weak new challengers are not credible. But again, both fail to reach statistical significance. Figure 5.13 depicts nevertheless the relationship between the petition requirement and the formation of new political parties. The expected number of new parties decreases with a higher number of signatures required both in elections where a weak new party is credible and in those where a weak challenger is not credible. But the effect is considerably stronger when weak challengers are not credible.

These findings resonate in part with empirical cases. For instance, Day and Degenhardt (1988, 277f) report that the German *Aktion Soziale Gemeinschaft, die Partei der Sozialversicherten Arbeitnehmer und Rentner (ASG)* (Social Community Action (Party of Socially Insured Employees and Pensioners)) failed to collect the necessary 20,000 signatures to participate at its first Bundestag election. Given that they received only 1,834 votes in their participation in 1987, this can hardly surprise. Hence, electoral participation may sometimes be rendered more difficult by high ballot access requirements, but in the present case this only resulted in a delayed emergence of this party. Similarly, the careful study by Cole (1992) on the increase from 150 to 500 pounds of the British electoral deposit in 1985 suggests that it barely affected the number of candidates in by-elections. However, he notes a shift from independent and "other" candidates toward candidates from minor or major parties. Interest-

36. A log-likelihood ratio test does not allow to reject the hypothesis, that the coefficients in elections when weak new challengers are non-credible are 0.

Fig. 5.13. Petition signatures required and the number of new parties

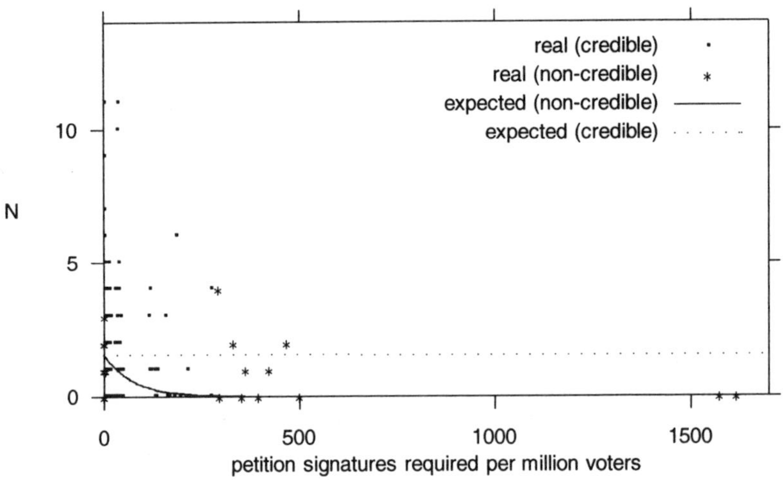

ingly, for the elections considered here, namely the elections since 1985, my classification characterizes them as allowing for credible threats by weak challengers. Hence, according to my implication the effect should be present, but as my results and those of Cole (1992) suggest, ballot access hardly diminishes party formation.

Hence, the results reported here only partly support my implication that increasing costs of party formation should decrease the number of new parties only if the weak potential new party is a credible threat. But only public party financing has the expected positive effect on the number of new parties in both specifications. This same effect is weaker in elections where weak challengers are not credible. The other variables have either the wrong sign or are larger in elections where weak new challengers are not credible. The standard errors attached to these coefficients are, however, quite important and make it hard to distinguish the effects from randomness. Nevertheless, the differences in the two sets of coefficients might explain why Harmel and Robertson (1985) do not find any significant relation between the difficulty of ballot access and the number of new parties. Since the effect is only noticeable when weak new parties are credible, looking at the relation in all elections is likely to lead to inconclusive results.[37]

37. When the cutoff point to determine situations where weak new parties are credible

Benefits of High Demands

The benefits of high demands are at the center of the third implication. This theoretical variable is practically absent in the literature on new political parties. Implicitly, arguments on the impact of the centralization of a given country on the emergence of new parties come close to this variable. Harmel and Robertson (1985), for instance, argue that in centralized countries the likelihood of new parties emerging should be smaller. A similar argument appears in Chhibber and Kollman (1998), who show that the effective number of parties decreases in the United States and India as a function of increasing centralization. Figure 5.14 gives weak support to this view.[38] It relates the degree of centralization measured as the percentage of taxes that the central government receives, compared to the total taxes for the entire country,[39] with the number of new political parties. The relationship is slightly negative, as Harmel and Robertson (1985) hypothesize, but, as in their analysis, is rather weak.

Also related to the benefits of high demands is the composition of government. Both Kitschelt (1988) and Müller-Rommel (1993) argue that, in the case of the Green parties, an important factor was the presence of socialists in government and the length of their tenure. If such parties did not share government responsibility, the likelihood of appearance of Green parties diminishes. This indicates that a longer presence in government makes it harder to implement new policies. Naturally, when looking at new parties in general, the presence of socialists in government can have both a positive and a negative effect on party formation. Instead I will look at a more general indicator, which basically measures whether there has been a government change since the last election. If Kitschelt's (1988) and Müller-Rommel's (1993) argument can be extended, a recent government change should diminish the likelihood of a new party. Using as source information provided by Lane, McKay, and Newton (1991), I coded each election whether it was preceded by a change in government. Contrary to the underlying hypothesis I fail to find a decrease of party formation after a government change. On average, in elections after a government change, one finds 1.44 new parties. In elections where the same

---

is changed, some results change. If the number of such elections increases, the effects of all variables decrease when weak new parties are credible. Hence the support for my implication is even stronger with other cutoff points. The results reported here also fail to undergo any significant changes if the analysis is restricted to genuinely new parties.

38. The results from a negative binomial regression are the following estimated coefficients (standard errors in parentheses): Intercept 0.86 (0.49), centralization -0.69 (0.63), and α 0.82 (0.15) $n = 261$.

39. Lane, McKay, and Newton (1991, 81f) report the data that is used here. Additional sources and interpolations used are documented in the appendix.

Fig. 5.14. Centralization (central government's tax share) and the emergence of new political parties

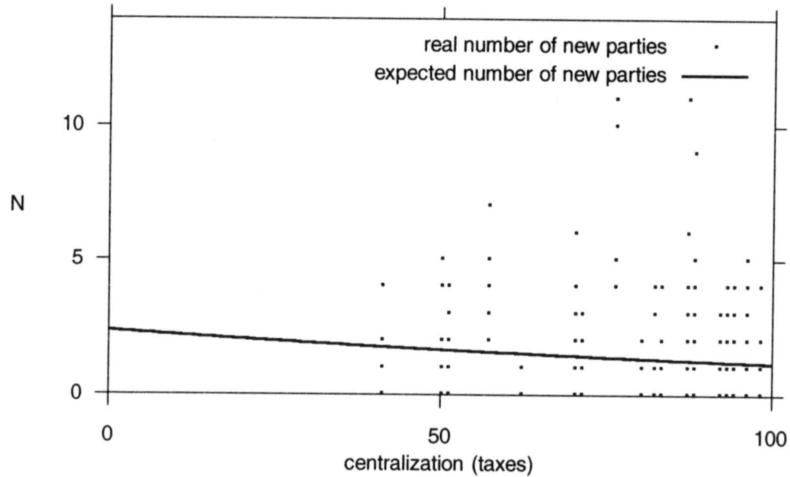

government presents itself to the voters this average is only 1.29,[40] a difference that is not statistically significant.

Finally, Müller-Rommel (1993, 120ff, 1996) argues that the presence of provisions for referendums diminish the likelihood of party formation. According to him, referendums allow potential new parties to formulate their griefs in an arena other than the electoral one. In the case of Green parties, however, he finds a positive relationship (Müller-Rommel 1993, 122, 1996). For the case of the extreme right parties no relationship is detectable. Employing data from Lijphart (1984), Austen, Butler, and Ranney (1987), and Nohlen (1990) I find a negative relationship, as hypothesized by Müller-Rommel (1996). In countries with referendums at the national level one can expect 1.27 new parties per election. In all other countries this average increases to 1.83.[41]

My theoretical implication predicts that if the benefits of high demands increase, they should invariably lead to a bigger number of new political parties.

40. The results from a negative binomial regression are the following: Intercept 0.25 (0.13) government change 0.11 (0.16) α 0.83 (0.15) $n = 261$.

41. The results from a negative binomial regression are the following: Intercept 0.61 (0.21) referendum -0.37 (0.23) α 0.80 (0.14) $n = 261$.

TABLE 5.8. Benefits of high demands, weak contenders, and new parties

independent variable	base model all elections b (s.e.)	complete model all elections b (s.e.)	complete model only credible b (s.e.)
majoritarian	0.53	0.66	0.11
government	(0.20)	(1.13)	(1.15)
number of parties	0.12	0.86	-0.79
in government	(0.09)	(0.67)	(0.67)
government change	0.26	-0.52	0.77
	(0.17)	(0.64)	(0.67)
centralization	-0.83	-2.81	2.27
(taxes)	(0.70)	(2.35)	(2.28)
referendum	-0.22	0.02	-0.23
	(0.26)	(0.78)	(0.84)
constant	0.55		0.47
	(0.53)		(0.52)
α	0.73		0.59
	(0.14)		(0.13)
n	261		261
log-likelihood	-416.16		-405.16

I argue that these benefits depend largely on how quickly a high demand can be implemented. Hence, using Kitschelt's and Müller-Rommel's argument, I assume that a recent government change decreases the benefits of high demands. Similarly, if the government is majoritarian, or if on average there are few parties in the government, changes are more likely to be adopted. Here, governmental parties do not need to take as much notice of opposing views, since they have no or only a limited number of partners to listen to. Referendums according to the argument discussed above should decrease the benefits of high demands, since the same benefits can be achieved by launching a referendum. Finally, in highly centralized countries, benefits from important demands are most likely higher. High demands often require decisions which are taken at the center; if a country is highly centralized, the effect of such decisions is much stronger. These five indicators serve as measures of the benefits of high demands.

The results in table 5.8 give little support to my implication. The results for the base model suggest that as expected the presence of majoritarian governments increases the likelihood of party formation. This effect is, however, counteracted by the impact of the number of parties in government. As this number increases, new parties also become more likely. Changes in government preceding the election also increase slightly the chances of seeing a new competitor on the ballot. Since such changes decrease the benefits of high demands, the effect contradicts my implication. It is likely, however, that this measure for these benefits is too crude. A simple case in point is the emergence of the National Democratic Party (Nationaldemokratische Partei Deutschlands, NPD) in Germany (Fisher 1974, 141-151; Mackie and Rose 1991, 161; Day and Degenhardt 1988, 226f). Its emergence and rise are often linked to the first grand government coalition between the social-democrats (SPD) and the conservatives (CDU). Hence, a government change was instrumental in this party's rise, but for reasons that differ from those underlying the present implication. Contrary to my implication the degree of centralization decreases the likelihood of party formation. Finally, in support of my implication I find that allowing for referendums in a given polity decreases party formation.

Comparing these results to those of the complete specification suggests that the effects of the various variables are different in elections where weak new challengers are credible.[42] My implication suggested otherwise. Interestingly enough, in the complete specification again two variables have the expected effect. Majoritarian governments increase and government changes decrease the likelihood of party formation. In elections where weak new parties are not credible, the effect of majoritarian governments even increases, while the latter effect largely disappears. Referendums, according to the results of the complete specification appear to decrease party formation mostly in elections where weak challengers are credible, but not so in all other elections. While the direction of the effect is as expected, it should not differ between the two types of elections. A possible explanation might be found in a country where referendums are used heavily, namely Switzerland. Several authors (e.g., Gruner 1977) argue that the formation of parties in Switzerland is strongly related to the development of direct democracy in the past.[43] Referendums required organizations capable of organizing campaigns, and these transformed themselves later into political parties participating in elections. However, in more recent times research has shown that referendum campaigns also drain the resources of social movements that they could devote to other activities (e.g., Kriesi 1995, 96f). Consequently, they may intervene less frequently in elections. This view, in support of my implication, stems from a country where all elections have weak credible challengers. Thus the expected effect of the referendum variable in this context might be in part due to the Swiss cases.

Finally, the two remaining variables also appear to have their major effect in elections where weak challengers are not credible. Increasing numbers of parties in government lead to more new parties, while stronger centralization decreases the likelihood of party formation. These effects largely disappear when weak challengers are credible. Figure 5.15 illustrates this for the centralization measure. The effect of this variable is almost nonexistent in elections where weak new parties are credible, while the effect of the same variable is

42. This is based on a log-likelihood ratio test between the two models.

43. Jost (1986), however, questions this link between direct democracy and the emergence of parties in Swiss history.

Fig. 5.15. Centralization and the number of new parties

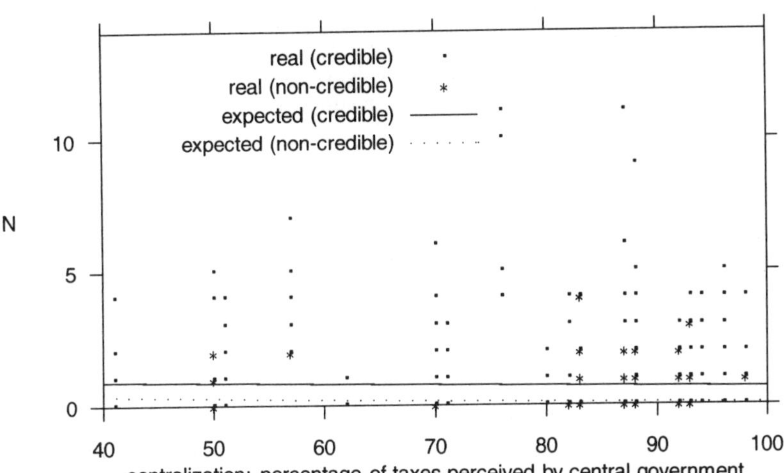

much more strongly negative in all other elections. This, as the results for the other variables, leaves us with a mixed picture for the empirical tests of this implication.[44]

Costs of Electoral Fight and Benefits of Weak Potential New Party

The last two implications concern the costs an established party has to bear when fighting a newcomer on the electoral scene and the benefits of a weak new party. These two theoretical variables are two sides of the same coin. If it is hard for an established party to fight a newcomer, it is almost inevitable that the benefits of the weak challenger are higher. Consequently, indicators related to the former theoretical variable are also likely to be linked with the latter. In addition, since the two implications predict similar relationships, we shall test them together.

Like the first two implications, these last two also find several parallels in the literature. The costs that an established party has to bear in an elec-

44. Interestingly enough, if the analysis focuses only on genuinely new parties the results of the base model suggest stronger effects for the centralization measure and for the presence of referendums in a country. In the complete specification of the model these differences disappear, however.

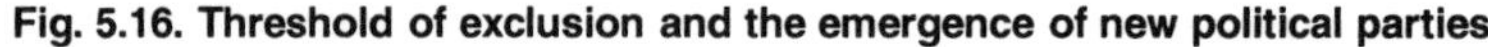

Fig. 5.16. Threshold of exclusion and the emergence of new political parties

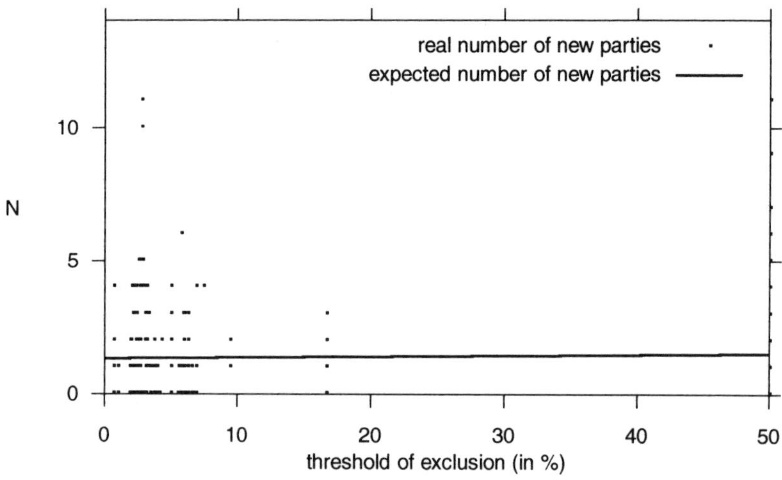

toral fight are often linked to the electoral system and its implicit thresholds. Harmel and Robertson (1985, 505) hypothesize that in proportional representation systems new parties should be more frequent. The same argument appears in Müller-Rommel (1993, 1996). While Harmel and Robertson (1985, 515) find a statistically significant relationship, it is of the wrong sign. More precisely, new parties appear more frequently in countries with plurality rule. Müller-Rommel (1996), however, finds that both extreme right and Green parties emerge more frequently in proportional representation systems. At the same time he also finds a negative relationship between their success and the proportionality of the electoral system for the latter parties (Müller-Rommel 1993, 117).

Figures 5.16 and 5.17 reflect some of these ambiguities. They relate two electoral thresholds to the number of new political parties. The threshold of representation corresponds to the lowest percentage with which a political party can achieve representation in parliament. In the Netherlands, for instance, this percentage corresponds to two-thirds of a percent, while in Germany the *Sperrklausel* sets it at five percent. The threshold of exclusion, on the other hand, corresponds to the percentage up to which a party can be excluded from a parliament. In a plurality electoral system a party may fail to win a seat as long as it wins less than 50 percent of the vote. Only with a vote share exceeding this threshold is a party assured of winning a seat. Both thresholds

Fig. 5.17. Threshold of representation and the emergence of new political parties

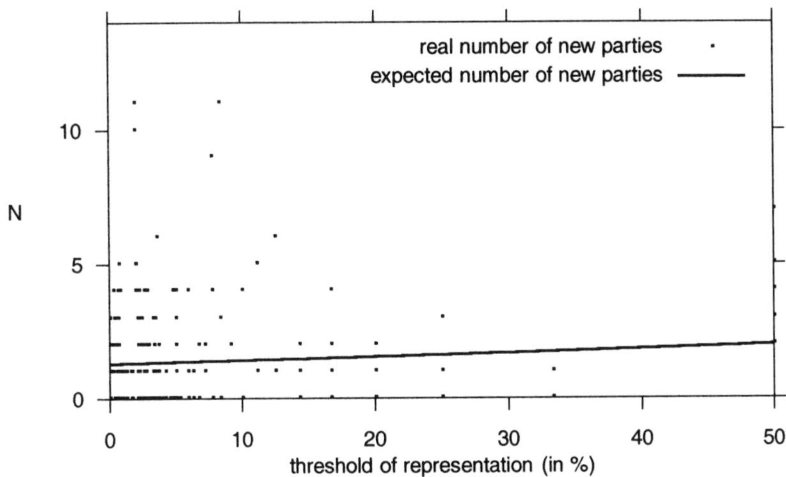

depend on the electoral formula used in a particular election and the number of parties competing in the election.[45] Despite strong theoretical reasons for expecting fewer new parties where electoral thresholds are high, the relationships turn out to be positive. Hence, as the threshold of exclusion increases, new parties become marginally more likely (figure 5.16).[46] The relationship is slightly stronger for the threshold of representation, but again in the wrong direction (figure 5.17).[47]

One of the reasons why the relationship between these electoral thresholds and the emergence of new political parties is positive might be the presence of the United States in the sample. As previously discussed, in presidential elections, which we consider here, new parties appear quite frequently. This happens despite rather high electoral thresholds. Consequently, the results based

---

45. The main sources for information on the electoral system employed are Sternberger and Vogel (1969) and Nohlen (1978, 1990). In the appendix I discuss in more detail these sources and the way these electoral thresholds are computed for various electoral systems.

46. The results from a negative binomial regression are the following estimated coefficients (standard errors in parentheses): Intercept 0.27 (0.10), threshold of exclusion 0.27 (0.33), and α 0.83 (0.12) $n = 261$.

47. The results from a negative binomial regression are the following estimated coefficients (standard errors in parentheses): Intercept 0.25 (0.09), threshold of representation 0.87 (0.72), and α 0.81 (0.14) $n = 261$.

Fig. 5.18. Threshold of exclusion and the emergence of new political parties (without the United States)

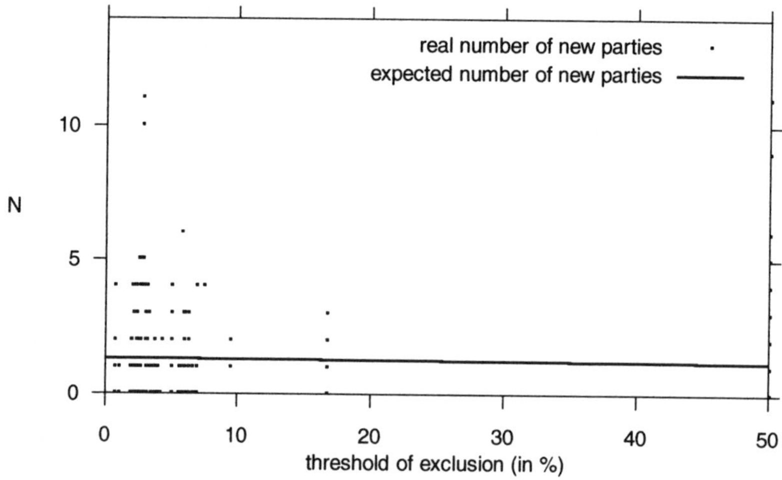

on the complete sample might be strongly affected by the observations from the United States. Figures 5.18 and 5.19, by omitting the United States from the sample, show that this is partly the case. For the threshold of exclusion the relationship becomes negative, though very weakly (Figure 5.18).[48]

The emergence of new political parties appears to be more strongly related to the threshold of representation (figure 5.19). As this threshold increases the likelihood of party formation decreases steadily.[49] For the analyses that follow, the result that the United States are in some sense an outlier will be crucial.[50]

In addition to these electoral thresholds, the benefits of a weak new party are to a large extent dependent on the parties already present in a political system. Harmel and Robertson (1985, 503) argue that in multiparty system the need for new parties is probably lowest. But if a new party should succeed

48. The results from a negative binomial regression are the following estimated coefficients (standard errors in parentheses): Intercept 0.29 (0.10), threshold of exclusion -0.20 (0.35), and α 0.85 (0.15) $n = 251$.

49. The results from a negative binomial regression are the following estimated coefficients (standard errors in parentheses): Intercept 0.43 (0.11), threshold of representation -3.02 (1.41), and α 0.81 (0.14) $n = 251$.

50. All other analyses presented in this chapter were also carried out without the United States, but no significant changes appeared in the results.

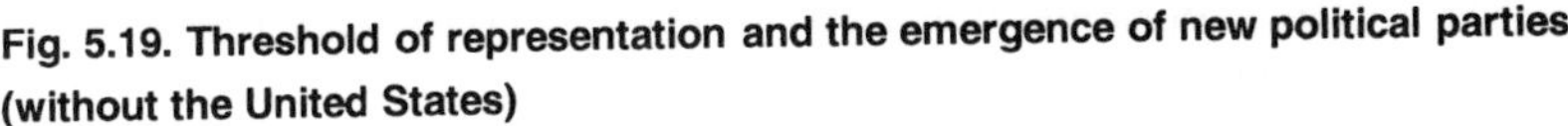

Fig. 5.19. Threshold of representation and the emergence of new political parties (without the United States)

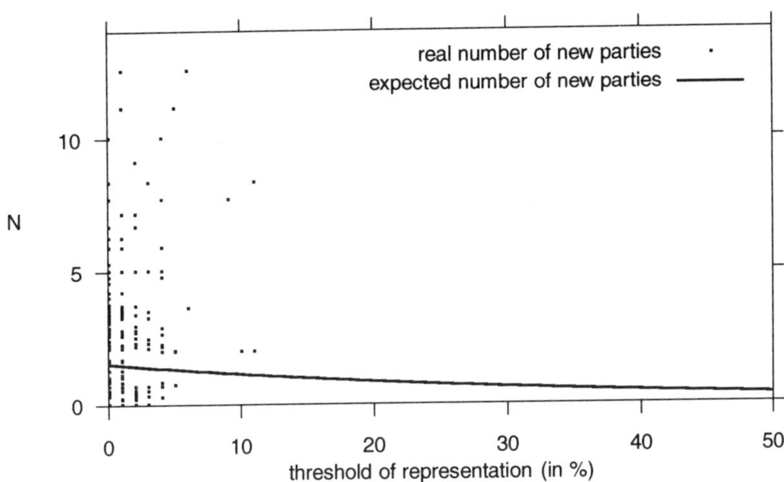

in a two-party system, its benefits might be considerable. Similarly, Müller-Rommel (1993, 137) makes the point that in a fragmented party system Green parties are more likely to succeed. At the same time, however, he also argues that the likelihood that an existing party has already picked up a certain issue is higher in fragmented party systems. Hence, if these arguments are right, it is not surprising that both Harmel and Robertson (1985, 514) and Müller-Rommel (1993, 138) fail to find even a weak relationship between the level of fragmentation (Müller-Rommel), respectively the number of effective parties (Harmel and Robertson) and the emergence of new parties.

Despite these mixed results of the preliminary explorations, I attempt to test this fourth implication, which not surprisingly predicts that the number of new parties should decrease if the costs of fighting a new party go up. But this relation should fail to materialize if weak new parties are not credible. Similarly, new parties should become more frequent if the benefits of a weak new party increase. Again, this relationship should only hold in situations where weak new parties are credible.

I measure the costs of fighting a new party through characteristics of the electoral system and of government. If the electoral laws provide for high electoral thresholds, the electoral system effectively keeps out an important number of new parties. Hence, the costs of fighting a new party decrease

TABLE 5.9. Costs of electoral fights, benefits of weak new party, weak contenders, and new parties

	base model	complete model	
	only credible	only credible	only non-credible
independent	b	b	b
variable	(s.e.)	(s.e.)	(s.e.)
threshold of	0.96	0.74	-0.84
exclusion	(0.53)	(0.53)	(2.24)
threshold of	1.77	1.72	0.64
representation	(1.57)	(1.54)	(3.56)
number of parties	0.10	0.03	0.23
in government	(0.09)	(0.09)	(0.34)
number of	0.00	-0.03	-0.21
governments	(0.04)	(0.04)	(0.23)
federal	-0.37	-0.47	0.13
	(0.24)	(0.24)	(0.71)
constant	0.01		0.42
	(0.16)		(0.23)
α	0.69		0.64
	(0.14)		(0.14)
n	261		261
log-likelihood	-414.01		-409.79

with the two electoral thresholds, namely the threshold of exclusion and the threshold of representation. It is obvious that the benefits of a weak new party also depend heavily on these thresholds. If the thresholds increase, a weak new party is much less likely to find representation; this will decrease its benefits.

The benefits of a weak new party are also likely to be higher in federal systems. There, even small parties might gain access to executive power, albeit at a lower level than the central government (Chandler and Chandler 1987). Similarly, as the number of parties in government increases or governments change frequently, it is much more likely that a new party can expect to join a government. This increases the benefits which a weak new party might anticipate when forming. By extension, these variables affect in a similar way the fighting costs of the established party.

The results for this combined test of two implications are only partially encouraging (table 5.9). Contrary to my implication higher electoral thresholds increase the likelihood of party formation in the whole sample. The threshold of representation shows the strongest impact. As this threshold increases, the expected number of new parties becomes significantly higher, if the weak ones are credible (figure 5.20). The effect is still positive, but smaller, in elections where a weak new party is not credible. Also, in contradiction to my implication are the results for the threshold of exclusion. Here the effect is positive in elections with credible weak challengers, while it becomes negative in all remaining elections. These results relate strongly to the findings of Harmel and Robertson (1985), who also found a relationship between the electoral system and the formation of new parties in contradiction to their expectations.

Fig. 5.20. Threshold of representation and the number of new parties

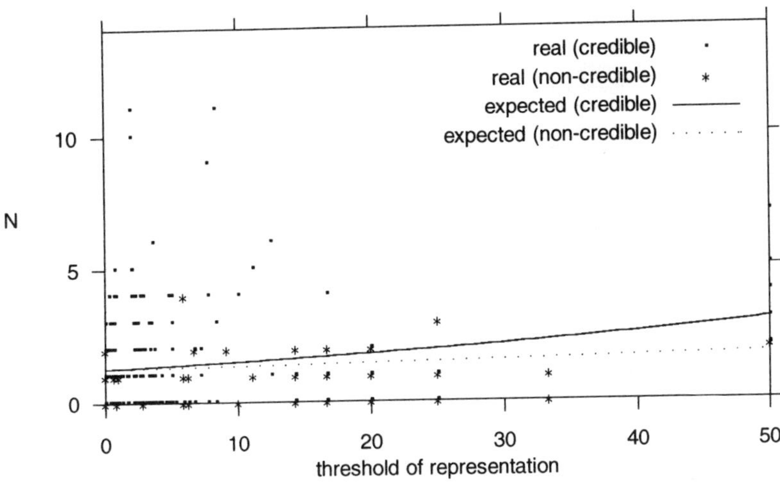

Excluding the United States from the sample, however, leads to results much more in line with my implication (table 5.10). While the effect of the threshold of exclusion is still positive, the effect for the threshold of representation is large and negative. As predicted by my implication, this effect is stronger if weak new challengers are credible than in the remaining elections (Figure 5.21).

The estimated coefficients for the number and composition of governments have the expected signs in the sample excluding the United States, but are comparatively small. In addition, in the complete specification it appears that the effect in elections, where weak new challengers are not credible, is larger. Finally, contrary to my implication, federalism leads to fewer new parties, whether the United States is included in the sample or not. On average in the sample without the United States, the expected number of new parties equals 1.28 in unitary systems. If a country is federal and the election allows for credible weak new parties, the expected number drops to 1.02. If the latter condition does not hold in a federal system, it only increases to 1.23. This effect is contrary to the implication, since I assumed that the benefits for a weak new party should be higher in a federal country. But the effect is quite small. Similarly, increasing the number of governments by one per decade or adding another party to government only slightly changes the expected number of new parties. An additional party in government in a credible situation

TABLE 5.10. Costs of electoral fights, benefits of weak new party, weak contenders and new parties (without the United States)

	base model	complete model	
	only credible	only credible	only non-credible
independent	b	b	b
variable	(s.e.)	(s.e.)	(s.e.)
threshold of	2.99	2.70	0.29
exclusion	(0.92)	(0.89)	(2.55)
threshold of	-8.79	-8.56	-2.62
representation	(4.37)	(4.23)	(4.87)
number of parties	0.07	-0.00	0.23
in government	(0.10)	(0.10)	(0.35)
number of	0.04	0.01	-0.20
governments	(0.04)	(0.05)	(0.23)
federal	-0.11	-0.21	-0.03
	(0.27)	(0.26)	(0.73)
constant	-0.04		0.39
	(0.17)		(0.24)
α	0.71		0.66
	(0.15)		(0.15)
n	251		251
log-likelihood	-386.69		-382.59

increases fails to change the expected number of new parties in a significant way, but in all other situations it leads to an increase to 1.51. The respective numbers for an additional government per decade are 1.21 and 0.99.[51]

Summing Up

It is obvious that these isolated tests of my implications only partially reveal the importance of the different theoretical variables. Since the latter stem from a single theoretical framework and derive from comparative statics results, it is important to control simultaneously for the other variables. To carry out such a joint test I only use the variables that, according to my theoretical model, should influence the likelihood of seeing new parties.[52] In table 5.11 I present in the first column (Model 1) the estimated coefficients for all variables that should influence the emergence of new parties according to my theoretical model. In order to assess whether each theoretical variable of my model con-

51. If the analysis discussed here focuses on genuinely new parties no important differences appear for the whole sample. If the cases from the United States are omitted, however, the coefficient for the threshold of representation decreases and fails to reach statistical significance.

52. Due to serious multi-collinearity problems, it was not possible to include both sets of variables for each implication. The multi-collinearity problems mostly stem from variables that only vary across space and not across time. With a considerable number of independent variables, such country-specific measures become increasingly problematic. In the appendix I present results from an additional analysis, where for each implication separately the second set of explanatory variables was added. The results suggest, that none of these additional variables contribute significantly to the explanation of the emergence of new parties.

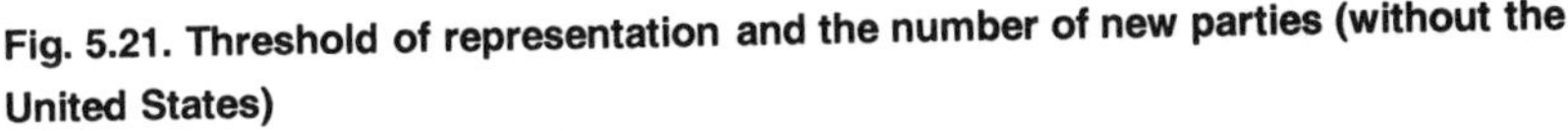

Fig. 5.21. Threshold of representation and the number of new parties (without the United States)

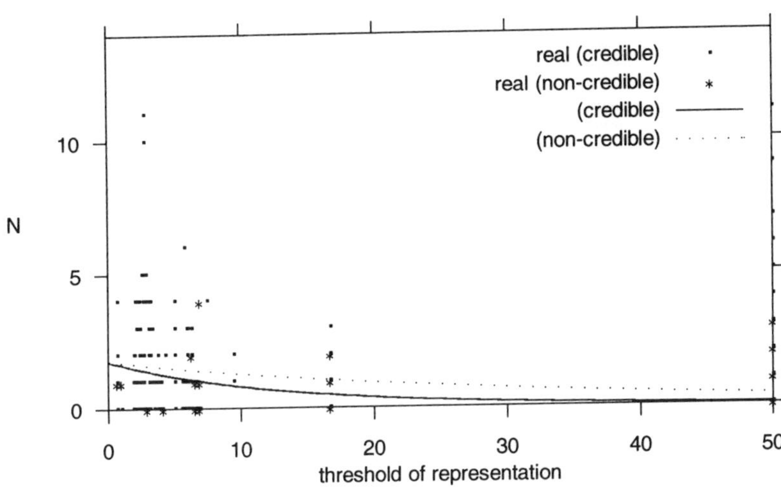

tributes to the explanation of the formation process, I estimate four additional sets of coefficients (Table 5.11, Models 2-5). In each of the four estimations, one theoretical variable together with its indicators was dropped from the equation.

Table 5.11 reemphasizes again the central role new issues play in the formation of new political parties. Their overall impact is strongly significant.[53] Among the variables employed to measure the importance of new issues few changes appear in comparison to the individual test. Again, linguistic homogeneity appears to diminish strongly the average of new parties per election. In heterogeneous countries one expects an average of 2.13 new parties at each election. In homogeneous countries this average drops to 0.92. This obviously again relates to the Spanish case discussed above.

The effect of religious homogeneity is of the wrong sign, but much smaller. Also of the wrong sign, but much stronger, is the effect of ethno-linguistic fragmentation. As this type of fragmentation increases, the average number of new parties decreases. Again, the effect of this variable has to be consid-

53. Based on the differences in log-likelihoods between the joint model and the other estimated equations, I carried out simple χ^2 tests. If not mentioned, I used a 0.05 level for statistical significance.

TABLE 5.11. Explaining party formation

independent variable	Model 1 b (s.e.)	Model 2 b (s.e.)	Model 3 b (s.e.)	Model 4 b (s.e.)	Model 5 b (s.e.)
New issues					
plural	0.24		0.40	-0.02	-0.22
	(0.36)		(0.32)	(0.30)	(0.25)
semiplural	-0.29		-0.31	-0.08	0.06
	(0.30)		(0.30)	(0.25)	(0.27)
religious homogeneity	0.20		0.23	0.15	-0.01
	(0.29)		(0.28)	(0.25)	(0.28)
linguistic homogeneity	-0.84		-0.73	-1.00	-0.45
	(0.47)		(0.43)	(0.42)	(0.41)
ethno-linguistic	-1.38		-1.37	-1.50	-0.81
fragmentation	(1.12)		(0.95)	(1.07)	(1.02)
growth rate	-0.22		-0.20	-0.24	-0.23
	(0.07)		(0.07)	(0.07)	(0.07)
unemployment rate	0.03		0.03	0.02	0.05
	(0.02)		(0.02)	(0.02)	(0.02)
population	1.56		1.53	1.59	0.84
	(0.39)		(0.37)	(0.37)	(0.30)
Formation costs (credible)					
public party financing	0.05	0.29		0.07	0.02
	(0.22)	(0.20)		(0.22)	(0.21)
electoral deposit	2.53	-0.59		2.98	3.73
	(2.31)	(2.51)		(2.25)	(2.06)
petition signatures	0.36	0.16		0.34	0.32
	(0.15)	(0.17)		(0.14)	(0.16)
Benefits from high demands					
centralization (taxes)	-1.15	-1.81	-1.26		-0.65
	(0.94)	(0.85)	(0.84)		(0.65)
majority government	0.08	0.44	0.10		0.09
	(0.23)	(0.20)	(0.22)		(0.25)
number of parties in government	0.17	0.09	0.11		0.09
	(0.18)	(0.16)	(0.18)		(0.10)
government change	0.05	0.14	0.06		0.07
	(0.18)	(0.19)	(0.18)		(0.18)
referendum	-0.22	-0.29	-0.24		0.18
	(0.29)	(0.28)	(0.30)		(0.25)
Fighting costs (credible)					
threshold of representation	-4.77	-0.04	-4.53	-4.54	
	(1.73)	(1.77)	(1.72)	(1.56)	
threshold of exclusion	2.59	1.91	2.62	2.20	
	(0.72)	(0.72)	(0.69)	(0.64)	
number of governments	0.02	0.01	0.02	-0.01	
	(0.05)	(0.04)	(0.04)	(0.04)	
number of parties in government	-0.09	0.10	-0.01	0.04	
	(0.18)	(0.16)	(0.18)	(0.09)	
federal	-0.20	-0.75	-0.34	0.01	
	(0.37)	(0.36)	(0.34)	(0.25)	
Constant	1.74	1.09	1.82	1.17	0.88
	(0.95)	(0.80)	(0.79)	(0.69)	(0.78)
α	0.20	0.53	0.24	0.22	0.28
	(0.09)	(0.14)	(0.10)	(0.09)	(0.09)
n	261	261	261	261	261
log-likelihood	-373.45	-403.88	-376.80	-375.11	-380.92
Δ log-likelihood		-30.43	-3.35	-1.66	-7.48

ered together with those of the other variables measuring the characteristics of society. Important effects also come from the economic variables, especially

Fig. 5.22. Growth rate and the number of new parties

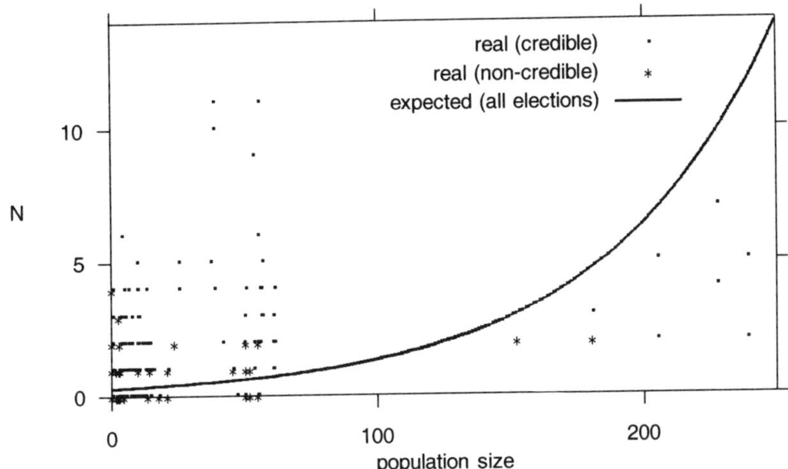

from the growth rate. As figure 5.22 shows, high growth rates heavily decrease the likelihood of seeing new parties. The unemployment rate, as expected, increases this likelihood, while the population size continues to relate positively to the formation of new parties. The large countries with important numbers of new parties discussed above illustrate this finding. Similarly, parties of the extreme right like the NSDAP discussed in chapter 3 and the Poujade movement in France provide examples for the effects of economic variables on the emergence of new parties.

The formation costs only contribute slightly to the explanation of new political parties. Controlling the different relationships for other variables also leads to changes for several effects. The required petition signatures have a positive and significant effect on the formation of new parties, while an increase in the electoral deposit continues to stimulate, though not significantly, the emergence of new challengers. The presence of public party financing as expected increases the likelihood of seeing new parties emerge. But compared to the individual test of this implication, the effect is much smaller. Overall the empirical support for this implication is limited. Formation costs fail to have a strong direct impact on the emergence of new political parties. It has to be noted, however, that the effect of these theoretical variables might be mostly of an indirect nature. Since the formation costs are an integral part of the credibility measure, any effect of the latter is related to the formation costs.

Contrary to the two previous theoretical variables, the impact of benefits from high demands overall is hardly significant. Some individual coefficients almost reach statistical significance, but together they cannot be distinguished from 0. The presence of referendums decreases as expected the frequency of new parties. The Swiss case with a high usage of referendums and relatively few new parties, provides illustration for this finding.

Among the other variables of this third implication, several have much smaller coefficients than in the individual test. The presence of a majoritarian government, for instance, has less of an effect on the expected number of new parties. It increases this number from 1.08 to 1.17, which is much smaller than the effect reported above. Similarly, an additional party in government increases the expected number of new parties from 1.10 to 1.31. The direction of this effect also contradicts my implication. The degree of centralization continues to have a negative impact on the number of new parties.

Finally, when controlling for the other implications, the link between the formation of new parties and the costs of fighting electoral challengers appears as a significant contribution. The threshold of representation considerably decreases the number of new parties, while the threshold of exclusion achieves the opposite (Figure 5.23). These opposite effects are largely due to the fact that these two measures are intimately related. The effects of the other variables undergo only few changes with respect to the individual test. An additional government per decade increases the expected number of new parties from 1.10 to 1.12. Still in contradiction to my implication is the impact of a federal system. In unitary systems the expected number of new parties is equal to 1.16, and it is only 0.95 in federal countries. Since I assumed that federal systems increase the benefits of weak new parties, my implication predicts that the relationship would take the opposite direction.[54]

This joint test strengthens the conclusion that new issues are central to the explanation of the emergence of new parties. If new issues are important, new parties emerge much more frequently. New issues are related with economic indicators, the size of the population, and the characteristics of society. The effect of the costs of forming a new party is rather puzzling in the joint tests. It appears that increasing the petition signatures and the electoral deposit stim-

54. Dropping the cases from the United States only marginally alters the results presented here. The most significant difference is that the effect of the threshold of representation becomes much smaller. Given that the direction of this change is opposite to the one found for the individual test of the relevant implication, I do not consider this change in more detail. It is likely that controlling for the other implications, the United States is no longer an outlier. Hence, omitting it from the analyses only reduces the number of cases. When focusing the analysis on genuinely new parties in the whole sample no significant changes appear. But, in parallel with the previous remark, dropping the United States from the analysis decreases the effect of the fighting costs on the emergence of new parties.

Fig. 5.23. Electoral thresholds and the number of new parties

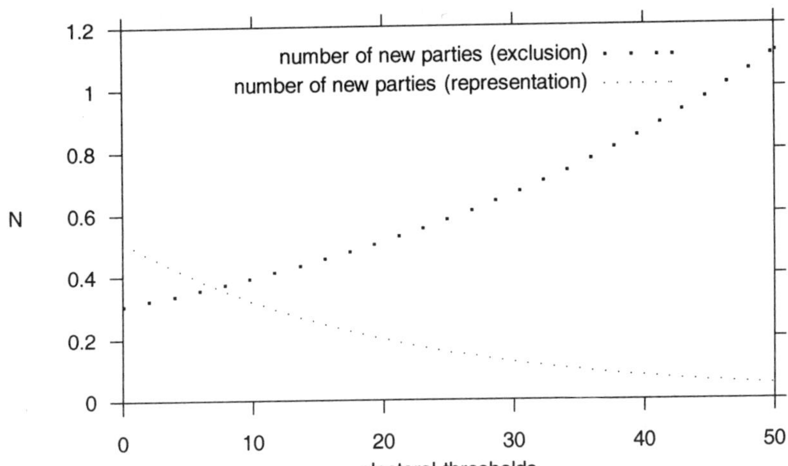

ulates party formation. This goes squarely against my implication and most stances in the literature. It rejoins, however, the finding of Cole (1992) on the impact of the increased electoral deposit adopted in Great Britain in 1985.

More in line with my implication is the fact that public financing of parties diminishes the costs of forming a new party and consequently stimulates party formation. However, it is unclear whether the effect of the public funding of parties is stronger in elections where weak new challengers are credible, as my implication predicts, than in all other elections. These weak results for the impact of the formation costs on the emergence of new parties have to be taken, however, with some caution. As discussed above, the formation costs also influence the credibility of weak new challengers. Since the implication relating the fighting costs with the emergence of new parties only holds when weak new challengers are credible, it is obvious that the formation costs have at least an indirect effect. At least for this last implication they appear to be an important mediating factor explaining the formation of new parties.

The results for the implication on the benefits from high demands are largely disappointing. These benefits appear to be hardly related to the emergence of new parties. While some coefficients have the expected sign, they fail to contribute significantly to the explanation of party formation. More support appears for the implications concerning the benefits of weak new parties and the costs of fighting a new party in an election. The results show that the costs and benefits are strongly influenced by the electoral thresholds. Some other factors also play a certain role, but they pale with respect to the effects of the electoral system. Especially the threshold of representation decreases significantly the likelihood of party formation in elections where weak challengers are credible.

Conclusion

New political parties, contrary to an important stance in the literature, arise frequently in Western democracies. At almost every election a new party makes its appearance and disturbs the competitive game between established parties. To show the importance of this phenomenon was the first aim of the present chapter. More central goals of the chapter were the tests of the theoretical model, through estimations based on the implications presented in the theoretical chapter. These implications relate variables from the theoretical model to the frequency of new political parties.

In the present conclusion I summarize the insights of the empirical results. Empirical support is greatest for the first implication, which relates the importance of new issues with the emergence of new parties and their initial success. For the explanation of the emergence I showed that the problem "push" (Rüdig 1990) is crucial. Independent of whether or not weak new parties are credible, the number of new parties consistently increases with the importance of new issues.

Empirical support for the theoretical framework is more mixed for the other implications. Concerning the costs of forming a new party, these do appear to have an impact on the emergence of new actors on the electoral scene. Contrary to my implication, however, the importance of the petition requirement actually increases the number of new parties when weak ones are credible challengers. When controlling for the other explanatory factors, it still appears that public party financing decreases formation costs, and thus leads to more new parties; however, the other indicators display results contradicting the theoretical framework. On both the empirical and theoretical level the relationship between formation costs and the emergence of new parties is a contribution to the literature on new parties. The effect of the formation costs consistently varies according to the credibility of weak new challengers. This aspect is, however, completely absent from the literature on new political parties.

On a similar note, the effect of the benefits of weak new parties and the costs of fighting them on the electoral scene is of both theoretical and empirical interest. The substantive literature advances the hypothesis that these costs and benefits increase the likelihood of seeing new parties. The theoretical framework suggests, and the empirical results underpin, that this effect should only hold if weak new parties are credible. If they are not, this effect should disappear. This contribution is most likely at the basis of most of the conflicting results on the relationship between the electoral system and the emergence of new parties. Only with the help of my theoretical model was I able to highlight this intervening factor, which is the credibility of the challenge by a weak new party.

The tone is more mixed for the relationship between the benefits that a potential new party gets from an accepted high demand and the formation of new parties. Most effects are rather small, when controlling for the other explanatory factors of the emergence of new parties. In addition only the referendum variable and the indicator whether the government is majoritarian have the expected effects.

Despite the less than perfect quality of the data used here and the considerable number of potential problems, the results lend considerable support to my theoretical model. In the concluding remarks of my study I will discuss these results in this more general context and relate them to possible extensions.

CHAPTER 6

The Initial Success of New Parties

The implications derived from the theoretical model mostly relate a series of theoretical variables with the likelihood of new political parties. But some implications also give hints at the relative frequency of weak and strong new parties. Consequently, some limited information is available on the initial strength of the newcomers on the electoral scene. The implications that yield this information appear in table 6.1. They correspond to implications 1, 3, and 4 discussed in chapter 3.[1] The first of them suggests that the increasing importance of new issues should lead to more new parties, both of the strong and weak type, as long as the latter are credible. If the weak parties are not a credible challenge, the increasing importance of new issues only leads to more strong new parties. Consequently, on average, new parties should be stronger when new issues become more important.

The third implication discussed in chapter 3 suggests that weak new parties, provided that they are credible, arise more frequently if the benefits of high demands increase. In parallel, strong new parties emerge less frequently under such circumstances. Hence, as the benefits of high demands increase, the average strength of new parties should go down. If the weak challengers are not credible threats, however, the relationship is reversed. Then increasing benefits do not change the frequency of weak new parties, but do so for the strong ones. Hence the average strength should increase with higher benefits.

Finally, the fourth implication presented in chapter 3 predicts that weak new parties arise more frequently if the costs of fighting a newcomer in the electoral arena increases. But this relationship only holds if weak new parties are credible challengers. If they are not, changes in the costs of fighting an electoral battle do not alter the frequency of weak and strong new parties. Consequently, the average strength of new parties should not change.

These implications rely, as mentioned above, on the relative strength of the potential new parties. The initial success at the ballot, while certainly related to this relative strength, depends also on another set of actors, namely voters.

---

1. Implications 2 and 5 of chapter 3 fail to give indications on the strength of new parties. Consequently, they do not appear in table 6.1.

TABLE 6.1. Implications for initial strength of new parties

	implication	direction of relationship	
		if credible	if non-credible
1	new issues	weak +	weak 0
		strong +	strong +
		strength 0	strength +
3	benefits of high demand	weak +	weak 0
		strong -	strong +
		strength -	strength +
4	costs of electoral fight	weak +	weak 0
		strong 0	strong 0
		strength -	strength 0

However, these do not appear in the theoretical model. Consequently, the following tests of the implications have to be taken with a grain of salt. They reveal certainly one aspect of the initial strength of new parties. But strategic behavior, like tactical voting and coordination among voters (Cox 1997), might reduce considerably the link between the relative strength of a potential new party and its first electoral result.

Following the discussion in chapter 4, it is obvious that compared to the empirical analyses on the emergence of new parties in chapter 5, I have to switch my observational unit to test these implications. From now on I will focus on the new political parties that presented candidates at an election. As table 5.2 in chapter 5 shows, overall 361 new parties emerged in the 261 elections under consideration. For each of these parties I attempted to determine the vote share that they received in the first national election where they fielded candidates. Despite considerable effort it proved impossible to obtain exact electoral returns for all of these new parties. Most likely, a considerable number of these parties obtained so few votes that they appeared in official electoral statistics under the heading of "others." Overall, I was able to determine the exact first electoral result for 260 new parties. This implies that for a considerable number of new parties I fail to have information on the dependent variable that I wish to explain, namely their initial electoral success. Despite the fact that these parties with missing electoral returns are likely to have had only marginal electoral success, omitting them from the analyses that follow might lead to biases. This especially, since the accuracy of electoral statistics is likely to vary from country to country. And since some of my explanatory variables are country-specific, simply omitting the parties with missing data is likely to lead to biases (e.g., Achen 1986). Table 6.2 reports the results of a simple analysis attempting to explain the presence or absence of information on the initial electoral success of new parties. The dependent variable is simply whether or not I have such information for a given party. As independent variables I employ dichotomous variables for the countries under consideration,[2]

2. Given that for some countries I have information on all parties, some dichotomous vari-

TABLE 6.2. Predicting the availability of the initial electoral result of new parties

independent variables	b (s.e.)
election year	-0.01 (0.01)
Austria	-1.44 (0.61)
Belgium	-1.01 (0.56)
Finland	-0.78 (0.66)
France	-2.39 (0.47)
Germany	-1.86 (0.48)
Greece	-1.48 (0.53)
Iceland	-0.60 (0.63)
Ireland	-1.98 (0.50)
Italy	-1.31 (0.51)
Netherlands	-1.29 (0.53)
Norway	-0.87 (0.67)
Portugal	-1.20 (0.59)
Spain	-1.75 (0.47)
Sweden	-1.62 (0.63)
Switzerland	-1.08 (0.57)
Great Britain	-3.24 (0.49)
Canada	-2.12 (0.51)
Australia	-1.49 (0.56)
Constant	2.69 (0.81)
log-likelihood	-158.14
correctly predicted	282
mode	260
n	361

as well as the year of the election when the party appeared. This latter variable should pick up the effect of improving electoral statistics over time.

Table 6.2 shows that there are some considerable differences among countries when it comes to having exact electoral returns for new parties. Exact initial electoral results are more often missing for new parties appearing in Great Britain, France and Canada than for those in other countries. Interest-

ables had to be omitted. The countries omitted are Denmark, Luxembourg, the United States, and New Zealand. Consequently, these four countries form the base category, against which the results reported in table 6.2 can be interpreted.

ingly enough, the effect of time is negative but negligible. For more recent elections the likelihood of missing information on the initial electoral success of new parties is thus slightly larger. While these results are interesting by themselves, they also serve as instrument for a correction of the missing data problem in the analyses that follow. More precisely, the results reported in table 6.2 allow correcting for the problem of the missing information on the dependent variable. This is done by introducing in the subsequent analyses an additional independent variable, namely the inverse Mills-ratio (λ).[3] Adding this variable corrects for the systematic bias that is introduced by the missing data problem (e.g., Heckman 1976 and 1979; Achen 1986).

While this missing data problem will prove less consequential, another one is more central. As I argued above, simple analyses of the initial electoral strength are bound to lead in error. The problem occurs because the set of new political parties is a self-selected sample drawn from all groups that have ever considered forming a new party. Neglecting the selection mechanism leads almost inevitably to biased results. Consequently, using my second research design we shall study the initial success of new political parties in the following way. The previous chapter made it possible to highlight the crucial factors which determine whether or not new parties emerge. Exactly the same factors should determine the selection into the sample of new political parties. When studying the relationship between one of the theoretical variables and the initial success of new parties, we must take into account that the decision to form a new party is partially related to the same variables. To separate the influence of the variables on the success from the one on the sample selection, I will use a nonstandard Tobit model (Maddala 1983; Muthen and Jöreskog 1983; Bloom and Killingsworth 1985; King 1989a, 213f; Greene 1990; Breen 1996). Despite the fact that we do not have information on the units that are absent from the sample, it is possible to propose a statistical model which integrates the so-called truncation mechanism:

$$y_i = \beta_0 + \sum_{j=1}^{k} (\beta_{j1} * (1 - x_{ci}) + \beta_{j2} * x_{ci}) x_{ji} + \varepsilon_i \qquad (6.1)$$

$$t_i = \delta_0 + \sum_{j=1}^{k} (\delta_{j1} * (1 - x_{ci}) + \delta_{j2} * x_{ci}) x_{ji} + \theta_i \qquad (6.2)$$

$$if\ t_i > 0 \qquad y_i \ and\ x_{ji}\ are\ observed \qquad (6.3)$$

$$if\ t_i \leq 0 \qquad y_i \ and\ x_{ji}\ are\ not\ observed \qquad (6.4)$$

3. This corresponds to the "hazard-rate" of a given case appearing in the sample (Brehm 1993, 106).

Fig. 6.1. Initial strength of the new parties

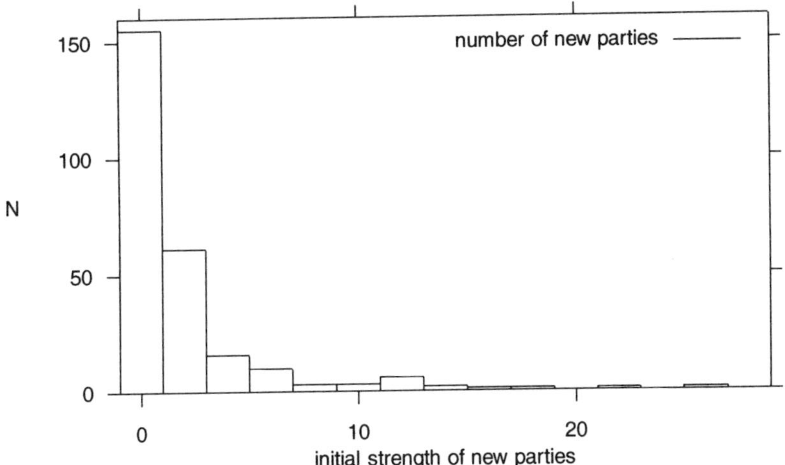

In this model, a separate selection equation is modeled with a latent variable t. If the value of this variable exceeds 0, both the dependent and the independent variables are observed. On the other hand, if the latent variable has a value below 0, none of the variables is observed. Again, I introduce all variables for situations where weak new parties are credible and where they are not. x_c is equal to 1 for elections in the former case and equal to 0 in the latter one.[4]

Such a statistical model can be estimated by maximum-likelihood methods (MLE).[5] The results can easily be compared to those of a simple regression analysis based on the observed cases. The comparison is possible, since, if the correlation between the error-terms ($\rho(\varepsilon, \theta)$) of the two equations above becomes 0, the estimation of the outcome equation collapses to a simple linear regression.

4. In addition I add λ both to the selection and outcome equation, however, without interacting it with the credibility measure. Strictly speaking this solution is problematic, since this correction for selection bias fails to work if the dependent variable is dichotomous, as in the selection equation (Dubin and Rivers 1990). Brehm (2000), in a similar situation estimates the relevant equation as a linear probability model. Sartori (1999) proposes an estimator which directly addresses this problem. In the present context, however, adopting Sartori's solution would require considerable adjustments.

5. Muthen and Jöreskog (1983) transform such a model into a structural equation model,

Fig. 6.2. Probit of initial strength of new parties

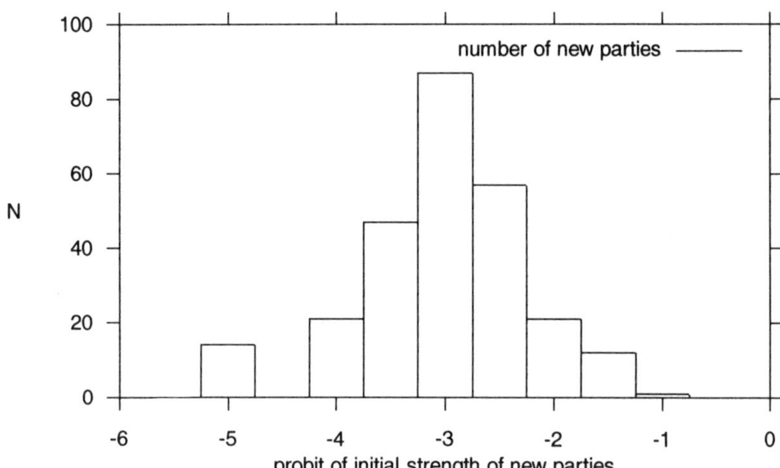

The dependent variable in this statistical model should reflect the initial success of the new parties in my sample. Not surprisingly, this variable is badly skewed (Figure 6.1). Most values are very close to 0, while a few observations are dispersed at higher levels. The highest initial electoral success appears for the Spanish Partido Democrata Popular (PDP). This party presented for the first time in 1982 candidates at the Spanish national election and received 26.5 percent (Day and Degenhardt 1988, 496f and Mackie and Rose 1991, 391f). Compared to most other new parties, this party's initial success is considerable. Most new parties are in the same category as for instance the Austrian *Europäische Föderalistische Partei (EFP)* which obtained only 535 votes or 0.007 percent in the 1962 election (McHale and Skowronski 1983, 36). Given this skewed distribution I transformed the dependent variable by simply taking the probit of the initial success measured as a proportion of the total vote. This leads to a variable that is nicely distributed (Figure 6.2).

Ideally, we would use the same independent variables as in the previous section to test the implications of the model concerning the initial success of new parties. Each set of independent variables would appear on the selection and the outcome equation, and their coefficients should be estimated. Unfortunately, the estimation of such models is "nontrivial, since the shape

---

which could be estimated in other ways, but in almost all cases the MLE method is used.

of the likelihood function can be complicated" (Muthen and Jöreskog 1983, 157).[6] In addition, since the independent variables imperfectly measure the theoretical variables, the estimation becomes even more difficult. Despite this, I proceeded to several estimations in order to illustrate the consequences of the selection mechanism. Instead of using the whole set of independent variables for each implication, I chose the most important one, for both the case where a weak new party is credible and where it is not.[7] Following the results discussed in chapter 5 I introduce these same variables also in the selection equation. Since according to my theoretical model the formation costs should only influence the emergence but not the success of new parties, I introduce also the petition signature requirement in the selection equation. While I also employ the electoral deposit and whether a country has public party financing as indicators for this theoretical variable, table 5.11 suggests that the petition requirement has the most important effect on party formation.

Among the four variables appearing on the selection equation two are interacted with the credibility measure, namely the petition requirement and the threshold of representation. This reflects both the predictions of the theoretical model and the empirical results presented in chapter 5. The four variables employed in the selection equation also share the characteristic that they relate strongly with the formation of new parties (Table 5.11 in chapter 5).

In the next sections I present analyses based on the three implications presented above. To introduce these analyses I first discuss some results from other authors who have studied the success of new political parties. This allows us to relate my independent variables to the ones used by other scholars. In addition, I can illustrate more forcefully that the selection bias is a serious problem and that the theoretical model is of use, since it gives much clearer indications on the relationships to be expected.

New Issues

The first implication to be tested suggests a positive impact of new issues on the initial strength of new parties, provided weak new challengers fail to be credible. In chapter 5 I employed a series of variables characterizing a given

---

6. Hug (1998) reports Monte-Carlo simulations illustrating the estimation difficulties for this statistical model and the conditions under which it performs well.

7. I simply chose the pair of variables that in a simple OLS regression yielded the smallest standard error of the regression. Among the variables measuring new issues, the size of the population appears most strongly related to the initial success. The possibility of referendums and the threshold of representation are most heavily linked to this same success among the variables measuring the benefits of high demands and the costs of fighting a new challenger on the electoral scene.

Fig. 6.3. Population size and the success of new political parties

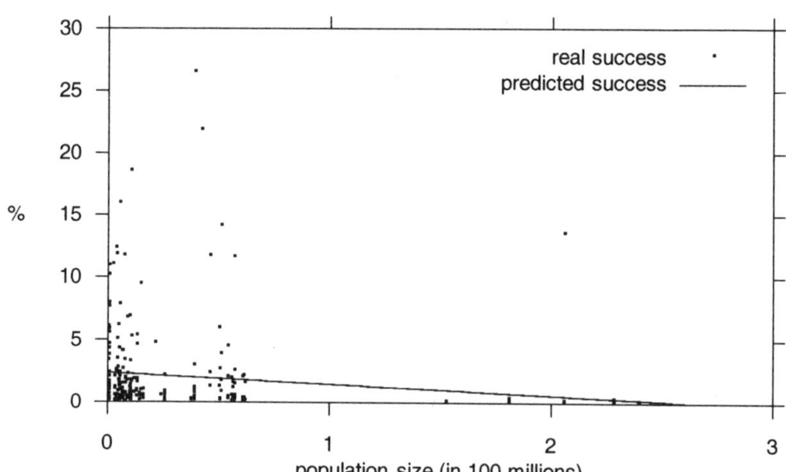

polity as having few or numerous new issues. These referred to the linguistic and religious homogeneity, the country's degree of pluralism and ethnic fragmentation, the population size, and two economic variables, namely the growth and unemployment rate.

New issues also play a significant role in the explanation of new parties' success by other authors. Harmel and Robertson (1985, 502-507) hypothesize that their social variables should influence the success of newcomers on the electoral scene.[8] For instance, they expect a positive relationship between the size of a country and the success of a new party. In their dataset they fail to find support for this contention, as is the case in mine (Figure 6.3).[9] The relatively strong relationship is largely due to outliers stemming from the American party system. But even when eliminating these cases from the dataset the relationship remains negative but becomes much weaker.

Similarly disappointing results appear for the other measures of the social context in Harmel and Robertson's (1985, 517) model: No variable has a statistically significant impact. Results based on my dataset come to almost

---

8. I discussed these different variables in chapter 6 and will come back to them only briefly here.

9. This curved line is based on a linear regression on the probit transformed initial success with the following results: constant -2.22 (0.05) population -0.80 (0.06)

identical conclusions. All of the variables that are close to the ones proposed by Harmel and Robertson fail to explain the success of new parties. The variation around the overall average of success of 1.95 percent cannot be accounted for by these variables. The theoretical model suggests two possible explanations for these disappointing results. First, in these simple bivariate analyses the interaction among different explanatory factors is omitted. But as the model shows, several variables should influence together the success of new parties. Hence, bivariate tests have to be taken with some caution. Second, the problem of sample selection can bias significantly the results if the estimation procedure does not take into account this complicating feature.

To illustrate these problems for the first implication I use the size of the population to measure the importance of new issues. This variable appears in both the outcome and selection equation presented above. In the latter appear, as discussed, measures for the different other implications studied in chapter 5. The first column of table 6.3 presents the results of an OLS estimation of the population size's impact on the transformed initial success of new parties. According to these estimations, I would conclude that an increasing size in the population leads to a smaller initial success of new parties if the weak ones are credible. The effect is positive in all other elections but much more difficult to distinguish from 0. The results lend only partial support to the implication. The latter effect is in line with the predictions of implication 1, but in elections with credible weak challenger the effect should equal zero.[10]

When controlling for the selection mechanism, however, the support for my implication becomes stronger. According to the results appearing in the second column of table 6.3, if the weak challengers are credible, an increasing size of the population leads to stronger parties. In elections where weak challengers fail to be credible, this positive effect is much stronger. While the coefficients are of the expected size and direction, they fail to reach statistical significance. Nevertheless, this result lends some empirical support to my implication.

While the party with the biggest initial electoral success in my sample, namely the Spanish PDP, appeared in an election in which weak new challengers were credible challengers, other strong new parties in big countries appeared in other elections. For instance, France saw the emergence of the *Centre du progrès et de la démocratie moderne* in the 1967 election, which according to table 5.5 is an election where weak challengers fail to be credible. The party's leader, Jean Lecanuet, took the party to an important electoral success, gaining 14.1 percent of the total vote. The party later merged with other

10. While the estimated coefficient for λ is of interest from a technical standpoint, its interpretation is far from intuitive. For this reason I refrain here and below from discussing this coefficient.

TABLE 6.3. New issues and strength of new parties

	OLS	MLE
independent variables	b (s.e.)	b (s.e.)
	outcome	
population (credible)	-0.80	0.61
	(0.06)	(1.16)
population (not credible)	1.01	2.53
	(0.92)	(1.82)
λ	-0.03	1.64
	(0.15)	(1.44)
constant	-2.22	-5.61
	(0.07)	(2.96)
	selection	
population (all elections)		1.76
		(0.66)
petition signatures (credible)		0.04
		(0.13)
referendum (all elections)		-0.12
		(0.15)
threshold of representation (credible)		0.15
		(0.97)
λ		1.85
		(1.04)
constant		-2.91
		(2.14)
σ_ε	0.67	1.15
		(0.29)
$\rho(\varepsilon, \theta)$		0.92
		(0.04)
log-likelihood	-263.38	-246.81
n	260	260

centrist parties (McHale and Skowronski 1983, 253ff; Mackie and Rose 1991, 141f).

The results also clearly illustrate the problem of self-selection present in a sample of newly formed new parties. Based on the initial OLS estimations, my conclusion on the effect of the population size on the initial success of new parties would have been noticeably different. These results suggest a negative relationship when weak challengers are credible. When controlling for the self-selection bias, this effect largely disappears. In large part this is due to the effect of the population variable on the selection equation. There this variable displays, as in the analyses of chapter 5, a strong and positive impact on the likelihood of party formation. Similarly, the effects of petition requirement and the presence of referendums correspond to the ones reported above. The only change appears for the threshold of representation which in this analysis affects slightly positively the selection into the sample of newly formed parties.

A final piece of information appearing in table 6.3 is the correlation between the error terms of the two equations ($\rho(\varepsilon, \theta)$). The estimated coefficient is rather large and positive, while the associated standard error is small. Consequently, together with the differences in the estimated coefficients of the outcome equation, this suggests clearly that the selection mechanism cannot be ignored.[11]

Benefits from High Demands

The third implication from the theoretical model relates the initial success of new parties to the benefits of high demands. Such higher benefits should diminish the average strength in situations where weak new parties are credible, while leading to the opposite in all other elections. In chapter 5 I employed a series of indicators on the government structure to measure the benefits of high demands. These were whether the government in place was majoritarian, the number of parties in government, whether a government change preceded the election, the degree of centralization as measured by the taxes collected by the central government, and whether the country allows for referendums.

Among these variables one also appears in the writing of other authors as explanatory factor for the success of new parties. Harmel and Robertson (1985, 505) venture that in two-party systems the success of new parties should be higher.[12] In their empirical analysis, however, they find a significant relationship of the opposite sign. In my dataset the average success of new parties formed under a majoritarian government is equal to 1.47 percent but increases to 2.20 percent for all other new parties. Thus, also in my dataset the relationship contradicts Harmel and Robertson's hypothesis, despite the fact that the relationship in my dataset fails to reach statistical significance.

To test this implication I use as proxy-measure whether the country in question employs referendums. If this is so, the benefits from a high demand should be reduced as argued above. Thus, the presence of referendums should increase the strength of new parties if the weak challengers are credible and have an opposite effect in all other elections.

In the results of the initial OLS estimation we find results which partly support the theoretical framework (Table 6.4). If new challengers are credible, the presence of referendum institutions increases the success of newly formed

11. Dropping the new parties from the United States from the analysis leads to only minor changes in the results. Restricting the analysis to the initial success of genuinely new parties suggests that the size of population still affect positively the initial success of new parties, provided the weak challengers fail to be credible. This coefficient has, however, a huge standard error, and in addition, the effect in all other elections is strongly negative. Dropping both the cases from the United States and all fissions leads to even weaker results. These changes are, however, likely to be related with the significant drop in the number of cases. While in the complete sample there are 260 observations, focusing on genuinely new parties reduces it to 177. The respective numbers with the new parties from the United States are 225 and 143.

12. While the existence of a two-party system is not equivalent to a majoritarian government, the link is sufficiently strong to suppose that both variables measure the same thing.

TABLE 6.4. Benefits from high demands and strength of new parties

independent variables	OLS b (s.e.)	MLE b (s.e.)
	outcome	
referendum (credible)	0.70	-0.34
	(0.11)	(0.72)
referendum (not credible)	1.17	-0.19
	(0.16)	(0.72)
λ	0.45	1.26
	(0.17)	(0.61)
Constant	-3.28	-4.15
	(0.10)	(0.30)
	selection	
population (all elections)		1.31
		(0.50)
petition requirement (credible)		0.00
		(0.16)
referendum (all elections)		-0.56
		(0.92)
threshold of representation (credible)		0.26
		(1.35)
λ		1.67
		(0.82)
constant		-1.63
		(0.43)
σ_ε	0.77	1.01
		(0.12)
$\rho(\varepsilon, \theta)$		0.90
		(0.04)
log-likelihood	-298.17	-248.12
n	260	260

parties. On the other hand, this effect is also positive if new challengers are on average so weak that they are noncredible. This latter effect, according to my implication, should be negative. Controlling for the selection mechanism weakens the support for my theoretical framework. Both effects become negative, but fail to reach statistical significance. This time it is the sign of the coefficient for elections with credible weak challengers that contradicts my implication.

An illustration for this result again appears in the data covering Switzerland. As mentioned above, all elections in this country allow for credible weak challengers, and thus the initial success of new parties should be higher on average, since referendums are possible in this country. While the average success of new parties in my sample is of 1.95 percent, it is only of 1.33 for the Swiss new parties. Hence, the bivariate effect in Switzerland contradicts my implication, and thus might partly explain the negative result reported in table 6.4. Nevertheless, it is likely that controlling for the other explanatory variables might change this result.

In the selection equation one again notes the positive influence of the population size on the chances of forming a new party. As the population size increases, the likelihood of seeing a new party becomes more important. The effect of the petition requirement drops to 0, while referendums still affect negatively the formation of new parties, as hypothesized above. Finally, the threshold of representation remains positively related to the selection variable, contrary to expectancy. Nevertheless, these latter effects fail to reach statistical significance.[13]

Fighting Costs

The fourth implication relates the costs of fighting a new party on the electoral scene to the new party's initial strength. These costs diminish when the electoral thresholds increase, as I argued in chapter 5. These costs also increase in federal systems, with more numerous parties in government and high number of governments per decade.

My theoretical framework suggests that an increasing electoral threshold should lead to more successful new parties. This implication goes squarely against most stances in the literature. Harmel and Robertson (1985, 505) hypothesize that the success of new parties should be higher in proportional representation systems than in majoritarian ones. Their empirical analysis supports this hypothesis.[14] Müller-Rommel (1993, 116f), however, hypothesizes a negative relationship between the degree of proportionality and the success of Green parties. He finds support for this hypothesis, which runs counter to the hypothesis discussed here.

A simple bivariate analysis of the relationship between the threshold of representation and the initial success of new parties in my dataset also lends support to this hypothesis. Figure 6.4 depicts this relationship as a linear trend together with the observed initial success.[15] Remembering that the case of the United States caused some problems in the previous chapter when relationships with the electoral system were estimated, the question arises whether this is also the case here. Dropping the cases stemming from the United States does indeed make the relationship slightly positive, but it fails to reach any substantial or statistical significance.

The initial OLS estimates of the relationship between the threshold of representation and the initial success of new parties (Table 6.5) invalidates my

---

13. Restricting the sample to genuinely new parties or eliminating all new parties from the United States leads to a few changes, but none of them affect the substantive conclusions presented here.

14. Of all hypotheses on the success of new political parties, this is the only one for which Harmel and Robertson (1985, 517) find empirical evidence.

15. The coefficients for the linear relationship are as follows: constant -2.25 (0.05) threshold of representation -3.00 (0.27).

Fig. 6.4. Threshold of representation and the success of new political parties

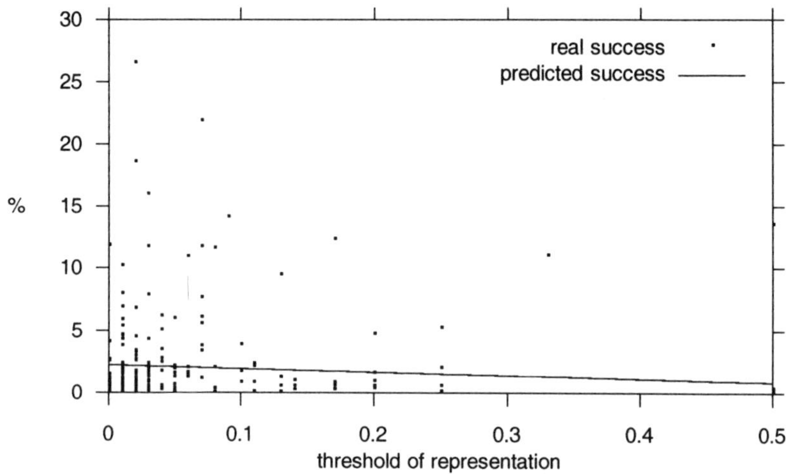

implication, but also questions the simple hypothesis of other scholars. This relationship is strongly negative, as long as weak new challengers are credible. If they fail to be credible, the relationship becomes positive. Consequently, the sometimes mixed results reported in the literature on the effect of electoral systems on the formation of new parties might find part of an answer in this result. Simple bivariate relationships seem to overlook interactions which seem to play a crucial role.

Controlling for the selection mechanism alters the relationship considerably. As predicted by my implication the effect of the threshold of representation on the initial success of new parties is positive if the latter are credible. This same effect is much smaller in all remaining elections. The intuition behind this result is that only those new parties form, which are sure to clear electoral hurdles. Thus, in the Netherlands with a low hurdle even largely unsupported groups may decide to compete in an election. The discussion of the emergence of the Dutch Green party and the NSDAP in chapter 2 illustrate this perfectly. In that latter case the 1920s the Weimar Republic saw a tremendous number of small splinter parties emerging and disappearing almost as fast. In countries with higher thresholds such groups would be wasting their time when knowing that they would never win representation in an election. Hence, in such countries like for instance Great Britain, parties self-select themselves

TABLE 6.5. Costs of electoral fight and strength of new parties

	OLS	MLE
independent variables	b (s.e.)	b (s.e.)
	outcome	
threshold of representation (credible)	-3.15 (0.28)	2.38 (3.41)
threshold of representation (not credible)	0.75 (1.08)	0.05 (0.67)
λ	-0.07 (0.16)	1.73 (1.12)
constant	-2.26 (0.08)	-5.43 (1.98)
	selection	
population (all elections)		1.06 (0.46)
petition requirement (credible)		0.04 (0.13)
referendum (all elections)		-0.10 (0.14)
threshold of representation (credible)		3.14 (3.36)
λ		1.98 (0.92)
constant		-2.80 (1.50)
σ_ε	0.70	1.13 (0.21)
$\rho(\varepsilon,\theta)$		0.92 (0.03)
log-likelihood	-273.62	-248.59
n	260	260

only if they expect reasonable success.[16] The tale about the SDP reported in chapter 2 illustrates this nicely. In the statistical analysis reported here, this effect appears when controlling for the selection mechanism, even though the coefficients fail to reach statistical significance.

On the selection equation, one notes again a strong and positive relationship for the population size. Compared to the previous analyses, the effect of the threshold of representation increases, but accompanied by a similar increase in the standard error. The remaining coefficients are similar to those discussed above. One might suspect that the inclusion of the American new parties in this analysis leads to similar biases as in the previous chapter. Dropping these observations from the dataset, alters some of the results of the previous analysis, as shown in table 6.6.

Contrary to the results appearing in table 6.5 the effect of the threshold of representation in the sample without the United States is negative if weak challengers are credible. This result contradicts my implication. Interestingly, the simple linear regression would lend more support to my implication. This

16. Obviously, Berrington's (1985) assessment that the British political landscape is littered with new parties runs partly against this reasoning.

TABLE 6.6. Costs of electoral fight and strength of new parties (without the United States)

independent variables	OLS b (s.e.)	MLE b (s.e.)
	outcome	
threshold of representation (credible)	1.23	-1.15
	(0.98)	(2.32)
threshold of representation (not credible)	1.18	-0.07
	(0.92)	(0.59)
λ	-0.39	0.29
	(0.15)	(0.23)
constant	-2.26	-2.69
	(0.07)	(0.16)
	selection	
population (all elections)		10.91
		(6.24)
petition requirement (credible)		0.07
		(0.32)
referendum (all elections)		0.78
		(0.60)
threshold of representation (credible)		-11.74
		(7.73)
λ		2.27
		(1.44)
constant		-1.44
		(0.83)
σ_ε	0.59	0.66
		(0.03)
$\rho(\varepsilon, \theta)$		0.80
		(0.10)
log-likelihood	-199.83	-190.32
n	225	225

is largely due to considerable changes in the coefficients for the selection equation. The effect of the population size increases dramatically, while the threshold of representation exerts a strong negative effect on the likelihood of selection. This reflects results reported in the previous chapter. Also the effect of referendums becomes positive, contrary to expectancy. While there might be a whole set of reasons for these considerable changes worth discussing, I postpone this discussion till after the presentation of a joint test of the three implications under scrutiny.[17]

17. Restricting the analysis to genuinely new parties leads to erratic results for this implication. If the cases from the United States are included the threshold of representation has a huge negative effect on the initial success of new parties, provided the weak new challengers are credible. This effect is accompanied by a similarly huge positive effect of this threshold on the selection equation. If the cases from the United States are dropped, the results come close to those reported for the whole sample in table 6.5. Again, the small number of cases in these latter analyses is partly to blame for these erratic results.

Summing Up

The results of these different individual tests are partially disappointing. Only one implication finds strong support in the estimation results. When new issues become more important new parties become stronger, provided that weak new parties are not a credible threat. In all other elections the effect is also positive, but much smaller. Mixed support appears for the implication relating the initial success of new parties with the costs of an electoral fight. In the whole sample the counterintuitive implication finds support in the results, which suggest that increasing electoral thresholds leads to stronger parties, provided the weak challengers are credible. This effect is largely absent when the latter condition fails to hold. But if the cases from the United States are dropped from the analyses, this partial support for my implication vanishes. Then, increasing thresholds of representation seem to decrease the initial strength of new parties.

Again, however, it is obvious that these different implications are related and that individual tests only provide a partial picture. Combining the independent variables of the three implications allows a more detailed look at the determinants of the initial success of new parties. The initial OLS estimates suggest that the size of the population increases the initial strength of new parties, if weak challengers are not credible (Table 6.7). This finding is largely in support of my implication, but the coefficient fails to reach statistical significance. In addition, the effect in all other elections is negative and significant, despite the fact that my implication predicted it to be 0. Referendums appear to affect positively the initial strength of new parties, while this is also the case for the threshold of representation if weak challengers are credible. This effect is tiny and becomes large and negative if all other elections.

Taking into account the selection mechanism partly changes the picture. As Table 6.7 shows, the support for implication 1 found in the individual test largely disappears in this joint test. Larger population sizes are associated with weaker new parties, if the latter are credible. In all other elections the effect is slightly positive, as predicted by my implication. The former effect, however, should be small and negligible. More disappointing results appear for the other implications. The referendum variable, despite my implication, has almost identical negative effects in both types of elections. Both of the effects of the threshold of representation are also negative. These negative results extend also to the selection equation, where the effect of the population size fails to reach statistical significance and the threshold of representation has a strong and positive effect. At the same time it appears that the correlation between the error terms of the two equations ($\rho(\varepsilon, \theta)$) is negative. In all previous tests this coefficient is positive. Again, the usual suspects are the cases stemming from the United States. Dropping these cases leads to results much more in

TABLE 6.7. New issues, benefits of high demands, costs of fighting, and strength of new parties

independent variables	OLS b (s.e.)	MLE b (s.e.)
	outcome	
population (credible)	-0.76	-1.03
	(0.18)	(0.73)
population (not credible)	0.86	0.26
	(1.00)	(1.31)
referendum (credible)	0.10	1.68
	(0.12)	(2.47)
referendum (not credible)	0.37	2.08
	(0.19)	(2.50)
threshold of representation (credible)	0.17	-4.50
	(0.78)	(4.84)
threshold of representation (not credible)	-1.01	-0.88
	(1.32)	(0.81)
λ	0.06	-2.24
	(0.16)	(2.45)
constant	-2.37	0.57
	(0.14)	(2.46)
	selection	
population (all elections)		0.99
		(0.98)
petition signatures (credible)		0.00
		(0.15)
referendum (all elections)		-2.06
		(2.93)
threshold of representation (credible)		8.69
		(5.40)
λ		2.70
		(2.77)
constant		-3.21
		(2.79)
σ_ε	0.67	1.00
		(0.13)
$\rho(\varepsilon.\theta)$		-0.86
		(0.05)
log-likelihood	-261.53	-240.11
n	260	260

line with my theoretical model (Table 6.8).[18]

While the effects are not terribly strong, the results appearing in table 6.8 show again a positive effect of the size of population on the initial success of new parties, provided that weak challengers fail to be credible. In all other elections this effect is largely 0, which strongly supports implication 1. While referendums, as predicted, lead to stronger new parties in elections with credible weak parties, the corresponding effect in all other elections is also positive

18. Eliminating also the fissions from the analyses leads again to erratic results, most likely due to the small number of cases. The estimation based on a sample excluding the cases from the United States leads to inflated standard errors. In the larger sample, some changes in the coefficients appear, but all of them have large standard errors. This makes it hard to interpret whether these differences are substantively significant or not.

TABLE 6.8. New issues, benefits of high demands, costs of fighting, and strength of new parties (without the United States)

	OLS	MLE
independent variables	b (s.e.)	b (s.e.)
	outcome	
population (credible)	-0.31 (0.25)	-0.17 (0.31)
population (not credible)	1.47 (0.90)	1.16 (1.24)
referendum (credible)	0.11 (0.10)	0.18 (0.12)
referendum (not credible)	0.43 (0.17)	0.50 (0.22)
threshold of representation (credible)	1.91 (0.98)	0.05 (1.68)
threshold of representation (not credible)	-1.06 (1.14)	-1.11 (1.03)
λ	-0.25 (0.19)	-0.13 (0.18)
constant	-2.40 (0.12)	-2.51 (0.13)
	selection	
population (all elections)		14.49 (35.86)
petition signatures (credible)		-0.49 (0.96)
referendum (all elections)		2.17 (2.46)
threshold of representation (credible)		-16.02 (12.12)
λ		-0.26 (11.01)
constant		-0.18 (2.09)
σ_ε	0.58	0.61 (0.03)
$\rho(\varepsilon, \theta)$		1.00 (0.01)
log-likelihood	-192.71	-184.85
n	225	225

and even stronger. According to my implication the effect should be negative. Finally, the coefficients for the threshold of representation can hardly be considered to be in support of my theoretical framework. While the coefficient in elections with credible weak challengers is positive, it is tiny. The other coefficient is much larger and negative, despite the fact that my implication predicts it to be close to 0.

On the selection equation the coefficients are much larger than in the previous analyses.[19] Nevertheless the direction of the effects is in support of various of my implications. Population size appears to increase the likelihood of becoming part of the sample of newly formed parties. Higher thresholds of representation diminish this prospect considerably. Also, higher signature

19. This is likely due to the fact that the estimated $\rho(\varepsilon, \theta)$ is almost equal to 1.

requirements diminish slightly the chances of party formation. Finally, referendums appear to encourage party formation, contrary to my implications.

Conclusion

Explaining the success of new political parties is not an easy task. Harmel and Robertson (1985) noted this in their own study. Despite touching this question only at the margin, the theoretical framework used here allowed for some insights and especially for some additional guidance in the study of new parties. Directly from the theoretical framework stems the idea that the relationships between certain variables and the success of new parties depend on the latter's credibility. This insight finds strong support in all basic analyses which have been presented in this chapter.

The theoretical framework also stresses the need for an appropriate research design. In the context of studying the success of new parties, the model emphasizes the fact that new parties are a self-selected sample. This chapter proposed a procedure for studying the new parties' success in spite of this complicating factor. The empirical results clearly demonstrated that controlling for the selection mechanisms several relationships are considerably altered.

The results also lend support to parts of my implications. Several of the tests appearing above underline the role played by new issues in explaining the success of new parties. The latter appear to be more successful with increasing importance of new issues, but only provided that weak challengers fail to be credible. The impact of the costs of fighting a new party in an election on the latter's success is harder to assess based on the results reported here. While there appears to be an effect of the threshold of representation on the initial success of new parties, its importance and direction vary with the sample considered. What seems clear is that the effect of electoral thresholds is not as simple and direct as often described in the literature. There appears even some limited support for my counterintuitive implication, namely that increasing thresholds should increase the initial strength of new parties, provided weak challengers are credible.

The explanation for the mixed results for the various implications resides in two factors. First, the theoretical framework does not explicitly address the success of new political parties. It does not include any elements which would allow it to take into account the electoral competition that follows the arrival of a new competitor on the electoral scene. Hence, the mixed results concerning the costs of fighting a new party are most likely linked to the partiality of the theoretical framework, which does not directly address the electoral competition that inevitably follows the formation of a new party. In particular, the crucial actors in this last stage, namely voters, are not included in the model.

Hence, any strategic calculation of these actors, resulting in tactical voting, for example, is completely neglected. This might account for the weak performance of this implication.

Second, the combination of a demanding estimation procedure and error-prone measures of the theoretical variables is also problematic. It is likely that the disappointing variables are largely due to this lethal combination, and with better measures the implications would find much better support. But given the demands of the estimation procedures error-prone measures are likely to lead to errors.

Consequently, future research has to focus on providing better theoretical models allowing for more precise insights into the success of new political parties. The results reported here, however, seem to give sufficient support to my main claims. More precisely, the self-selection of new parties is likely to be at the heart of any serious theoretical model attempting to explain the success of new parties. Such new models could then be tested, preferably with better empirical measures, using the estimation procedures presented here.

CHAPTER 7

Conclusion

Despite the neglect that new political parties experience in the literature on parties and party systems, it is my contention that it is crucially important to understand this phenomenon. It is not only the numerical importance of new political parties (which I documented in the empirical part) which justifies a closer look at new parties. To understand their substantive impact on political systems is also of great interest.

Thus, the present study attempted to provide a new look at new political parties in Western democracies. Three goals were at the center of this study. First, I attempted to develop a general framework for the study of new parties. The argument was that all new parties, whether they are addressing new or old issues, whether they are concerned about problems of immigration or pollution, or whether they are on the left or the right, emerge in a heavily structured environment. This environment is strongly influenced by institutional constraints and the behavior of existing parties. While both elements play a central role in the existing literature on new political parties, they have never been addressed in their strategic context. The importance of the behavior of established parties in explaining the emergence of new parties calls for special attention to these strategic interactions.

Consequently, I proposed a game-theoretic model which describes the interaction between an established party and a potential new party. One possible outcome of the game is the formation of a new political party. On the theoretical level, I have shown that one requirement for the emergence of new parties is uncertainty. More precisely, in my model new parties only appear if the established parties are not completely sure how strong their adversary is. The presence of uncertainty and the problems of adopting new issues also figure prominently in the literature on party system change, but less so in models on the emergence of new parties.

The model provides a certain number of testable implications, which mostly relate the likelihood of new political parties to theoretical variables of the model. Some of these are identical or close to hypotheses of other theoretical frameworks. Nonetheless, the implications are often more precise, and provide conditions under which certain relationships should hold. Hence, while encompassing most theoretical arguments from the substantive literature, my game-theoretic model provides more detailed and precise insights into the process of party formation.

In addition to implications on the formation of new parties, the model gives some limited insights into their initial success. Here, the game-theoretic approach is very advantageous, since it highlights a crucial problem in empirical studies of the success of new political parties: The model shows that, since the formation of a new party is the result of a conscious decision, the set of new parties is a self-selected sample. Selection into the sample, however, depends partly on the expected success of the new party. Hence, this selection mechanism has to be considered when studying the success of new parties.

This shows the importance of the second goal of this study concerning research designs in the study of new political parties. These questions are often neglected in the field of comparative politics, but are of crucial importance in the study of new political parties. While the explanation of the emergence of new parties is distinct from the explanation of their subsequent success, the two research questions are intimately linked. The link is formed by the selection mechanism, which decides whether or not a group takes the step to form a new party. On this basis, the twofold research design presented here allows the study of both the emergence of new parties and their initial success.

The twofold research design finds application in the empirical study of new political parties in 22 Western democracies since the end of World War II. This part reports on the third goal of the present study, which consists of testing the theoretical model and illustrating the importance of both adequate research designs and a consistent theoretical framework. A first insight of the empirical study is the sheer numerical importance of new political parties. In almost every election at least one new party appears in the 22 democracies under consideration. Their average initial electoral success of almost 2 percent of the total vote is also respectable. Especially, since most of these newcomers start their electoral career with very small percentages, succeeding only to attract a handful of votes. But some parties, like the British SDP discussed in chapter 2, or the Spanish Partido Democrata Popular manage to obtain double-digit vote shares from the very start.

Apart from showing this numerical and sometimes also electoral importance, the empirical tests lend considerable support to my theoretical model. Central to this, as in most other theoretical and empirical work on new parties, is the importance of new issues or the problem "push" (Rüdig 1990). New parties arise more frequently if new issues are important. Here, both on the empirical and theoretical level, my study rejoins the substantive literature, which finds similar results. Where my approach improves on existing work is in relation to the link between new issues and the initial success of new parties.

My theoretical framework provides a rationale for a more complicated relation, specifically, where new issues increase the initial success only if weak new parties are credible. This claim finds some support in the empirical analysis, even when considering the selection mechanism.

The theoretical model also rejoins the existing literature in other areas, while at the same time providing more precise insights. For example, the costs of forming a new party should decrease the likelihood of new party formation, but only if weak new parties are credible. The qualification of this relationship is absent in all other work. The impact of formation costs is assumed to diminish the number of new parties in all situations. But the empirical results lend some support to my model, showing that the impact of formation costs differs according to context.

Similarly, in the literature the costs of fighting a new party, which are heavily determined by the electoral system, are consistently linked with the emergence of new parties. Again, however, my framework suggests that increasing these costs should lead to more new parties only if weak political parties are credible in a given political system. In individual tests, which come close to what is popular in the substantive literature, this implication does not hold up very well. Only if the United States is dropped from the analyses do we find support for my implication. The implication also finds stronger support when the relationship is controlled for the impact of the variables from the other implications. Here again, my theoretical model improves on the existing literature.

This is less the case if one considers the impact of these costs on the initial success of new parties. The model predicts that new parties become stronger on average when the costs decrease. Hence, higher electoral thresholds, which diminish the costs of fighting a new party, should lead to stronger new parties on average. While this claim finds support in some results of the substantive literature, it fails to do so in the empirical tests. Higher costs of fighting new parties hardly affect or slightly diminish the average initial success of the latter.

In explaining the initial success of new political parties, another implication also results in a mixed picture. The relevant implication suggests that new parties should be more successful if the benefits from a high demand are important, provided that a weak new party is not a credible challenge. If it were credible, the relationship should be negative. This precise implication finds no parallel in the substantive literature, but finds some mixed support in the empirical tests. The same theoretical variable, namely the benefits of high political demands by potential new parties, does not, however, sufficiently explain the emergence of new parties. Higher such benefits should lead to more new parties under all circumstances. However, this does not always hold.

This empirical part of my study strongly underlines the importance of my two previous goals. In the study of new political parties it is useful to have a precise theoretical framework at hand. Such frameworks, especially when the subject of investigation is embedded in a strategic situation, preferably stem from game-theoretic models. By taking into account interdependent choices and permitting rigorous deductions from basic premises, these models have important advantages. They also highlight, as I have been able to show, questions of research design, which can prove crucial in empirical research.

Despite these achievements, the present study also includes shortcomings which lend themselves to extensions. One of the most important ones concerns the limited insights that the theoretical model provides for the success of new parties. Obviously, this success involves additional actors than the two considered in my theoretical framework. Apart from established parties and the new political party, voters play an important role in the fate of new political parties: To a large extent they determine their fate.

Hence, by omitting voters the model can only provide limited insights into the initial success of new parties. This omission explains some results which contradicted the theoretical model. This suggests a possible extension and avenue for future research. The theoretical model should attempt to integrate the third actor, which was omitted from this work. A more complete theoretical framework should address how a new party is accepted on the electoral scene. In this context, spatial models of electoral competition would be very helpful. Such a model could then be tested adequately with the help of this study's twofold research design.

CHAPTER 8

Appendix

In the present appendix the reader finds additional material on three elements of the main text: First, the game-theoretic model on which the theoretical framework of the present study is based; second, additional details on the data used in the empirical analysis; and in the last section I discuss the estimation procedures which were used in the empirical part of this study.

Game-theoretic Model

In this section I present first additional assumptions of my game-theoretic model. Second, I derive and prove the equilibria for both the complete and the incomplete information versions of the model. Third, I will present the comparative statics analyses on which my implications are based before discussing in more detail the payoff structure of the model.

Additional Assumptions

I impose three additional assumptions concerning the relationship between the benefits and the costs to the potential new party:

Assumption 4

$$c_{hw} - c_{lw} < b_h - b_l \tag{8.1}$$

Assumption 5

$$c_{hs} - c_{ls} < b_s - b_l - c \tag{8.2}$$

Assumption 6

$$c_{hs} - c_{ls} < b_h - b_s + c \tag{8.3}$$

The first assumption (4) of this set, simply states that the weak type prefers making a high demand to a low one, provided that both of them are accepted. If this were not the case the weak type would always make low demands, hereby reveal its type to the established party. Consequently, even with incomplete information, complete separation would occur, leading to an equilibrium in which no new parties would appear.[1]

The second assumption (5) implies that the strong type is better off forming a new party after making a high demand than in making a low demand which is accepted. Should this not be the case the established party, by accepting all low demands, could prevent the occurrence of all high demands, and also the emergence of all new parties. Furthermore, it would imply that all potential new parties could be bought off with small concessions. This is hardly the case, as is proved by the formation process of most new parties.

The third assumption (6) shows that the strong type prefers making a high demand that is accepted to making a low demand and then having to form a new party. Consequently, for all strong potential new parties there is a basis for a compromise concerning the integration of new policies into the programs of established parties. Again, this assumption is quite intuitive, since established parties are ready to change their programs considerably, provided that they perceive a threat from a potential newcomer.

Strategies and Equilibrium Concepts

Here I briefly discuss the beliefs and strategies adopted by the two actors in the game (Table 8.1). Both actors share the same prior belief $b(s)$, which corresponds to the probability that Nature chooses a strong type. Since this information is immediately revealed to the potential new party, only the established party will have the opportunity to update its beliefs. The updated beliefs of the established party are designated by $b_e(.|.)$.The process of updating is dependent on the kind of demand that the established party receives. Consequently, the established party can form two posterior beliefs. The first one is $b_e(s|h)$, which corresponds to the probability that the established party faces a strong type, given that the potential new party has made a high demand. The second posterior ($b_e(s|l)$) is the corresponding belief after a low demand.

The strategies of the potential new party correspond to the probabilities of making high demand, conditional on being either a weak or a strong type. The complement of these probabilities is obviously the probability of making a low demand. As noted above, the last decision node of the potential new party can be folded back to last decision node of the established party, since

1. This will become clear below, when I discuss the different equilibria.

TABLE 8.1. Beliefs and strategies in the signaling game

beliefs		
$b(s)$	$prob(strong)$	prior
$b_e(s\|h)$	$prob(strong\|high\ demand)$	posterior
$b_e(s\|l)$	$prob(strong\|low\ demand)$	posterior
strategies		
$p_s(h)$	$prob(high\ demand\|strong\ type)$	
$p_w(h)$	$prob(high\ demand\|weak\ type)$	
$p_e(a\|h)$	$prob(accept\ demand\|high\ demand)$	
$p_e(a\|l)$	$prob(accept\ demand\|low\ demand)$	

no more strategic interaction is taking place. Consequently, strong challengers will always form a new party if their demand is rejected. Weak challengers will only form if their benefits (b_w) exceeds the cost of formation.

The strategies of the established party correspond to the probabilities of accepting a demand, conditional on this demand being high or low. Again, the complement of these probabilities corresponds to the probabilities of rejection.[2]

In the analysis of my model I will use two equilibrium concepts, which are both refinements of the Nash equilibrium. The Nashequilibrium requires that "each player's strategy is an optimal response to the other players' strategies." (Fudenberg and Tirole 1991, 11).[3] The first equilibrium concept I will use to analyze the complete information version of my model is the subgame-perfect equilibrium. This concept requires that the strategy combination induces a Nash equilibrium not only in the whole game tree, but also in each of its subgames. Strategy combinations that fulfill this requirement form a subgame-perfect equilibrium. Subgame-perfection is, however, often powerless in games of incomplete information. Since subgames cannot cut across information sets, frequently the only subgame is the entire game-tree. Consequently, I will use a stronger equilibrium concept for the incomplete information version of my game, namely the D1 criterion (Cho and Kreps 1987, 205f and Banks 1991, 16f). This is a mild refinement of the perfect Bayesian equilibrium concept, which requires that each player acts optimally, given his or her beliefs. Wherever possible these have to be updated according to Bayes' rule. The D1 criterion adds a weak additional requirement for these beliefs. When-

2. In the complete and perfect information case the established party conditions its strategy also on the type of challenger. Since I discuss this case only briefly, I refrain from specifying it completely.

3. Fudenberg and Tirole (1991) discuss in great detail the different equilibrium concepts that I will use below.

ever an information set is never reached in equilibrium, the perfect Bayesian equilibrium allows any beliefs at such decision nodes, since the updated beliefs according to Bayes' rule are not defined. Since these beliefs often have a strong impact on what happens on the equilibrium path, some equilibria may rely on odd out-of-equilibrium beliefs. The D1 criterion, by imposing conditions on these beliefs, rules out some of these implausible equilibria. It requires that a player put 0 weight on that type which only weakly prefers defecting from the equilibrium path, while there is another type that has a strict preference for doing so. This means that the out-of-equilibrium beliefs should reflect the fact that one type is more likely to defect from the equilibrium path, since it can be strictly better off, while the other type is indifferent.[4]

Equilibria and Proofs

In this part I will present the equilibria and proofs for both the complete and incomplete information versions of my model.

Complete Information Equilibria

Proposition 1 *Under complete information the only subgame-perfect equilibria are the following:*

1. *if* $b_w > c$
   $p_s(h) = 1,\ p_w(h) = 0,\ p_e(a|h) = 1,\ p_e(a|l) = 1$
2. *if* $b_w \leq c$
   $p_s(h) = 1,\ p_w(h) = 0,\ p_e(a|h) = 1,\ p_e(a|l) = 0$

Proof of proposition 1: Under complete information, I can easily solve the game by backward induction. If $b_w > c$, then both types will challenge the established party after a rejected demand. Consequently, the established party accepts high demands from the strong type and low demands from the weak type ($p_e(a|h) = 1$ and $p_e(a|l) = 1$), since $-f_s < -a_h$ and $-f_w < -a_l$. High demands by the weak type, however, are not accepted by the established party, because $-a_h < -f_w$. Thus, the strong type will always make high demands ($p_s(h) = 1$), while the weak type will always make low demands ($p_w(h) = 0$). If $b_w < c$, then the established party has no incentive to accept low demands,

4. One can note that the D1 criterion collapses to subgame perfection under complete information. In that sense I could use the same solution concept, namely D1, for both versions of my model. To simplify the presentation of the equilibria of the complete information version, I will use subgame perfection as solution concept.

so that $p_e(a|l) = 0$. All other strategies remain the same. Finally, if $b_w = c$, then the weak potential new party is indifferent between challenging and acquiescing with respect to a rejected demand. This becomes important only after a rejected low demand, since high demands by weak types are always rejected. If the weak type adopts a strategy in which he challenges a rejected low demand with a probability higher than $\frac{a_l}{f_w}$, the established party will accept the low demands with probability 1. If the probability of challenging is smaller, the established party will reject all demands made by the weak type. Since $-c_{lw} < b_l - c_{lw}$, a probability of challenging a rejected demand bigger than $\frac{a_l}{f_w}$ can be part of an equilibrium.[5] *Q.E.D.*

Incomplete Information Equilibria

Under incomplete information two sets of equilibria can be distinguished. I present these in propositions 2 and 3, before proving them with the help of two lemmas (1, 2).

Proposition 2 *If $b_w > c$ the only equilibria satisfying the D1 criterion are the following:*[6]

1. *if* $b(s) < \frac{a_h - f_w}{f_s - f_w}$
   $p_s(h) = 1$, $p_w(h) = \frac{b(s)(f_s - a_h)}{(1-b(s))(a_h - f_w)}$, $p_e(a|h) = \frac{b_l - b_w + c + c_{hw} - c_{lw}}{b_h - b_w + c}$ *and* $p_e(a|l) = 1$.
2. *if* $b(s) = \frac{a_h - f_w}{f_s - f_w}$
   $p_s(h) = 1$, $p_w(h) = 1$, $p_e(a|h) \geq \frac{b_l - b_w + c + c_{hw} - c_{lw}}{b_h - b_w + c}$, $p_e(a|l) = 1$ *and* $b_e(s|l) = 0$.
3. *if* $b(s) > \frac{a_h - f_w}{f_s - f_w}$
   $p_s(h) = 1$, $p_w(h) = 1$, $p_e(a|h) = 1$, $p_e(a|l) = 1$ *and* $b_e(s|l) = 0$.

Looking at the situation where a weak potential new party might actually challenge a rejected demand ($b_w > c$). As Proposition 2 shows, there are two types of equilibria. If the prior belief is high enough ($b(s) \geq \frac{a_h - f_w}{f_s - f_w}$) only pooling equilibria are possible (Figure 8.1). Here, the likelihood of facing a strong

5. To simplify, I did not specify in the proposition of the main text the complete strategy of the potential weak party. I excluded the action taken after a rejected demand. This does not have any substantive consequences, and additionally only concerns a knife-edge case.

6. In all propositions and lemmas I have only specified out-of-equilibrium beliefs and omitted beliefs that are updated according to Bayes' rule. These can easily be computed with the information contained in the propositions. Omitting them leads to a more concise presentation of the results.

Fig. 8.1. Equilibria with strong and weak credible potential new parties

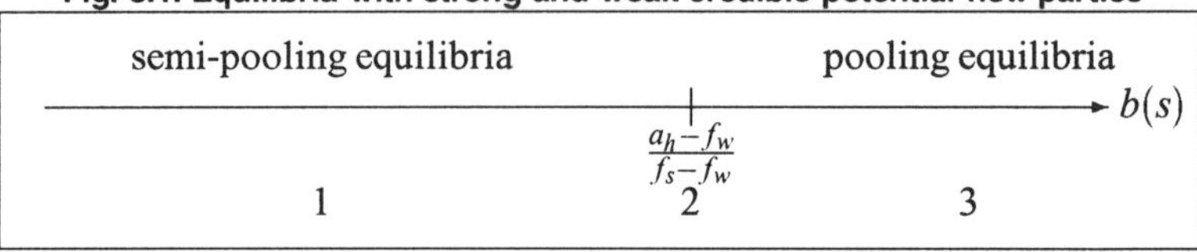

type is so high that the established party is happy to accept some high demands from weak types, as long as it does not have to fight a strong challenger in an election. Consequently, since the weak types do not fear having their bluffs called, they all make high demands. What the established party would do with low demands is without consequence for the equilibrium because they are never made.

If the prior belief is sufficiently low ($b(s) < \frac{a_h - f_w}{f_s - f_w}$), semi-pooling equilibria exist. While the strong type always makes high demands, the weak type only bluffs from time to time. Since it is likely that a weak challenger will be behind a high demand, the established party rejects these demands with a certain probability. It accepts, however, all low demands. But the probability, with which it accepts high demands, sometimes leads the weak types to make such demands. Whenever the threat from the weak type to form a new party is not credible, the equilibria show a similar structure, with details that differ slightly (Proposition 3). Again, if the prior belief is high enough ($b(s) \geq \frac{a_h}{f_s}$), the established party will not take the risk of fighting a strong challenger and accepts all high demands.[7] But the weak type will always make high demands in this situation, because in equilibrium all low demands face rejection. Consequently, with these prior beliefs, only pooling equilibria exist (Figure 8.2).

Proposition 3 *If $b_w < c$ the only general*[8] *equilibria satisfying the D1 criterion are the following:*

1. *if* $b(s) \leq \frac{a_h}{f_s}$ *and* $\frac{c_{hw} - c_{lw}}{c_{hs} - c_{ls}} \geq \frac{b_h}{b_h - b_s + c}$
   $p_s(h) = 1$, $p_w(h) = \frac{b(s)(f_s - a_h)}{(1 - b(s))a_h}$, $p_e(a|l) = 0$, $p_e(a|h) = \frac{c_{hw} - c_{lw}}{b_h}$.
2. *if* $b(s) = \frac{a_h}{f_s}$
   $p_s(h) = 1$, $p_w(h) = 1$, $p_e(a|h) \geq \frac{(b_l - b_s + c) + c_{hs} - c_{ls}}{b_h - b_s + c}$, $p_e(a|l) = 0$, *and* $b_e(s|l) = 0$.
3. *if* $b(s) > \frac{a_h}{f_s}$

7. Only if $b(s) = \frac{a_h}{f_s}$ will the established party reject high demands with a certain probability.

8. Under very specific conditions an additional semi-pooling equilibrium exists. Given its specificity I have not included it in this proposition and will present it only below in the proofs.

Fig. 8.2. Equilibria with only strong credible potential new parties

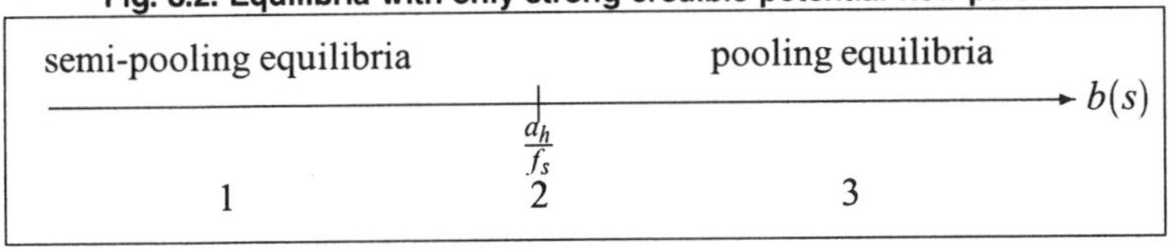

semi-pooling equilibria		pooling equilibria	
	$\frac{a_h}{f_s}$		$\rightarrow b(s)$
1	2	3	

$p_s(h) = 1,\ p_w(h) = 1,\ p_e(a|h) = 1,\ p_e(a|l) = 0,\ \textit{and}\ b_e(s|l) = 0.$

Semi-pooling equilibria exist if the prior belief is sufficiently low ($b(s) < \frac{a_h}{f_s}$). In this situation, the strong type continues to make high demands, but the weak type will only bluff with a certain probability. The established party accepts the high demands with a given probability, but never with certainty. Low demands again face outright rejection, since the weak type cannot credibly threaten to form a new party.

It is useful to start the proof of propositions 2 and 3 by stating the two following lemmas $(1, 2)$, which present all perfect Bayesian equilibria for the signaling game. Before attacking the task of proving the two lemmas, I will present two threshold beliefs which make the established party indifferent between accepting high or, respectively, low demands. These two threshold beliefs will prove central for the analysis that follows. In order to derive them I will set the utilities of accepting and rejecting a high or, respectively, low demand equal to each other. Solving for the two beliefs $(b(h|s), b(l|s))$ will give me the two threshold values.

$$\begin{aligned} E(a|h) &= b_e(s|h)(-a_h) + (1 - b_e(s|h))(-a_h) \\ &= -a_h \end{aligned} \tag{8.4}$$

$$\begin{aligned} E(r|h) &= b_e(s|h)(-f_s) + (1 - b_e(s|h))(-f_w) \\ &= b_e(s|h)(f_w - f_s) - f_w \end{aligned} \tag{8.5}$$

Setting the two expected utilities equal to each other yields the threshold belief.

$$E(a|h) = E(r|h) \tag{8.6}$$

$$-a_h = b_e(s|h)(f_w - f_s) - f_w \tag{8.7}$$

$$b_e(s|h) = \frac{f_w - a_h}{f_w - f_s}$$

$$= \frac{a_h - f_w}{f_s - f_w} \qquad (8.8)$$

For beliefs higher than this threshold value, the established party will accept all high demands. If the belief is lower, then high demands are always rejected. In a similar fashion the second threshold belief can be derived.

$$\begin{aligned}
E(a|l) &= -a_l && (8.9)\\
E(r|l) &= b_e(s|l)(-f_s) + (1 - b_e(s|l))(-f_w) &&\\
&= b_e(s|l)(f_w - f_s) - f_w && (8.10)\\
E(a|l) &= E(r|l) && (8.11)\\
-a_l &= b_e(s|l)(f_w - f_s) - f_w && (8.12)\\
b_e(s|l) &= \frac{f_w - a_l}{f_w - f_s} && (8.13)
\end{aligned}$$

The value of this expression for $b_e(s|l)$ is always negative, since $f_w > a_l$ and $f_s > f_w$. Consequently, the established party is better off by accepting low demands under all beliefs.

Lemma 1 *Under incomplete information if $b_w > c$ the following are all perfect Bayesian equilibria:*

1. *if* $b(s) < \frac{a_h - f_w}{f_s - f_w}$
   $p_s(h) = 1$, $p_w(h) = \frac{b(s)(f_s - a_h)}{(1-b(s))(a_h - f_w)}$, $p_e(a|h) = \frac{b_l - b_w + c + c_{hw} - c_{lw}}{b_h - b_w + c}$ *and* $p_e(a|l)$ $= 1$.
2. *if* $b(s) = \frac{a_h - f_w}{f_s - f_w}$
   $p_s(h) = 1$, $p_w(h) = 1$, $p_e(a|h) \geq \frac{b_l - b_w + c + c_{hw} - c_{lw}}{b_h - b_w + c}$, $p_e(a|l) = 1$ *and* $b_e(s|l)$ $\in [0,1]$.
3. *if* $b(s) > \frac{a_h - f_w}{f_s - f_w}$
   $p_s(h) = 1$, $p_w(h) = 1$, $p_e(a|h) = 1$, $p_e(a|l) = 1$ *and* $b_e(s|l) \in [0,1]$.

Proof of lemma 1: I will prove this lemma in two parts. First, I will show that the strategy combinations in lemma 1 are in equilibrium. Secondly, I will show that all other strategy combinations cannot be part of an equilibrium. Before proceeding, I can note that every rejected demand will be challenged by the potential new party, since $b_w > c$.

- The first equilibrium is semi-pooling. Since, in equilibrium, only the weak type makes low demands with a certain probability, the belief $b_e(s|l) = 0$. Since $-a_l > -f_w$ the established party accepts all low demands ($p_e(a|l) = 1$). The weak potential new party only uses mixed strategies if making high demands yields the same payoff as making low demands. Consequently, $p_e(a|h) = \frac{b_l - b_w + c + c_{hw} - c_{lw}}{b_h - b_w + c}$, which is smaller than 1 by assumption 4. This implies that this can only be an equilibrium if the established party is indifferent between accepting high and low demands. As shown above, this is only the case if $b_e(s|h) = \frac{a_h - f_w}{f_s - f_w}$. But this belief has to be the result of updating according to Bayes' rule, so that $b_e(s|h) = \frac{a_h - f_w}{f_s - f_w} = \frac{b(s)}{b(s)+(1-b(s))p_w(h)}$. Solving for $p_w(h)$ yields $\frac{b(s)(f_s - a_h)}{(1-b(s)(a_h - f_w)}$. This insures that both the actions of the established party and the weak potential new party are in equilibrium. The strong potential new party, however, will only make high demands with certainty if $p_e(a|h) \geq \frac{b_l - c_{ls} - b_s + c_{hs} + c}{b_h - b_s + c}$, which holds for all $p_e(a|h)$, since the fraction is negative by assumption 5. This establishes the second equilibrium, which can only hold as long as $b(s) \leq \frac{a_h - f_w}{f_s - f_w}$, since, by the strategy combination of the potential new parties, $b(s) \leq b_e(s|h)$.

The second equilibrium is pooling. Both types make high demands with certainty, which implies that $b_e(s|h) = b(s)$. The prior belief is such that the established party is indifferent between accepting and rejecting high demands. By $-a_l > -f_w$ and $-a_l > -f_s$ it will accept low demands under all out-of-equilibrium beliefs, which implies that the strong type will make high demands, as long as $p_e(a|h) \geq \frac{b_l - b_s + c + c_{hs} - c_{ls}}{b_h - b_s + c}$. By assumption 5, this fraction is negative, so that it holds for all $p_e(a|h)$. The weak type will also make high demands only if $p_e(a|h) \geq \frac{b_l - b_w + c + c_{hw} - c_{lw}}{b_h - b_w + c}$. Since this fraction is, by assumption 4, always smaller than 1, this establishes the equilibrium.

The third equilibrium is, again, a simple pooling one. Since no updating can take place, the established party adopts its priors after a potential new party has made a high demand. Since its prior belief is sufficiently high ($b(s) \geq \frac{a_h - f_w}{f_s - f_w}$) it will accept all high demands. Given this, both the weak and the strong potential new parties are better off making high demands, and this independent of the out-of-equilibrium action of the established party. This is true since both $\frac{b_h - c_{hw} - b_w + c_{lw} + c}{b_l - b_w + c} \geq p_e(a|l)$ and $\frac{b_h - c_{hs} - b_s + c_{ls} + c}{b_l - b_s + c} \leq p_e(a|l)$ are always fulfilled. The first fraction is, by assumption 4, strictly greater than 1, while the second is negative by assumptions 5 and 6.

- In order to prove that no other strategy combination can be part of an equilibrium, I will proceed by strategy pairs of the two types of potential new parties.

i) If $p_s(h) = 1$, $p_w(h) = 1$ then $b(s) = b_e(s|h)$, which implies that $p_e(a|h) = 1$ if $b_e(s|h) > \frac{a_h - f_w}{f_s - f_w}$. This establishes the first equilibrium discussed above. If $b_e(s|h) < \frac{a_h - f_w}{f_s - f_w}$, then $p_e(a|h) = 0$. The weak type will then make high demands only if $p_e(a|l) \leq \frac{c_{lw} - c_{hw}}{b_l - b_w + c}$. But this fraction is, by assumptions 1 and 2, always negative, implying that there can be no equilibrium. Finally, if $b_e(s|h) = \frac{a_h - f_w}{f_s - f_w}$, then $p_e(a|h) \in [0, 1]$ which leads to the second equilibrium as shown above.

ii) If $p_s(h) = 1$ and $p_w(h) = 0$, then $p_e(a|h) = 1$, since the established party suffers less from integrating a high demand than from fighting a strong type. But then the weak contender will also make high demands, making it impossible for this strategy combination to be part of an equilibrium.

iii) If $p_s(h) = 0$ and $p_w(h) = 1$, then $p_e(a|h) = 0$, since $-f_w > -a_h$, and $p_e(a|l) = 1$. But then the weak potential new party will prefer making low demands ($p_w(h) = 0$), by assumptions 1 and 2, so there is also no equilibrium.

iv) If $p_s(h) = p_w(h) = 0$, then the posterior belief $b_e(s|l)$ is equal to the prior $b(s)$. By assumption 3, $p_e(a|l) = 1$ for all prior beliefs $b(s)$. In that case, the strong type will make low demands only if $p_e(a|h) \leq \frac{b_l - c_{ls} - b_s + c_{hs} + c}{b_h - b_s + c}$. By assumptions 5 and 6, this expression is always negative, implying that there can be no equilibrium.

v) If $p_s(h) = 1$ and $0 < p_w(h) < 1$, this implies that $p_e(a|l) = 1$, since $-a_l > -f_w$. With the other strategies derived above, this defines the third equilibrium.

vi) If $0 < p_s(h) < 1$ and $p_w(h) = 1$, then $p_e(a|l) = 1$ since $-a_l > -f_s$. Furthermore, for the strong type to adopt a mixed strategy requires that $E_s(h) = E_s(l)$, which implies that $p_e(a|h) = \frac{b_l - b_s + c_{hs} - c_{ls} + c}{b_h - b_s + c}$. But, according to assumption 6, this fraction is always bigger than 1, implying that no equilibrium can exist.

vii) If $0 < p_s(h) < 1$ and $0 < p_w(h) < 1$, then, both $p_e(a|h) = \frac{p_e(a|l)(b_l - b_s + c) + c_{hs} - c_{ls}}{b_h - b_s + c}$ and $p_e(a|h) = \frac{p_e(a|l)(b_l - b_w + c) + (c_{hw} - c_{lw})}{b_h - b_w + c}$. Since, by assumption 3, $p_e(a|l) = 1$ the two conditions only hold under a very particular set of payoffs. It requires that $\frac{b_l - b_s + c + c_{hs} - c_{ls}}{b_h - b_s + c} = \frac{b_l - b_w + c + c_{hw} - c_{lw}}{b_h - b_w + c}$. But by assumption 5 the first expression is negative, implying that this strategy combination cannot form an equilibrium.

viii) If $p_s(h) = 0$ and $0 < p_w(h) < 1$, then $p_e(a|h) = 0$, since $-a_h < -f_w$. But, since the weak type uses a mixed strategy, it must be true that $E_w(h) = E_w(l)$, which implies that $p_e(a|l) = \frac{c_{lw} - c_{hw}}{b_l - b_w + c}$. According to assumption 2, this expression is negative, proving that this is not an equilibrium.

ix) If $0 < p_s(h) < 1$ and $p_w(h) = 0$, then $p_e(a|h) = 1$, since $-a_h > -f_s$. But since $p_e(a|l) = 1$, the strong type assumptions 5 and 6, $b_h - c_{hs} > b_l - c_{ls}$. So no equilibrium exists.

Since no other strategy combination is possible, this concludes the proof and shows that the equilibria specified in lemma 1 are the only ones that are perfect Bayesian. *Q.E.D.*

Lemma 2 *Under incomplete information, if $b_w < c$, the following are all perfect Bayesian equilibria:*

1. *if* $b(s) < \frac{a_l}{f_s}$
   $p_s(h) = 0,\ p_w(h) = 0,\ p_e(a|h) \leq \max[\frac{c_{hs}-c_{ls}}{b_h-b_s+c}, \frac{c_{hw}-c_{lw}}{b_h}],\ p_e(a|l) = 0$ *and* $b_e(s|h) \leq \frac{a_h}{f_s}$.
2. *if* $b(s) = \frac{a_l}{f_s}$
   $p_s(h) = 0,\ p_w(h) = 0,\ p_e(a|h) \leq min[\frac{p_e(a|l)(b_l-b_s+c)+c_{hs}-c_{ls}}{b_h-b_s-c}, \frac{p_e(a|l)b_l+c_{hw}-c_{lw}}{b_h}],\ p_e(a|l) \leq \frac{c_{hs}-c_{ls}}{b_s-b_l-c}$ *and* $b_e(s|h) \leq \frac{a_h}{f_s}$.
3. *if* $b(s) \in [\frac{a_l}{f_s}, \frac{a_h}{f_s}]$ *and* $\frac{c_{hw}-clw}{c_{hs}-c_{ls}} \leq \frac{b_h}{b_h-b_s+c}$
   $p_s(h) = \frac{a_h(b(s)f_s-a_l)}{b(s)(a_h-a_l)f_s},\ p_w(h) = \frac{(b(s)f_s-a_l)(f_s-a_h)}{(1-b(s))(a_h-a_l)f_s},\ p_e(a|h) = \frac{(b_s-b_l+c)(c_{hw}-c_{lw})+b_l(c_{hs}-c_{ls})}{(b_s-c)(b_h-b_l)}$ *and* $p_e(a|l) = \frac{(c_{hw}-c_{lw})(b_h-b_s+c)-(c_{hs}-c_{ls})b_h}{(b_l-b_h)(b_s-c)}$.
4. *if* $b(s) \leq \frac{a_h}{f_s}$ *and* $\frac{c_{hw}-clw}{c_{hs}-c_{ls}} > \frac{b_h}{b_h-b_s+c}$
   $p_s(h) = 1,\ p_w(h) = \frac{b(s)(f_s-a_h)}{(1-b(s))a_h},\ p_e(a|l) = 0,\ p_e(a|h) = \frac{c_{hw}-c_{lw}}{b_h}$.
5. *if* $b(s) = \frac{a_h}{f_s}$
   $p_s(h) = 1,\ p_w(h) = 1,\ p_e(a|h) \geq \frac{p_e(a|l)(b_l-b_s+c)+c_{hs}-c_{ls}}{b_h-b_s+c},\ p_e(a|l) \leq \frac{c_{hs}-c_{ls}}{b_s-b_l+c}$, *and* $b_e(s|l) \in [0, 1]$.
6. *if* $b(s) > \frac{a_h}{f_s}$
   $p_s(h) = 1,\ p_w(h) = 1,\ p_e(a|h) = 1,\ p_e(a|l) \in [0, 1]$, *and* $b_e(s|l) \in [0, 1]$.

Proof of lemma 2: Again, I will prove this lemma in two parts. First, I will show that the strategy combinations in lemma 2 are in equilibrium. Second, I show that all other strategy combinations cannot be part of an equilibrium. Before proceeding, I can note that no rejected demand will be challenged by the weak potential new party, since $b_w < c$.

- In the first equilibrium, the prior belief is such that low demands face rejection by the established party, given that both types make them with certainty. Under these circumstances, the strong type make low demands only if $p_e(a|h) \leq \frac{c_{hs}-c_{ls}}{b_h-b_s+c}$. Similarly, for the weak type, $p_e(a|h) \leq \frac{c_{hw}-c_{lw}}{b_h}$ has to hold. Since high demands are accepted with a probability lower than 1, it follows that the out-of-equilibrium belief must satisfy the condition that $b_e(s|h) \leq \frac{a_h}{f_s}$.[9]

In the second equilibrium, the prior belief $b(s)$ is such that the established party is indifferent between accepting and rejecting low demands if both types make these demands with certainty. The strong type would make low demands only if $p_e(a|h) \leq \frac{p_e(a|l)(b_l-b_s+c)+c_{hs}-c_{ls}}{b_h-b_s+c}$. Similarly, $p_e(a|h) \leq \frac{p_e(a|l)b_l+c_{hw}-c_{lw}}{b_h}$ must be the case for the weak type to make low demands. The second fraction is positive for all values of $p_e(a|l)$, while the first one requires $p_e(a|l) \leq \frac{c_{hs}-c_{ls}}{b_s-b_l+c}$. Only if both conditions are fulfilled can this strategy combination form an equilibrium. Since the established party would accept the high demands only with a probability lower than 1, the out-of-equilibrium belief $b_e(s|h) \leq \frac{a_h}{f_s}$.

In the third equilibrium, both types use mixed strategies. This implies that they are both indifferent between making high and low demands. Solving simultaneously the two equations $E_s(h) = E_s(l)$ and $E_w(h) = E_w(l)$ yields $p_e(a|h) = \frac{(b_s-b_l+c)(c_{hw}-c_{lw})+b_l(c_{hs}-c_{ls})}{(b_s-c)(b_h-b_l)}$ and $p_e(a|l) = \frac{(c_{hw}-c_{lw})(b_h-b_s+c)-(c_{hs}-c_{ls})b_h}{(b_l-b_h)(b_s-c)}$. Since both probabilities are strictly smaller than 1, it must be true that the beliefs $b_e(s|h)$ and $b_e(s|l)$ are equal to the corresponding thresholds of $\frac{a_h}{f_s}$ and $\frac{a_l}{f_s}$. Using Bayes' rule and solving for $p_s(h)$ and $p_w(h)$ yields respectively $p_s(h) = \frac{a_h(b(s)f_s-a_l)}{b(s)(a_h-a_l)f_s}$ and $p_w(h) = \frac{(b(s)f_s-a_l)(f_s-a_h)}{(1-b(s))(a_h-a_l)f_s}$. This equilibrium only exists if $b(s) \in [\frac{a_l}{f_s}, \frac{a_h}{f_s}]$. This can be easily shown by plugging these values into the formula for $p_s(h)$ and $p_w(h)$. If the prior belief is at the upper limit, both $p_s(h)$ and $p_w(h)$ are equal to 1, while they are equal to 0 if the prior is at its lower limit. In addition, it only holds if $\frac{c_{hw}-c_{lw}}{c_{hs}-c_{ls}} \leq \frac{b_h}{b_h-b_s+c}$; in all other cases $p_e(a|l)$ should be negative to maintain an equilibrium.

In the fourth equilibrium, the prior belief is such that the established party would reject high demands if both types would make them with certainty. If the weak type only makes high demands with a certain probability while the strong type makes them with certainty, the established party will reject all low demands, since $-a_l < 0$. For the weak type to use a mixed strategy implies that $E_w(h) = E_w(l)$, or more precisely that

9. I do not explicitly derive this and the other threshold beliefs, since they are similar to the ones presented above, with the exception that the challenge of the weak type is no longer credible.

$p_e(a|h)(b_h - c_{hw}) + (1 - p_e(a|h))(-c_{hw}) = -c_{lw}$. Solving for $p_e(a|h)$ yields $\frac{c_{hw}-c_{lw}}{b_h}$, which is strictly smaller than 1, by assumption 4. Consequently, the established party is indifferent between accepting and rejecting high demands, which requires that $b_e(s|h) = \frac{a_h}{f_s}$. Setting this equal to the formula for updating beliefs according to Bayes' rule and solving for $p_w(h)$ yields $\frac{b(s)(f_s-a_h)}{a_h(1-b(s))}$. Given the probability of acceptance of high demands, the strong type will prefer to make high demands if $\frac{c_{hs}-c_{ls}}{b_h-b_s+c} \leq \frac{c_{hw}-c_{lw}}{b_h}$. Consequently, this defines an equilibrium.

In the fifth equilibrium, which is again pooling, the prior belief is such that the established party is indifferent between accepting and rejecting high demands. Now, the probability of acceptance for high demands $p_e(a|h)$ has to be high enough to assure that both types make high demands. For the strong type this is the case if $p_e(a|h) \geq \frac{p_e(a|l)(b_l-b_s+c)+c_{hs}-c_{ls}}{b_h-b_s+c}$. The weak type will make high demands as long as $E_w(h) \geq E_w(l)$, which implies that $p_e(a|l) \leq \frac{p_e(a|h)(b_h)+c_{lw}-c_{hw}}{b_l}$. Combining the two conditions shows that the out-of-equilibrium action $p_e(a|l) \in [0,1]$, which can be supported by beliefs $b_e(s|l) \in [0,1]$. For $p_e(a|h) \geq 0$ it is necessary that $p_e(a|l) \leq \frac{c_{hs}-c_{ls}}{b_s-b_l+c}$, which establishes the second equilibrium.

In the sixth equilibrium the prior belief is so high that the established party accepts all high demands when it cannot update its belief after such a demand. In such a case, the strong potential new party will always make high demands, since, by assumption 6, $b_s - c_{ls} - c < b_h - c_{hs}$. Similarly, for the weak type, it holds for all $p_e(a|l)$ that $p_e(a|l)(b_l - c_{lw} - c) + (1 - p_e(a|l))(-c_{lw}) < b_h - c_{hw}$ (by assumption 4). Consequently, this is an equilibrium for all out-of-equilibrium actions $p_e(a|l)$ and, by extension, all out-of-equilibrium beliefs $b_e(s|l)$.

- In the second part of the proof I check whether any other equilibria exist. I proceed again in steps defined by the strategies that the two types of potential new parties can adopt.

  i) If $p_s(h) = p_w(h) = 1$, then $b_e(s|h) = b(s)$. If this belief exceeds $\frac{a_h}{f_s}$, then $p_e(a|h) = 1$. This leads to the first equilibrium, as shown above. If the belief $b_e(s|h) = \frac{a_h}{f_s}$, then $p_e(a|h) \in [0,1]$, which, again, allows for an equilibrium as proved in the first part. If $b_e(s|h) < \frac{a_h}{f_s}$, then $p_e(a|h) = 0$ and the weak type will make high demands only if $p_e(a|l) < \frac{c_{lw}-c_{hw}}{b_l}$. By assumption, this expression is always negative, so there can be no equilibrium.

  ii) If $p_s(h) = 1$ and $p_w(h) = 0$, then $p_e(a|h) = 1$, since $-a_h > -f_s$ and $p_e(a|l) = 0$, since $-a_l < 0$. But then the weak type prefers to make high demands ($p_w(h) = 1$) by assumption 4, so this can be no equilibrium.

iii) If $p_s(h) = 0$ and $p_w(h) = 1$ then $p_e(a|h) = 0$ since $-a_h < -f_w$ and $p_e(a|l) = 1$ since $-a_l > -f_s$. But then the weak type will make low demands ($p_w(h) = 0$), since $-c_{hw} < b_l - c_{lw}$. Consequently, this strategy for the potential new party cannot be part of an equilibrium.

iv) If $p_s(h) = 0$ and $p_w(h) = 0$ $p_e(a|l) = 1$ if $b(s) > \frac{a_l}{f_s}$. In that case, the strong party will refrain from making high demands if $p_e(a|h) \leq \frac{b_l - c_{ls} - b_s + c_{hs} + c}{b_h - b_s + c}$. But, by assumption 5, this expression is negative, which implies that this can be no equilibrium. For the cases where $b(s) \leq \frac{a_l}{f_s}$, I have already shown above that equilibria exist.

v) If $p_s(h) = 1$ and $0 < p_w(h) < 1$, then $p_e(a|l) = 0$ since $b_e(s|l) = 0$ and $-a_l < 0$. Given that the weak type uses a mixed strategy, it has to be true that $E_w(h) = E_w(l)$, implying that $p_e(a|h) = \frac{c_{hw} - c_{lw}}{b_h}$. The strong type makes high demands only if $p_e(a|h) \geq \frac{c_{hs} - c_{ls}}{b_h - b_s + c}$. As shown above, this can only be part of an equilibrium if $\frac{c_{hw} - c_{lw}}{b_h} \geq \frac{c_{hs} - c_{ls}}{b_h - b_s + c}$.

vi) If $0 < p_s(h) < 1$ and $p_w(h) = 1$, then $p_e(a|l) = 1$, since $b_e(s|l) = 1$. Since the strong type is using a mixed strategy, $p_e(a|h)$ has to equal $\frac{b_l - c_{ls} - b_s + c_{hs} - c_{ls}}{b_h - b_s + c}$. But this last expression is negative by assumption 5. Thus, this strategy combination fails to be part of an equilibrium.

vii) If $0 < p_s(h) < 1$ and $0 < p_w(h) < 1$, then $p_e(a|h) = \frac{p_e(a|l)(b_l - b_s + c) + c_{hs} - c_{ls}}{b_h - b_s + c}$ and $p_e(a|h) = \frac{p_e(a|l)(b_l) + c_{hw} - c_{lw}}{b_h}$ in order for both types to use mixed strategies. As shown above, this implies certain values for $p_e(a|l)$ and $p_e(a|h)$. These can be part of an equilibrium as long as $b(s) \in [\frac{a_l}{f_s}, \frac{a_h}{f_s}]$. If this is not the case, it must be true that $p_e(a|l)$ and $p_e(a|h)$ exceed 1 or are negative.

viii) If $p_s(h) = 0$ and $0 < p_w(h) < 1$, then $p_e(a|h) = 0$, since $b_e(s|h) = 0$ and $0 > -a_h$. But the weak type only uses a mixed strategy if $p_e(a|l) = \frac{c_{lw} - c_{hw}}{b_h}$, which is negative by assumption 2. This implies that this strategy combination cannot be part of an equilibrium.

ix) If $0 < p_s(h) < 1$ and $p_w(h) = 0$, then $p_e(a|h) = 1$, since $b_e(s|h) = 1$ and $-a_h > -f_s$. But for the strong type to use a mixed strategy requires that $p_e(a|l) = \frac{b_h - c_{hs} - b_s - c_{ls} + c}{b_l - b_s + c}$. This expression is negative by assumption 5, implying that no equilibrium exists with this strategy combination.

Since no other strategy combinations exist, this concludes the proof and shows that the equilibria specified in lemma 1 are the only ones that are perfect Bayesian. *Q.E.D.*

Proof of proposition 2: To prove this proposition requires only to check the out-of-equilibrium beliefs of lemma 1. The D1 criterion requires that the established party puts zero probability on the type for which it is weakly less beneficial to deviate from the equilibrium path. To do this I will check one equilibrium after the other. In the first equilibrium, the D1 criterion has no bite, since there are no out-of-equilibrium beliefs. The second equilibrium is immune to this refinement, since the equilibrium is again independent of the out-of-equilibrium belief $b_e(s|l)$. These beliefs are only pinned down by the D1 criterion. The same is the case for the third equilibrium, since it is independent of the out-of-equilibrium action $p_e(a|l)$ and, consequently, also of the out-of-equilibrium belief $b_e(s|l)$. *Q.E.D.*

Proof of proposition 3: As for the previous proof, it is only necessary to check the out-of-equilibrium beliefs of lemma 2 to determine whether or not they fulfill the D1 criterion. The first equilibrium does not survive the D1 criterion. Since $p_e(a|h)$ is strictly smaller than 1, this implies that the established party is not certain as to whether or not it faces a strong type when a high demand is made. However, there are some best responses by the established party, which would lead the strong type to make high demands, while the weak type would continue making low demands. Consequently, the established party should adopt the belief $b_e(s|h) = 1$. This belief, and since $-a_h > -f_s$, destroys the equilibrium, because the established party would adopt a different strategy, namely $p_e(a|h) = 1$. The same happens to the second equilibrium, where the belief $b_e(s|h) = 1$, which conforms to the D1 criterion, destroys the equilibrium. The third equilibrium survives the application of the D1 criterion, since all information sets of the established party are reached with positive probability. This equilibrium, however, relies on very restrictive assumptions about the payoffs. More precisely, it implies that if low demands are rejected with certainty, there are some strategies for which the weak potential new party would prefer making high demands, while the strong one would prefer sticking to low demands. Consequently, I will exclude this equilibrium from the subsequent considerations. In the fourth equilibrium, all information sets of the established party are reached with strictly positive probability, so that the D1 criterion has no bite. The fifth equilibrium experiences the same modifications. There exist some out-of-equilibrium actions which would lead the weak type to a deviation, while the strong type would continue to make high demands. Consequently, the established party should adopt the out-of-equilibrium belief $b_e(s|l) = 0$. But then it would also reject all low demands ($p_e(a|l) = 0$), which defines the equilibrium which fulfills the D1 criterion. In the sixth equilibrium, the out-of-equilibrium belief $b_e(s|l)$, as the out-of-equilibrium action $p_e(a|l)$, has no impact on the equilibrium path. However, the D1 criterion requires that this belief reflect the fact that the weak type is more likely to defect to making low demands than the strong type. Consequently, the equilibrium survives the D1 criterion, but the out-of-equilibrium belief and action is more severly restrained. *Q.E.D.*

Comparative Statics

The equilibria of my model allow a certain number of insights. Before turning to more detailed comparative statics results I discuss two fundamental results. It is interesting that under two conditions new parties never appear in equilibrium. If the established party is perfectly informed on the strength of the potential new party, it will never face an electoral challenge. Hence, incomplete information is a necessary, but not sufficient, condition for the formation of new parties in my model. Similarly, if the established party's prior belief of facing a strong type is high, new parties will never form.[10] In both cases the established party accepts all high demands, which leads the potential new party to refrain from forming a new party. Low demands face rejection if the potential new party is likely to be not credible. According to my model, new parties appear only when established parties are uncertain about the strength of their opponent, and if their prior belief is not too high. This implies that the likelihood of facing a weak potential new party should not be too small.

Second, after the established party has decided to reject a demand, the potential new party makes a purposeful decision to form or to acquiesce. More precisely, it will only form if the benefits of running in an election exceed the costs of forming a new party. The benefits of running in an election are, however, very likely to be linked with the expected success of a new party. This has very serious consequences for the explanation of the success of new parties. Attempting such an explanation must take into account that strategic and purposeful decision. Consequently, new parties do not form a random subset of all groups that ever thought to form a new party. This important point appears in the chapter focusing on questions of research design.

Some interesting comparative statics results follow quite directly from the last two propositions and give insights into the formation process of new political parties. Among these, I will look only at those which allow me to make observations about the formation of new parties. More precisely, I will explore how changes in the payoff structure affect the likelihood of new parties appearing on the electoral scene.

To present these results I will essentially use three elements to judge the likelihood of new political parties: $p(snp)$ corresponds to the probability that a strong new party forms in a given situation, $p(wnp)$ corresponds to the probability that a weak new party appears on the electoral scene, while $p(np)$ is the sum of these two probabilities. To calculate them I introduce two new probabilities which are of only minor importance. $p_s(c|r)$ and $p_w(c|r)$ are the

10. If $b(s) > \frac{a_h}{f_s}$ then all types will make high demands which the established party will accept. They will do so also if $b(s) > \frac{a_h - f_w}{f_s - f_w}$ and simultaneously $b_w > c$.

TABLE 8.2. Comparative statics results

	$b_w > c$			$b_w < c$		
—	$\partial p(snp)$	$\partial p(wnp)$	$\partial p(np)$	$\partial p(snp)$	$\partial p(wnp)$	$\partial p(np)$
$\partial b(s)$	+	+	+	+	0	+
∂c	−	−	−	0	0	0
∂c_{hs}	0	0	0	0	0	0
∂c_{ls}	0	0	0	0	0	0
∂c_{hw}	−	−	−	−	0	−
∂c_{lw}	+	+	+	+	0	+
∂b_h	−	+	+	+	0	+
∂b_s	0	0	0	0	0	0
∂b_l	−	−	−	0	0	0
∂b_w	+	+	+	0	0	0
∂a_h	0	−	−	0	0	0
∂f_s	0	+	+	0	0	0
∂a_l	0	0	0	0	0	0
∂f_w	0	+	+	0	0	0

probabilities with which a strong, or respectively weak, potential new party challenges the rejection of its demand. While $p_s(c|r)$ is always equal to one, $p_w(c|r)$ is equal to one only if $b_w > c$.[11] Based on this, the probabilities with which weak and strong new parties form are relatively easy to determine:

$$p(snp) = b(s)(1 - p_e(a|h))p_s(c|r) \quad (8.14)$$
$$p(wnp) = (1 - b(s))p_w(h)(1 - p_e(a|h))p_w(c|r) \quad (8.15)$$
$$p(np) = p(snp) + p(wnp) \quad (8.16)$$

As already noted, if the probability of facing a strong challenger ($b(s)$) is considerably high, the model predicts that no new parties should form. Conversely, if this probability is low, new parties can emerge, and the likelihood varies as a function of $b(s)$. Consequently, we will only consider cases where new parties can actually appear.[12]

As table 8.2 shows, increasing $b(s)$ always leads to a higher probability of seeing both weak and strong parties appear on the electoral scene. This may

11. Here, I have neglected the difference between rejected high and rejected low demands. This is possible, since in equilibrium the strong type always makes high demands, and the weak type only challenges rejected high demands. If the weak type can credibly threaten to form a new party, all its low demands are accepted in equilibrium.

12. This is the case if $b_w > c$ and $b(s) < \frac{a_h - f_w}{f_s - f_w}$ or $b_w < c$ and $b(s) < \frac{a_h}{f_s}$.

TABLE 8.3. Comparative statics results with only strong credible potential new parties

		$b_w < c$	
$\div$	$\partial p(snp)$	$\partial p(wnp)$	$\partial p(np)$
$\partial b(s)$	$1 - \frac{c_{hw} - c_{lw}}{b_h}$	0	$1 - \frac{c_{hw} - c_{lw}}{b_h}$
∂c	0	0	0
∂c_{hs}	0	0	0
∂c_{ls}	0	0	0
∂c_{hw}	$-\frac{b(s)}{b_h}$	0	$-\frac{b(s)}{b_h}$
∂c_{lw}	$\frac{b(s)}{b_h}$	0	$\frac{b(s)}{b_h}$
∂b_h	$\frac{b(s)(c_{hw} - c_{lw})}{b_h^2}$	0	$\frac{b(s)(c_{hw} - c_{lw})}{b_h^2}$
∂b_s	0	0	0
∂b_l	0	0	0
∂b_w	0	0	0
∂a_h	0	0	0
∂f_s	0	0	0
∂a_l	0	0	0
∂f_w	0	0	0

appear counterintuitive, but it is easy to explain. As $b(s)$ increases, the number of potential challengers making high demands becomes bigger, while the probability of accepting a high demand remains independent of this. Consequently, the overall probability of new party formation increases.[13] A simple implication can be derived from this comparative statics result, since the prior belief on the distribution of types ($b(s)$) increases when new issues become more important.

In the main text I have only provided information on the direction of relationships between several variables and the likelihood of new political parties emerging. The comparative statics results, however, provide more precise indications on the types of relationships. Tables 8.3 and 8.4 present this additional information. They both represent the partial derivatives of the probability of party formation, with respect to all the variables that determine the payoffs of the two actors. The table 8.3 shows these results for the case where $b_w < c$, while table 8.4 illustrates the case where $b_w > c$.

13. Evidently these comparative statics results only hold as long as $b(s)$ does not exceed the threshold values of respectively proposition 2 and 3.

TABLE 8.4. Comparative statics results with strong and weak credible potential new parties

—	$\partial p(snp)$	$\partial p(wnp)$	$\partial p(np)$
$\partial b(s)$	$1-\frac{b_l-b_w+c_{hw}-c_{lw}+c}{b_h-b_w+c}$	$\frac{(f_s-a_h)(b_h-c_{hw}-b_l+c_{lw})}{(a_h-f_w)(b_h-b_w+c)}$	$\frac{(f_s-f_w)(b_h-c_{hw}-b_l+c_{lw})}{(a_h-f_w)(b_h-b_w+c)}$
∂c	$\frac{b(s)(b_l-c_{lw}-b_h-c_{hw})}{(b_w-b_h-c)^2}$	$\frac{b(s)(f_s-a_h)(b_l-c_{lw}-b_h+c_{hw})}{(a_h-f_w)(b_w-b_h-c)^2}$	$\frac{b(s)(b_l-c_{lw}-b_h+c_{hw})(f_s-f_w)}{(a_h-f_w)(b_w-b_h-c)^2}$
∂c_{hs}	0	0	0
∂c_{ls}	0	0	0
∂c_{hw}	$-\frac{b(s)}{b_h-b_w+c}$	$\frac{b(s)(f_s-a_h)}{(a_h-f_w)(b_w-b_h-c)}$	$\frac{b(s)(f_s-f_w)}{(a_h-f_w)(b_w-b_h-c)}$
∂c_{lw}	$\frac{b(s)}{b_h-b_w+c}$	$\frac{b(s)(f_s-a_h)}{(a_h-f_w)(b_h-b_w+c)}$	$\frac{b(s)(f_s-f_w)}{(a_h-f_w)(b_h-b_w+c)}$
∂b_h	$\frac{b(s)(b_l-c_{lw}-b_w+c_{hw}+c)}{(b_w-b_h-c)^2}$	$\frac{b(s)(f_s-a_h)(b_l-c_{lw}-b_w+c_{hw}+c)}{(a_h-f_w)(b_h-b_w+c)^2}$	$\frac{b(s)(f_s-f_w)(b_l-c_{lw}-b_w+c_{hw}+c)}{(a_h-f_w)(b_w-b_h-c)^2}$
∂b_s	0	0	0
∂b_l	$-\frac{b(s)}{b_h-b_w+c}$	$\frac{b(s)(f_s-a_h)}{(a_h-f_w)(b_w-b_h-c)}$	$\frac{b(s)(f_s-f_w)}{(a_h-f_w)(b_w-b_h-c)^2}$
∂b_w	$\frac{b(s)(b_h-c_{hw}-b_l+c_{lw})}{(b_w-b_h-c)^2}$	$\frac{b(s)(f_s-a_h)(b_h-c_{hw}-b_l+c_{lw})}{(a_h-f_w)(b_w-b_h-c)^2}$	$\frac{b(s)(f_s-f_w)(b_h-c_{hw}-b_l+c_{lw})}{(a_h-f_w)(b_w-b_h-c)^2}$
∂a_h	0	$\frac{b(s)(f_s-f_w)(b_h-c_{hw}-b_l+c_{lw})}{(a_h-f_w)^2(b_w-b_h-c)}$	$\frac{b(s)(f_s-f_w)(b_h-c_{hw}-b_l+c_{lw})}{(a_h-f_w)^2(b_w-b_h-c)}$
∂f_s	0	$\frac{b(s)(b_h-c_{hw}-b_l+c_{lw})}{(a_h-f_w)(b_h-b_w+c)}$	$\frac{b(s)(b_h-c_{hw}-b_l+c_{lw})}{(a_h-f_w)(b_h-b_w+c)}$
∂a_l	0	0	0
∂f_w	0	$\frac{b(s)(f_s-a_h)(b_h-c_{hw}-b_l+c_{lw})}{(a_h-f_w)^2(b_h-b_w+c)}$	$\frac{b(s)(f_s-a_h)(b_h-c_{hw}-b_l+c_{lw})}{(a_h-f_w)^2(b_h-b_w+c)}$

Payoffs

Given that the complete information version of the theoretical model yields as equilibrium outcome that new parties never appear on the electoral scene, an important question concerns whether this result is due to the assumed payoff structure. In this appendix, I present, both for the weak and strong type of potential new party, the conditions under which a new party might form if the complete information assumption is maintained. I do not present formal proofs for these conditions. They were obtained by working through all possible payoff orders, and a formal presentation would be tedious.

Strong Type

A strong new party becomes possible under complete information if the payoffs are changed in one of the following ways:

- $c_{ls} > c_{hs}$: If the costs of making a low demand are higher than the costs of making a high demand for the strong type, the latter can form a new party under complete information. In that case, the strong type will always make low demands, which, even when accepted, have a lower payoff than forming a new party.
- $a_l > f_s$ and $b_s - c_{ls} - c > b_h - c_{hs}$: In this case, the established party suffers more from accepting a low demand than from fighting a strong type in an election. In addition, the strong type prefers to form a new party after a rejected low demand, rather than to have a high demand accepted. Consequently, all strong types make low demands and form new parties after the rejection by the established party.
- $a_h > f_s$ and $b_s - c_{ls} - c > b_h - c_{hs}$: In this situation, the established party suffers more from accepting a high demand than from fighting a strong challenger. Thus, it rejects all high demands. Also, the strong type prefers to form a new party after a rejected low demand, rather than to have a high demand accepted. This again causes the formation of strong new parties.
- $a_l > f_s$ and $c_{ls} > c_{hs}$: Again, the costs of making a low demand exceed those of a high demand for the strong type. Consequently, the strong type makes low demands which are rejected by the established party, since an acceptance would hurt it very heavily.

Weak Type

A weak new party becomes possible under complete information only if the payoffs for the various actors are changed in one of the following four ways:

- $a_l > f_w$: If the established party suffers more from accepting a low demand than from fighting a weak challenger, new weak parties become possible.
- $f_w > a_h$ and $b_w - c_{lw} - c > b_h - c_{hw}$: In this situation, fighting a weak type is very costly, exceeding the costs of accepting a high demand. In addition, the weak type prefers to create a new party after a rejected low demand rather than to have high demand accepted.
- $b_w > b_l$: If the weak new party is always better off in fighting an election than in having a low demand accepted, weak new parties become logically possible.
- $c_{lw} > chw$: If making low demands exceeds the costs of making high demands for the weak potential new party, the latter will always make high demands. But these are too costly to be accepted by the established party, which leads to the formation of weak new parties.

The changes necessary in the payoff structure to produce complete information equilibria where new parties appear are implausible to varying degrees. Most require an important reversal of the payoff structure, which is incoherent on substantive grounds. All conditions which involve changes in the signaling costs are of this type. The other changes concern the benefits from accepted demands. All of these violate the assumption that for all potential new parties there is a possibility to find an agreement with an existing party. If this assumption is violated, every group considering the formation of a new party would do so automatically. Given the limited number of new parties, this is hardly a convincing argument.

Data Collection

In this section, I document the data used in the empirical part of this study, providing detailed information on the sources employed. For some instances, especially when different sources conflict, I cite them in detail to justify my coding decisions. The universe of countries and elections considered already figure in table 5.1 in the main text. As explained, the countries considered are the OECD countries (excluding Japan and Turkey). The elections considered are all regular national parliamentary elections since the end of World War II, except for the United States, where presidential elections are used. Since, in most countries, the war years have led to important changes in the structure of the party systems, new parties are only counted starting with the second regular election. I begin with the two independent variables, namely the number of new parties and their initial strength. After that, I proceed to the different variables that I use to measure the theoretical variables that are derived from my model. Finally, at the end I give a detailed description of the procedure I followed to construct my indicator for the credibility of a weak potential new party.

Number of New Parties

The number of new parties at each election corresponds to the number of organizations that proposed, for the first time, a list of candidates for the general parliamentary election. Only in the case of the United States were presidential elections chosen, since in those the entry of new parties is most notable. Even official sources do not often report all lists (e.g., Stöss 1975, 255), so my method probably underestimates the frequency of new party appearance. This bias can be diminished by using common sources, i.e. Mackie and Rose (1991), Mackie (1991, 1992), and the *Political Data Yearbook* (Mair and Koole 1992). I have also added all parties listed in the following books: Day and Degenhardt (1988), McHale and Skowronski (1983), Alexander (1982), Schapsmeier and Schapsmeier (1981), Coggins, Lewis, and Milia (1992), East and Bell (1990). For the United States, the main source was the ICPSR dataset *Candidate Name and Constituency Totals, 1788-1988.*[14] Both the names of the parties and their results were checked against the list provided by Rosenstone, Behr, and Lazarus (1984, 231ff).

For some parties, almost no information was available, which led me, for example, to drop all "other" parties for Germany. Regional parties, as long as they have not competed in national elections, have also been excluded. An important problem concerns regional parties that form when a given party splits along ethnic lines, as in Belgium and Spain, or regional ones, as in Great Britain. If a party divides and the resulting parties do not compete against each other, I assume that this does not change the competitive situation. Consequently, these types of new parties do not count as new ones, which is the case with the parties that formed in Belgium in the late sixties and at the beginning of the seventies. Consequently, inclusion as a new party requires essentially that the organization has proposed candidates for a general national election. A complete list of genuinely new parties and splits appears on the web at <http://uts.cc.utexas.edu/~simonhug/newparty/>

14. Inter-university Consortium for Political and Social Research. Candidate Name and Constituency Totals, 1788-1988 [Computer file]. 4th ICPSR ed. Ann Arbor, MI: Inter-university Consortium for Political Research [producer and distributor], 1990.

Success of New Parties

As discussed in the main text, I have adopted a simple measure of the success of new parties. Their initial success is simply the percentage of votes they garner in their first election. The data stem from the same source as the number of new political parties. Given the lack of information, some new parties could not be included in the analyses which focuses on their initial success. Out of the 361 genuinely new parties and splits, precise information on their initial success was available only for 260.

Pluralism and Semi-pluralism of Society

Harmel and Robertson (1985, 515) provide a classification according to whether a country is plural or semi-plural for almost all countries under consideration here. I have adapted this classification by coding the three missing countries, namely Greece, Portugal, and Spain, as neither plural nor semi-plural.

Linguistic and Religious Homogeneity

The source for these two variables, which measure the homogeneity of a given country, is the dataset by Banks and Textor (1968). They provide data for all countries except New Zealand. I have coded this country as being linguistically homogeneous and as religiously heterogeneous, based on information from the CIA World Factbook (1992) and Lane, McKay, and Newton (1991).

Ethno-linguistic Fragmentation

Lane, McKay, and Newton (1991, 20) provide several measures of ethno-linguistic fragmentation for all OECD countries. I have adopted their third measure, which originally stems from Taylor and Hudson (1972), for convenience (as it contains no missing data).

Size of Population

Lane, McKay, and Newton (1991, 8) provide population figures for all OECD countries. These figures correspond to midyear estimates for five decades. Accordingly, I took the figures for 1950 to cover all years preceding 1955, the 1960 figure to cover the years between 1955 and 1965, etc. The 1980 population figure covers then the period between 1975 and 1982, while the 1985 figure was used for all elections after 1982.

Economic Growth

Lane, McKay, and Newton (1991, 60) provide four figures for the growth of real GDP per capita. I have taken their figure for 1960-68 to cover all years before 1968, and their figure for 1979-85 for all elections after 1979. Between these years, I used the two other figures they provide.

Unemployment

The unemployment data that Lane, McKay, and Newton (1991, 60) present cover five years. I have used their 1960 figure for all elections before 1965, and their 1970 figure for elections between 1965 and 1972. Their 1975 figure covers the years between 1972 and 1977, the 1980 data covers the period between 1977 and 1982, while their 1985 figure covers the remaining elections. Data was missing for Iceland 1949-1963, Luxembourg 1948-1964, and Switzerland 1951-1963. Given their low and stable rate of unemployment in these years, I extrapolated the following values for the missing election years: Iceland 1 percent, Luxembourg 1 percent, and Switzerland 0.1 percent.

Public Financing of Parties

The source for this variable is Paltiel (1981, 164ff), who provides indications for most countries. I have coded all other countries as having no public financing of political parties, except for Portugal and Spain. This was supported by Delury (1987) and checked against the data provided in Katz and Mair (1992).

Number of Governments and Number of Parties in Government

Lane, McKay, and Newton (1991, 116ff) provide detailed information on the structure of government per decade in all OECD countries. I have employed their measures of number of governments per decade, and the average number of parties in government per decade.

Centralization

To measure the degree of centralization in a given country, I used the percentage of taxes that the central government receives, compared to the total taxes for the entire country. Lane, McKay, and Newton (1991, 81f) provide data at five-year intervals, in the period from 1950 to 1985. Here, I have used the 1950 figure for all years up to 1954, the 1955 figure for the period between 1955 and 1959, etc. The 1985 figures cover, consequently, all elections after 1985. This dataset has a series of missing datapoints. Most importantly there are no data for New Zealand. Thus, I resorted again to an extra/intrapolation, based on a simple linear regression for each country with missing data. For the

Swiss case I corrected all the datapoints before 1969, since the Lane, McKay, and Newton (1991) book seems to reproduce erroneous data (*Annuaire statistique suisse*, 1945-1970). I then ran regressions between the Lane, McKay, and Newton (1991) dataset and the three datapoints (1975, 1980, 1992) that I found in the OECD revenue statistics (*Revenue statistics of OECD member countries*, Organisation for Economic Co-operation and Development). This leads to very similar regression results for all three series. Hence, I averaged over all coefficients, which lead to the following results: -20.19 (intercept) 1.17 (slope for OECD measure). This suggests that the figures from Lane, McKay, and Newton (1991) are on average 20 points below the ones from the OECD revenue statistics. Hence, I computed the following figures for New Zealand: 88.6 (1975), 88.6 (1982), 89.8 (1992). Based on these figures I extrapolated to the other years: 86.5 (49), 86.6 (51), 86.8 (54), 87.1 (57), 87.3 (60), 87.5 (63), 87.8 (66), 88 (69), 88.2 (72), 88.4 (75), 88.7 (79), 88.9 (81), 89.1 (84), 89.4 (87), 89.6 (90).

Federalism

As source for whether a country is federal or not, I used the classification provided by Lijphart (1984). Spain and Portugal, which are not included in his classification, are coded as non-federal, based on information from the CIA World Factbook (1992).

Electoral Thresholds

The two electoral thresholds used in the empirical analysis correspond to the ones derived by Lijphart and Gibberd (1977). Below I present a table for the different electoral systems, and also add plurality rule (Rae, Hanby, and Loosemore 1971, 485), which is not included in Lijphart and Gibberd (1977, 225), as well as the Single Transferable Vote system (Gallagher 1992, 486).

TABLE 8.5. Thresholds of representation and exclusion

	Plurality	D'Hondt	Pure Saint-Laguë	Modified Saint-Laguë	Largest Remainder	Single Transferable Vote
threshold of exclusion						
if $n-1 \geq m$	$\frac{1}{2}$	$\frac{1}{m+1}$	$\frac{1}{m+1}$	$\frac{1}{m+1}$	$\frac{1}{m+1}$	$\frac{1}{m+1}$
if $\frac{m}{2} \leq n-1 \leq m$	$\frac{1}{2}$	$\frac{1}{m+1}$	$\frac{1}{2m-n+2}$	$\frac{1.4}{1.6m-0.2n+1.6}$	$\frac{n-1}{mn}$	$\frac{1}{m+1}$
if $n-1 \leq \frac{m}{2}$	$\frac{1}{2}$	$\frac{1}{m+1}$	$\frac{1}{2m-n+2}$	$\frac{1.4}{2m+n+2.4}$	$\frac{n-1}{mn}$	$\frac{1}{m+1}$
threshold of representation	$\frac{1}{n}$	$\frac{1}{m+n-1}$	$\frac{1}{2m+n-2}$	$\frac{1.4}{2m+1.4-2.4}$	$\frac{1}{mn}$	0

To determine the electoral thresholds for each election, three pieces of information are necessary. One has to know what electoral system is in use. The source for this information was essentially Sternberger and Vogel (1969), which discusses at length the different electoral systems and the changes that intervened in each country. This source was updated with information from Nohlen (1978, 1990) as well as the *Chronique des élections*. Second, the district magnitude (m) has to be known. Since in most systems this number varies from one district to the other, at least three possibilities arise. I could use the smallest, the largest, or the mean district magnitude. In the first two cases I would adopt the lowest, respectively highest electoral thresholds as representative for the whole country. In order to reflect the situation where entry is the easiest, I adopted this highest district magnitude, taking it from Lane, McKay, and Newton (1991). Finally, the last piece of information required is the number of parties (n) competing in the election. Again, most official sources do not report all the lists that presented candidates. To solve this I simply used the number of parties which received votes, according to Mackie and Rose (1991), Mackie (1991, 1992) and the *Political Data Yearbook* (Mair and Koole 1992). However, instead of using the number of parties getting votes in the current election, I used the information from the previous election. This measures the expected number of competitors that a newcomer must face. With these three pieces of information the calculation of the different thresholds becomes relatively easy.

Government Change

To measure the changes in government I adopted a simple measure. If between two elections the composition of the government involved a party being ejected or a new one being included, I coded the following election as being preceded by a government change. The source of the data is the country section in Lane, McKay, and Newton (1991). Their indications correspond largely to the indications in Gorvin (1989), though his are less precise.

Type of Government: Majoritarian

To measure the type of government I used the classification and the data of Woldendorp, Keman, and Budge (1993). For each election I selected the type of government which was in office up to election date. For two elections in Finland (1958 and 1975), and the elections in Greece, Ireland, Portugal, Spain, and the US, this source does not provide any information. For the US I assume that all governments are Single Party Governments. For the other cases I have consulted Lane, McKay, and Newton (1991). Governments were coded as majoritarian whenever a single party occupied all posts of ministers and as non-majoritarian in all other cases.

Referendum

I coded each country based on information from Lijphart (1984), Nohlen (1990), Austen, Butler, and Ranney (1987) whether it allows for referendums or not.

Costs of Forming a New Political Party: Electoral Deposit and Petition

A first measure of the costs of forming a new party essentially corresponds to the fees that are required for registering a party on the ballot. The primary source for this measure is the Interparliamentary Union (1976) and Sternberger and Vogel (1969). For individual countries, more precise information stems from several additional sources. The amount of the deposit in local currency was weighted by the corresponding GNP per capita of the election year. The data for the population and the GNP come from the *International Financial Statistics*.

The second measure for the costs of forming a new party comes from the number of signatures needed to have access to the ballot. This second measure of the difficulty in forming a new party is also taken from the Interparliamentary Union (1976), supplemented with information by Sternberger and Vogel (1969). Again, for individual countries, more precise information stems from several additional sources.

In order to determine the severeness of the number of signatures required to accede to the ballot, these numbers where divided by the size of the electorate. The source for this variable is also Mackie and Rose (1991), except for elections where the numbers are obviously false, for example, Denmark, 1988. Information was also taken from the same source on the number of people actually taking part at the election. For elections not covered in Mackie and Rose, either Mackie (1991, 1992), the *European Data Yearbook*, or the *Chronique des élections* were used. Below, I give more detailed information on the financial and administrative requirements for accessing to the ballot in individual countries. I do so, since some of these sources give contradictory information.

The number of signatures required to be able to participate in an election varies between 200 and 500 per district in Austria (Ohlinger 1983, 114). In addition, a party has to make a deposit of 6000 schilling. The Interparliamentary Union (1976, 75) shows the same figures, except that the electoral deposit is equal to $325. Müller (1992, 26) indicates that the "number of signatures for a nation-wide candidacy has varied from 2500 (1945-58) to 2800 (since 1971) to

5000 (1959-70)." Further on, Müller notes that in 1945, 100 petitions per electoral district were necessary for acceding to the ballot. This number passed to 200 in 1949, and starting in 1971, varied between 200 and 500 (Müller 1992, 40). Similarly, Müller mentions that the "financial contribution was introduced in 1959. . . . Then the cost of a nation-wide candidacy amounted to Ös 50000, and since 1971 it has been Ös 54000." Sternberger and Vogel (1969, 965) indicate that 200 signatures are required to accede to the ballot, as well as Ös 2000 starting 1959.

In Belgium, according to Dewachter (1983, 92), 600 signatures are required in big electoral districts, and 200 in small ones, in order to gain access to the ballot. The Interparliamentary Union (1976, 75) notes a range from 200 to 500, and indicates that no electoral deposit is required. Deschouwer (1992, 129f) notes the same range for the years 1960 to 1989. According to Sternberger and Vogel (1969, 116), between 200 and 500 signatures are required. Union Interparlementaire (1966, 52) reports 300 as the lowest number of signatures required.

For Denmark, the Interparliamentary Union (1976, 76; Union Interparlementaire 1966, 52) shows that the number of signatures necessary to get on the ballot varies between 25 and 50. An electoral deposit is not required. Bille (1992, 214), however, notes that a petition with 10000 signatures was required in 1960. Starting in 1965, 1/175 of the total valid votes cast in the last general election is required. Sternberger and Vogel (1969, 185) also note the requirement of 25 to 50 signatures per candidate and mention the absence of deposit.

In Finland an "electoral association must be formed for every candidate in parliamentary elections by at least 30 people eligible to vote in the constituency" (Sundberg and Gylling 1992, 285). This situation, which held from 1960 to 1967, was changed in 1969, after which only parties could propose candidates. To become a registered party at least 5000 adherents have to sign a petition. Starting in 1975, an "electoral association can be formed for every candidate in parliamentary elections by at least 100 persons eligible to vote in the constituency." (Sundberg and Gylling 1992, 285). The 30 signatures are also mentioned by Sternberger and Vogel (1969, 434f) and Union Interparlementaire (1966, 52).

The French electoral law only requires a deposit of $200 to get on the ballot for the National Assembly, but no signatures from voters (Interparliamentary Union 1976, 76). Similarly, Sternberger and Vogel (1969, 538) note a deposit of 1000 FF.

In Germany, a party has to present 200 signatures in an electoral district to access the ballot (Grimm 1983, 317). According to the Interparliamentary Union, however, no signatures are required, as long as the candidates are proposed by a party. A list can be put on the ballot if 1 percent of the voters of a given *Land* (or at most 2000 voters) sign a petition. Poguntke and Boll (1992, 331) note that from 1960 on, 1/1000 of those who are eligible to vote in the respective *Land* have to sign a petition, up to a maximum of 2000 signatures.

Sternberger and Vogel (1969, 710) indicate that at most 200 and at least 100 signatures are required to place a candidate on the ballot in Reikjavik. This requirement drops to 50, respectively 100 signatures for all other districts (Union Interparlementaire 1966, 52). These authors also mention that no deposit is required and that this is fixed in a 1959 law.

Only one signature, different from the candidate's, is required to gain access to the ballot in Ireland. A deposit of 100 pounds, however, is also required (Chubb 1983, 282). Sternberger and Vogel (1969, 684) note the same amount and mention the 1963 electoral law as its source. The Interparliamentary Union notes, however, that no signatures are required and shows that a deposit of $250 is necessary. Farrell (1992, 399) notes that no rules such as these existed in 1960 and 1962. But since that date, only parties can have their name put on the ballot. At the same time, rules were established for the recognition of a party which do not include any signatures or deposits. Union Interparlementaire (1966, 52) reports a requirement of 10 signatures.

According to the Interparliamentary Union (1976, 77), Italian parties have to collect between 500 and 1000 signatures to get on the ballot. A deposit is not required. Bardi and Morlino (1992, 478) note that from 1960 on for the Chamber of Deputies, lists of candidates have to be submitted with 500 signatures in each constituency. Sternberger and Vogel (1969, 745) indicate that the petition requirement was established in a 1948 law.

In Luxembourg, it is necessary to provide 25 signatures per district to accede to the ballot (Sternberger and Vogel (1969, 829f). This requirement was established in the electoral laws of 1924, 1932, and 1936.

In the Netherlands, access to the ballot requires 25 signatures in each electoral district and a deposit of 1,000 *Guilders* (Lijphart 1983, 250). Similar figures, namely 25 signatures and $325 figure in Interparliamentary Union (1976, 78). Sternberger and Vogel (1969, 886) note the same requirement and indicate that it was established in a law from 1951. Koole and van de Velde (1992, 635f) confirm these figures, but note that since 1989 only 10 signatures are required; these must be accompanied, however, by a deposit of 25,000 *Guilders*.

In Norway, parties are required to collect between 100 and 250 signatures, according to the Interparliamentary Union (1976, 78). This source is silent, however, on the electoral deposit. Svasand (1992, 743) indicates that 500 signatures were required in 1960 and in all elections from that year on. In 1990 this number was increased to 5000. Sternberger and Vogel (1969, 917) note that no deposit or signatures are required to accede the ballot, while Union Interparlementaire (1966, 52) mentions a requirement of between 50 and 100 signatures.

In Spain no deposit is required, but candidates have to be supported by at least five members of parliament, or seven provincial delegates, or at least 1000 heads of families or married women (Interparliamentary Union 1976, 79ff).

Sweden requires neither signatures from voters nor a deposit to accede the ballot (Interparliamentary Union 1976, 79). Pierre and Widfeldt (1992, 791) also note that no signatures are required to accede to the ballot. Parties, however, can protect their names by submitting 1000 signatures (until 1973), respectively 1500 (from 1973 on). Identical indications figure in Sternberger and Vogel (1969, 1107).

According to the Interparliamentary Union (1976, 79), 15 signatures are required to get on the ballot in Switzerland. This figure finds confirmation in Sternberger and Vogel (1969, 1136). Aubert (1983, 75) cites an identical figure, but notes that in the new law this number will be increased to 50 signatures.

In Great Britain, access to the ballot requires 10 signatures and a deposit of \$375 (Interparliamentary Union 1976, 79). Webb (1992, 840, 846f) notes that the deposit was increased from 150 pounds to 500 pounds in 1987. The amount of 100 pounds appears also in Sternberger and Vogel (1969, 624), while the number of signatures finds confirmation in Union Interparlementaire (1966, 52). Cole (1992, 78) notes that the 150 pound deposit was introduced in 1918.

Party candidates in the United States do not have to fulfill a requirement for signatures. Independent candidates have to be supported by at least one percent, sometimes 2 percent of the votes cast in a state. The electoral deposit also varies from state to state, ranging from 0 to 1,000 dollars (Interparliamentary Union 1976, 79).

In Canada 25 signatures are required to get access to the ballot (Union Interparlementaire (1966, 52).

Construction of Credibility Indicator

The credibility measure employed in this study relies on eight indicators, as discussed in chapter 5. Each of these indicators was standardized to have a mean value of 0 and a standard deviation of 1. Since the credibility measure should reflect whether the benefits of a weak new challenger exceed the formation costs, the indicators of the latter theoretical variable were subtracted from those of the former. Since I employ three measures for the formation costs, but five for the benefits of weak new challengers, I weigh these indicators accordingly. Table 8.6 describes this construction with the adequate signs and where $z(.)$ refers to the standardization of a variable.

The indicator constructed according to this formula has the following

TABLE 8.6. Construction of credibility measure

signed theoretical variables	standardized and signed indicators
+ benefits of weak challenger ($* \frac{3}{8}$)	- z(threshold of representation)
	- z(threshold of exclusion)
	+ z(federalism)
	+ z(number of parties in government)
	+ z(number of governments (per decade))
- formation costs ($* \frac{5}{8}$)	- z(public party financing)
	+ z(electoral deposit)
	+ z(petition signatures)
$\Sigma =$	degree of credibility of weak challenger

quintiles values: -1.18 (first quintile), -0.50 (second quintile), 0.73 (third quintile), and 1.27 (fourth quintile). Since I assume that in 20 percent of all elections weak challengers are not credible, cases where the indicator is smaller than -1.18 are assigned to the "non-credible" category. The classification of the elections according to this criterion appears in table 5.5.

Estimation Procedures

The empirical part of my work gives rise to several problems with the estimation procedures. Since the problems go very closely together with the two research designs, I will present and discuss them under separate headings. I will look initially at the estimations where the count of new political parties is the dependent variable. Then I will discuss the problems that appear with the selection mechanism when studying the success of new political parties.

Count of New Political Parties

In the first research design the dependent variable is the number of new parties that appeared in a given election. Consequently, the variable is a count and almost by definition not normally distributed. This constitutes the first problem in this research design. The second and third problems concern the units of analysis. Since the data points correspond to election years in several countries, the dependent variable varies both across space and across time. These two types of variations are seldom considered together in political science, as Stimson (1985) and Bartolini (1993) illustrate.

Variation over space might give rise to problems if some omitted variables are strongly correlated with certain countries. A common solution to this problem is an intercept, which varies across countries. Additional problems might be caused by spatial dependency, an aspect I have completely neglected in the empirical part of this work. Variation over time is quite standard and can give rise to autocorrelated errors. Since in my case there is additional variation across space, the interesting autocorrelations appear for each individual country in my dataset.

These three main problems are potentially hazardous for every inference drawn from my dataset. Thus, I adopted several estimation strategies to minimize the likelihood of erroneous inference. Each strategy attempted to take care of at least one of the three problems mentioned above. At the end of this section I report a last analyses which extends the final model reported in chapter 5.

As the dependent variable is a count, I estimated all my models as a negative binomial regression. This setup allows for overspersion, meaning that the variance, which is commonly set to the expected number of occurrences in Poisson-regression is set free to vary. The results from this estimation procedure differ slightly, when compared to simple OLS estimates.[15] For this reason I refrain from reporting these results here.

Nonetheless, these estimated models were used to check whether the second and third problem are serious. I saved residuals from the simple OLS estimations and checked their serial-correlations and their mean by country.[16] In general the residuals display no abnormal pattern. Some auto correlations appear in the residuals, but these are either rather weak or not systematic. Consequently, I refrained from seeking solutions to this problem. In addition, the average residual by country varied little, except for Spain. In this country the residuals are on average always very big, indicating a very poor fit of most estimates. But when controlling for this country-specific effect, only minor changes occurred in the estimated coefficients. Thus I do not present these alternative results. The problem was more serious for the case of the United States, where estimates for the link between party formation and the costs of fighting a new challenger change strongly when this country is dropped from the analysis. These changes were reported in the main text. Additional analyses also to referred suggest that no other analyses are affected by the presence of the United States in the sample.

Finally, I report here the results of an additional test. While table 5.11 in chapter 5 provides one type of a global test, it fails to give insights into whether the interactions highlighted in my theoretical model are really important. The ideal test for this aspect of the model would be to include all variables used in the individual tests presented above. If the implications were correct, only the interactions shown in table 5.3 should have a significant impact in the overall model. As noted above, serious problems of multicollinearity make such a test

15. For these estimations I resorted to a common transformation by taking the log of the count plus one half. Such a transformation leads to a variable which is distributed approximately normally. King (1988) criticizes this transformation.

16. I used residuals from the OLS regresssions since no equivalent to residuals are available for event-count regressions.

TABLE 8.7. Explaining party formation

	Model 1			Model 2			Model 3		
	all	cred.	non-cred.	all	cred.	non-cred.	all	cred.	non-cred.
variable	b	b	b	b	b	b	b	b	b
	(s.e.)	(s.e.)	(s.e.)	(s.e.)	(s.e.)	(s.e.)	(s.e.)	(s.e.)	(s.e.)
New issues									
plural	0.24			-2.44	2.34		0.40		
	(0.36)			(5.02)	(5.09)		(0.38)		
semiplural	-0.29			0.04	-0.20		-0.51		
	(0.30)			(1.86)	(1.92)		(0.32)		
religious	0.20			-1.03	1.09		0.13		
homogeneity	(0.29)			(2.47)	(2.50)		(0.30)		
linguistic	-0.84			-0.16	-0.16		-1.10		
homogeneity	(0.47)			(1.34)	(1.42)		(0.53)		
ethno-linguistic	-1.38			-3.33	3.77		-1.84		
fragmentation	(1.12)			(4.22)	(4.19)		(1.28)		
growth rate	-0.22			-0.16	-0.01		-0.19		
	(0.07)			(0.15)	(0.17)		(0.08)		
unemployment rate	0.03			0.09	-0.07		0.02		
	(0.02)			(0.20)	(0.20)		(0.02)		
population	1.56			0.63	1.26		2.15		
	(0.39)			(1.51)	(1.64)		(0.48)		
Formation costs									
public party		0.05			-0.05			-0.08	-1.28
financing		(0.22)			(0.24)			(0.23)	0.20
electoral		2.53			1.85			2.19	0.86
deposit		(2.31)			(2.26)			(2.26)	(0.22)
petition		0.36			0.40			0.39	-0.08
signatures		(0.15)			(0.15)			(0.16)	(0.31)
Benefits from high demands									
majority	0.08			0.08			0.10		
government	(0.23)			(0.23)			(0.22)		
number of parties	0.17			0.62			0.31		
in government	(0.18)			(0.85)			(0.31)		
government	0.05			0.01			0.06		
change	(0.18)			(0.19)			(0.18)		
centralization	-1.15			-1.23			-1.01		
(taxes)	(0.94)			(0.98)			(0.96)		
referendum	-0.22			-0.41			-0.30		
	(0.29)			(0.34)			(0.30)		
Fighting costs									
threshold of		-4.77			-7.53			-6.79	
representation		(1.73)			(2.30)			(2.14)	
threshold of		2.59			1.81			2.88	
exclusion		(0.72)			(1.04)			(0.79)	
number of		0.02			0.02			0.03	
governments		(0.05)			(0.05)			(0.05)	
number of parties		-0.09			-0.59			-0.25	
in government		(0.18)			(0.85)			(0.32)	
federal		-0.20			-0.46			-0.17	
		(0.37)			(0.39)			(0.38)	
Constant			1.74			1.68			2.03
			(0.95)			(1.06)			(1.02)
			0.20			0.15			0.18
			(0.09)			(0.09)			(0.09)
llik			-			-			-
			373.45			367.63			370.33
df llik						-5.82			-3.11

TABLE 8.7. Explaining party formation (cont'd)

	Model 4			Model 5		
	all	cred.	non-cred.	all	cred.	non-cred.
variable	b	b	b	b	b	b
	(s.e.)	(s.e.)	(s.e.)	(s.e.)	(s.e.)	(s.e.)
New issues						
plural	-0.16			-0.24		
	(0.42)			(0.48)		
semiplural	-0.16			-0.10		
	(0.34)			(0.36)		
religious	-0.08			0.04		
homogeneity	(0.30)			(0.30)		
linguistic	-0.28			-0.34		
homogeneity	(0.51)			(0.59)		
ethno-linguistic	0.46			0.39		
fragmentation	(1.31)			(1.56)		
growth rate	-0.21			-0.18		
	(0.08)			(0.07)		
unemployment rate	0.02			0.02		
	(0.02)			(0.02)		
population	1.73			1.68		
	(0.48)			(0.48)		
Formation costs						
public party		-0.01			-0.04	
financing		(0.23)			(0.23)	
electoral		1.74			2.25	
deposit		(2.22)			(2.24)	
petition		0.38			0.38	
signatures		(0.15)			(0.15)	
Benefits from high demands						
majority	0.11	0.03		0.12		
government	(1.18)	(1.20)		(0.23)		
number of parties	1.15	-1.11				
in government	(0.70)	(0.70)				
government	-1.05	1.20		0.03		
change	(0.69)	(0.71)		(0.18)		
centralization	-4.53	3.71		-1.24		
(taxes)	(2.65)	(2.39)		(0.97)		
referendum	1.19	-1.42		-0.30		
	(0.81)	(0.87)		(0.34)		
Fighting costs						
threshold of		-6.67			-6.51	-2.33
representation		(2.05)			(2.09)	(3.13)
threshold of		1.40			1.56	-0.40
exclusion		(0.87)			(0.97)	(2.01)
number of		0.01			0.00	-0.15
governments		(0.05)			(0.05)	(0.18)
number of parties					0.04	0.38
in government					(0.10)	(0.30)
federal		-0.33			-0.45	-0.98
		(0.37)			(0.37)	(0.84)
Constant		1.30				1.72
		(0.98)				(1.04)
		0.14				0.15
		(0.08)				(0.08)
		-368.73				-365.36
		-4.72				-8.08

impossible. Instead we test the interactions in the following way. In the first two columns of table 8.7 I reproduce the estimated coefficients of the global model from table 5.11. In the next twelve columns I present results for four other equations. In each of them I added one set of interactions linked to one theoretical variable, which should have no significant impact on the formation of new parties. Consequently, the alternative model presented in table 8.7 (columns 4-15) should fail to contribute significantly to the explanation of the emergence of new parties.

Table 8.7 largely supports my theoretical framework. Of all sets of additional interaction variables, none contributes significantly to the explanation of new political parties. I can interpret in more detail the global test appearing as model 1 in table 8.7.

Success of New Political Parties and Selection Bias

In the second research design, which attempts to explore the initial success of new parties, an important role is played by the selection mechanism. I argued above that the set of new political parties participating for the first time at a national election is far from a random sample. In effect, it is a self-selected sample of groups that considered forming a new party. Omitting the selection mechanism in the empirical study would almost certainly lead to significant biases in estimates of the effects of variables explaining new party success.

In order to take this problem into account, I proceeded to an estimation which directly models the selection mechanism. This was done by introducing an additional equation, which specifies the selection mechanism:

$$y_i = \beta_0 + \sum_{j=1}^{k} (\beta_{j1} * (1 - x_{ci}) + \beta_{j2} * x_{ci}) x_{ji} + \varepsilon_i \quad (8.17)$$

$$t_i = \delta_0 + \sum_{j=1}^{k} (\delta_{j1} * (1 - x_{ci}) + \delta_{j2} * x_{ci}) x_{ji} + \theta_i \quad (8.18)$$

$$if\ t_i > 0 \quad y_i\ and\ x_{ji}\ are\ observed \quad (8.19)$$

$$if\ t_i \leq 0 \quad y_i\ and\ x_{ji}\ are\ not\ observed \quad (8.20)$$

Assuming that y and t are multinormally distributed allows deriving a likelihood function of the following form:

$$L(\beta_y, \beta_t, \sigma_y^2, \sigma_t^2, \sigma_{yt} | y) = \Pi_{i=1}^{n} f_n(y_i | \mu_{y_i}, \sigma_y^2) \frac{[1 - F_n(0 | \delta_i, \phi^2)]}{[1 - F_n(0 | \mu_{t_i}, \sigma_t^2)]}$$

$$where\ \delta_i = \mu_{t_i} + \frac{\sigma_{yt}}{\sigma_y^2}(y_i - \mu_y)$$

$$\begin{aligned}
\phi^2 &= \sigma_t^2 - \frac{\sigma_{yt}^2}{\sigma_y^2} \\
\mu_{y_i} &= x_{1i}\beta_y \\
\mu_{t_i} &= x_{2i}\beta_t
\end{aligned} \tag{8.21}$$

Such a model is underspecified and, therefore, an additional restriction has to be included. King (1989a, 216) suggests imposing that the standard error of the selection equation (σ_t^2) is equal to 1. While this is a reasonable restriction, it can lead to serious problems in the estimations, since there is no guarantee that ϕ^2 is strictly positive, which is necessary for the likelihood function to be defined. I employed King's (1989a) solution, while using a series of starting values for the correlation among the error terms.

References

Achen, Christopher H. 1986. *Statistical Analysis of Quasi-Experiments*. Berkeley: University of California Press.

Aldrich, John H. 1995. *Why Parties? The Origin and Transformation of Party Politics in America*. Chicago: University of Chicago Press.

Alexander, Robert J. (ed.). 1982. *Political parties of the Americas: Canada, Latin America, and the West Indies*. Westport: Greenwood Press.

Aubert, Jean-François. 1983. La Suisse. In Cadart, Jacques (ed.) *Les modes de scrutin des dix-huit pays libres de l'Europe occidentale, leurs résultats et leurs effets comparés élections nationales et européennes*, 73-88. Paris: Presses Universitaires de France.

Austen, John; Butler, David; Ranney, Austin. 1987. Referendums, 1978-1986. *Electoral Studies* 6(2): 139-148.

Austen-Smith, David. 1983. The Spatial Theory of Electoral Competition: Instability, Institutions, and Information. *Environment and Planning C: Government and Policy* 1: 439-460.

Banks, Arthur S.; Textor, Robert B. 1968. *A Cross-polity Survey*. Cambridge: MIT Press.

Banks, Jeffrey S. 1991. *Signaling Games in Political Science*. Chur: Harwood Academic Publishers.

Bardi, Luciano; Morlino, Leonardo. 1992. Italy. In Katz, Richard S.; Mair, Peter (eds.) *Party Organizations. A Data Handbook*. London: Sage.

Bartolini, Stefano. 1993. On Time and Comparative Research. *Journal of Theoretical Politics* 5(2): 131-167.

Bartolini, Stefano; Caramani, Daniele; Hug, Simon. 1998. *Parties and Party Systems in Europe since 1945. Bibliography and Guide to the Literature*. London: Sage.

Bartolini, Stefano; Mair, Peter. 1990. *Identity, Competition, and Electoral Availability: The Stabilisation of European Electorates 1885-1985*. Cambridge: Cambridge University Press.

Beckwith, Karen. 1990. Book Review: 'Logics of Party Formation: Ecological Politics in Belgium and West Germany' by Herbert Kitschelt and 'Struggle, Politics and Reform: Collective Action, Social Movements, and

Cycles of Protest' by Syndey Tarrow. *West European Politics* 13(4): 158-161.

Berrington, Hugh. 1985. New Parties in Britain: Why Some Live and Most Die. *International Political Science Review* 6(4): 441-462.

Betz, Hans-Georg. 1990. Politics of Resentment: Right-Wing Radicalism in West Germany. *Comparative Politics* 23(1): 45-60.

Betz, Hans-Georg. 1994. *Radical Right-Wing Populism in Western Europe.* New York: St. Martin's Press.

Betz, Hans-Georg; Immerfall, Stefan. (eds.) 1998. *The New Politics of the Right. Neo-Populist Parties and Movements in Established Democracies.* New York: St. Martin's Press.

Bille, Lars. 1992. Denmark. In Katz, Richard S.; Mair, Peter (eds.) *Party Organizations. A Data Handbook.* London: Sage.

Bloom, David E.; Killingsworth, Mark R. 1985. Correcting for Truncation Bias Caused by a Latent Truncation Variable. *Journal of Econometrics* 27: 131-135.

Bogdanor, Vernon. 1981. The Social Democrats and the Constitution (Difficulties Confronting the Newly Formed Party). *Political Quarterly* 52: 285-294.

Boy, Daniel. 1981. Le vote écologiste en 1978. *Revue française de science politique* 22(avril): 394-416.

Brand, Karl-Werner. 1982. *Neue soziale Bewegungen. Entstehung, Funktion und Perspektive neuer Protestpotentiale.* Opladen: Westdeutscher Verlag.

Breen, Richard. 1996. *Regression Models: Censored, Sample Selected or Truncated Data.* Thousand Oaks: Sage.

Brehm, John. 1993. *The Phantom Respondents: Opinion Surveys and Political Representation.* Ann Arbor: University of Michigan Press.

Brehm, John, 2000. Alternative Corrections for Sample Truncation: Applications to the 1988 and 1990 Senate Election Studies. *Political Analysis* 1(2): 183-199.

Briquet, Jean-Louis; Courty, Guillaume; Legarve, Jean-Baptiste. 1990. Deux Verts en politique: Entretien avec A. Buchmann et Y. Cochet. *Politix* 9: 7-14.

Broszat, Martin. 1984. *Die Machtergreifung. Der Autstieg der NSDAP und die Zerstörung der Weimarer Republik.* München: Deutscher Taschenbuch Verlag.

Bullock, Alan. 1964. *Hitler – A Study in Tyranny.* New York.

Bürklin, Wilhelm P. 1984. *Grüne Politik.* Opladen: Westdeutscher Verlag.

Campbell, Donald T.; Ross, Herbert L. 1970. The Connecticut Crackdown on Speeding: Time Series Data in Quasi-Experimental Analysis. in Tufte,

Edward R. (ed.) *The Quantitative Analysis of Social Problems*. Reading: Addison-Wesley.

Campbell, Donald T.; Stanley, J.C. 1963. *Experimental and Quasi-Experimental Designs for Research*. Boston: Houghton Mifflin Company.

Caramani, Daniele; Hug, Simon. 1998. The Literature on Parties and Party Systems in Europe since 1945. A Quantitative Analysis. *European Journal of Political Research* 33(4): 497-524.

Chandler, William M.; Chandler, Marsha. 1987. Federalism and Political Parties. *European Journal of Political Economy* 3: 87-109.

Chhibber, Pradeep; Kollman, Ken. 1998. Party Aggregation and the Number of Parties in India and the United States. *American Political Science Review* 92(2): 329-342.

Cho, In-Koo; Kreps, David. 1987. Signaling Games and Stable Equilibria. *Quarterly Journal of Economics* 102: 179-221.

Chubb, Basil. 1983. L'Irlande. In Cadart, Jacques (ed.) *Les modes de scrutin des dix-huit pays libres de l'Europe occidentale, leurs résultats et leurs effets comparés élections nationales et européennes*, 279-304. Paris: Presses Universitaires de France.

Coggins, John; Lewis, D.S.; Milia, Giovanna. 1992. *Political parties of the Americas and the Caribbean: A Reference Guide*. Harlow: Longman.

Cole, Matthew. 1992. The Role of the Deposit in British Parliamentary Elections. *Parliamentary Affairs* 45: 77-91.

Cox, Gary W. 1990. Multicandidate Spatial Competition. In Enelow, James M.; Hinich, Melvin J. (eds.) *Advances in the Spatial Theory of Voting*. Cambridge: Cambridge University Press.

Cox, Gary W. 1997. *Making Votes Count*. Cambridge: Cambridge University Press.

Crewe, Ivor. 1986. Introduction: Electoral Change in Western Democracies: A Framework of Analysis. In Crewe, Ivor; Denver, Daniel (eds.) *Electoral Change in Western Democracies*, 1-22. London: Croom Helm.

Crewe, Ivor; King, Anthony. 1995. *SDP: The Birth, Life and Death of the Social Democratic Party*. Oxford: Oxford University Press.

Day, Alan J.; Degenhardt, Henry W. (eds.) 1988. *Political Parties of the World*. Harlow: Longman.

De Winter, Lieven. 1995. Regionalist Parties in Belgium: The Rise, Victory and Decay of the Volksunie. In De Winter, Lieven (ed.) *Non-State Wide Parties in Europe*, 23-70. Barcelone: Institut de Ciènces Politiques i Socials.

De Winter, Lieven; Türsan, Huri, (eds.) 1998. *Regionalist Parties in Western Europe*. London: Routledge.

Delury, George E. (ed.) 1987. *World Encyclopedia of Political Systems & Parties (2nd edition)*. New York: Facts of File Publications.

Denver, David T. 1983. The SDP (Social Democratic Party)-Liberal Alliance: The End of the Two-party System? *West European Politics*, 6: 75-102.

Deschouwer, Kris. 1992. Belgium. In Katz, Richard S.; Mair, Peter (eds.) *Party Organizations. A Data Handbook*. London: Sage.

Dewachter, Wilfried. 1983. La Belgique. In Cadart, Jacques (ed.) *Les modes de scrutin des dix-huit pays libres de l'Europe occidentale, leurs résultats et leurs effets comparés élections nationales et européennes*, 89-108. Paris: Presses Universitaires de France.

Dion, Douglas. 1998. Evidence and Inference in the Comparative Case Study. *Comparative Politics* 30(2): 127-145.

Dixit, Avinash; Nalebuff, Barry. 1991. *Thinking Strategically. The Competitive Edge in Business, Politics, and Everyday Life*. New York: W.W. Norton & Company.

Downs, Anthony. 1957. *An Economic Theory of Democracy*. New York: Harper and Row.

Drucker, Henry. 1986. 'All the King's Horses and All the King's Men': The Social Democratic Party in Britain. In Paterson, William ; Thomas, Alastair (eds.) *Social Democratic Parties in Western Europe*. London: Charterhouse.

Dubin, Jeffrey A.; Rivers, Douglas. 1990. Selection Bias in Linear Regression, Logit and Probit Models. In Fox, John; Long, Scott J. (eds.) *Modern Methods of Data Analysis*, 410-442. Newbury Park: Sage.

Duverger, Maurice. 1976. *Les partis politiques*. Paris: Colin.

Eagles, Munroe; Erfle, Stephen. 1993. Variations in Third/Minor Party Support in English Constituencies: One Party Dominance and Community Cohesion Perspectives. *European Journal of Political Research* 23(1): 91-116.

East, Roger; Bell, David. (eds.) 1990. *Communist and Marxist Parties of the World*. Chicago: St. James Press.

Eldersveld, Samuel J. 1982. *Political Parties in American Society*. New York: Basic Books.

Farrell, David M. 1992. Ireland. In Katz, Richard S.; Mair, Peter (eds.) *Party Organizations. A Data Handbook*. London: Sage.

Feddersen, Timothy J.; Sened, Itai; Wright, Steve G. 1990. Rational Voting and Candidate Entry under Plurality Rule. *American Journal of Political Science* 34(4): 1005-1016.

Fischer, Conan. 1995. *The Rise of the Nazis*. Manchester: Manchester University Press.

Fisher, Stephen L. 1974. *The Minor Parties of the Federal Republic of Germany: Towards a Comparative Theory of Minor Parties*. The Hague: Martinus Nijhoff.

Frankland, E. Gene. 1995a. *The Return of the Greens: Superwahljahr 1994 and Beyond*. Chicago: Paper prepared for presentation at the Annual Meeting of the American Political Science Association.

Frankland, E. Gene. 1995b. Germany: The Rise, Fall and Recovery of Die Grünen. In Richardson, Dick; Rootes, Chris (eds.) *The Green Challenge: The Development of Green Parties in Europe*. London: Routledge.

Franz-Willing, Georg. 1962. *Die Hitlerbewegung*. Hamburg; Berlin: R. v. Decker's Verlag G. Schenck.

Fudenberg, Drew; Tirole, Jean. 1991. *Game Theory*. Cambridge: MIT Press.

Gallagher, Michael. 1992. Comparing Proportional Representation Electoral System: Quotas, Thresholds, Paradoxes and Majorities. *British Journal of Political Science* 22(4): 469-496.

Geddes, Barbara. 1991. How the Cases You Choose Affect the Answers You Get: Selection Bias in Comparative Politics. In Stimson, James A. (ed.) *Political Analysis*, 131-152. Ann Arbor: University of Michigan Press.

Gorvin, Ian. (ed.) 1989. *Elections since 1945. A Worldwide Reference Compendium*. Essex: Longman.

Greenberg, John; Shepsle, Kenneth A. 1987. The Effect of Electoral Rewards in Multiparty Competition with Entry. *American Political Science Review* 81(2): 525-537.

Greene, William H. 1990. *Econometric Analysis*. New York: MacMillan Publishing Company.

Grimm, Dieter. 1983. La République Fédérale d'Allemagne. In Cadart, Jacques (ed.) *Les modes de scrutin des dix-huit pays libres de l'Europe occidentale, leurs résultats et leurs effets comparés élections nationales et européennes* 307-330. Paris: Presses Universitaires de France.

Gruner, Erich. 1977. *Die Parteien in der Schweiz*. Bern: Francke.

Harmel, Robert; Robertson, John D. 1985. Formation and Success of New Parties. *International Political Science Review* 6(4): 501-523.

Harmel, Robert; Svasand, Lars. 1997. The Influence of New Parties on Old Parties' Platforms – The Cases of the Progress Parties and Conservative Parties of Denmark and Norway. *Party Politics* 3(3): 315-340.

Harmel, Robert; Svasand, Lars; Gibson, Rachel. 1992. *New Parties on the Far Right: Contrasts and Similarities*. Chicago: Paper presented at the Annual Meeting of the Midwest Political Science Association.

Hauss, Charles; Rayside, David. 1978. The Development of New Parties in Western Democracies since 1945. In Maisel, Louis.; Cooper, Joseph (eds.) *Political Parties: Development and Decay*. Beverly Hills: Sage.

Hebel-Kunze, Barbara. 1977. *SPD und Faschismus. Zur politischen und organisatorischen Entwicklung der SPD 1932-1935*. Frankfurt a.M.: Röderberg-Verlag.

Heckman, James J. 1976. The Common Structure of Statistical Models of Truncation, Sample Selection and Limited Dependent Variables and a Simple Estimator for Such Models. *Annals of Economic and Social Measurement* 5(4): 475-492.

Heckman, James J. 1979. Sample Selection Bias as a Specification Error. *Econometrica* 47(1): 153-161.

Heijden, Hein-Anton van der. 1992. Niederlande. In Hey, Christian; Brendle, Uwe (eds.) *Umweltverbände und EG*. Freiburg: EURES – Institut für regionale Studien in Europa e. V.

Hermens, Ferdinand A. 1972. *Democracy or Anarchy? A Study of Proportional Representation*. New York: Johnson Reprint Corporation.

Hoffmann, Stanley. 1956. *Le mouvement Poujade*. Paris: Colin.

Horn, Wolfgang. 1972. *Führerideologie und Parteiorganisation in der NSDAP. 1919-1933*. Düsseldorf: Droste Verlag.

Hug, Simon. 1996. The Emergence of New Political Parties from a Game-theoretic Perspective. *European Journal of Political Research* 29(2): 169-190

Hug, Simon. 1998. *Selection Bias in Comparative Research. The Case of Incomplete Datasets*. Chicago: Paper prepared for presentation at the Midwest Political Science Association Annual Meeting, April 23-25.

Hug, Simon 2000. The Electoral Success of New Political Parties. A Methodological Note. *Party Politics* 6(2): 187-197.

Hülsberg, Werner. 1988. *The German Greens: A Social and Political Profile*. London: Verso.

Husbands, Christopher T. 1981. Contemporary Right-wing Extremism in Western Europe: A Review Article. *European Journal of Political Research* 9(1): 75-99.

Husbands, Christopher T. 1988. Extreme Right-Wing Politics in Great-Britain: The Recent Marginalisation of the National Front. *West European Politics* 11(2): 65-79.

Husbands, Christopher T. 1992a. The Netherlands: Irritants on the Body Politic. In Hainsworth, Paul (ed.) *The Extreme Right in Europe and the USA*, 95-125. London: Pinter.

Husbands, Christopher T. 1992b. The Other Face of 1992: The Extreme-Right Explosion in Western Europe. *Parliamentary Affairs* 45(3): 267-284.

Ignazi, Piero. 1992. The Silent Counter-Revolution: Hypotheses on the Emergence of Extreme Right-wing Parties in Europe. *European Journal of Political Research* 22(1): 3-34.

Ignazi, Piero. 1994. *L'estrema destra in Europa*. Bologna: Il Mulino.

Inglehart, Ronald. 1977. *The Silent Revolution*. Princeton: Princeton University Press.

Inglehart, Ronald. 1990. *Culture Shift in Advanced Industrial Societies*. Princeton: Princeton University Press.

Inglehart, Ronald; Andeweg, Rudy B. 1993. Change in Dutch Political Culture: A Silent or a Silenced Revolution. *West European Politics* 16(3): 345-361.

Inglehart, Ronald; Rabier, Jacques R. 1986. Political Realignement in Advanced Industrial Societies: From Class-based Politics to Quality-of-Life Politics. *Government and Opposition* 21: 456-481.

Interparliamentary Union. 1976. *Parliaments of the World. A Reference Compendium*. London: MacMillan Press.

Jamison, Andrew; Eyerman, Ron; Cramer, Jacqueline; Laessoe, Jeppe. 1990. *The Making of the New Environmental Consciousness. A Comparative Study of the Environmental Movements in Sweden, Denmark and the Netherlands*. Edinburgh: Edinburgh University Press.

Janda, Kenneth. 1980. *Political Parties*. New York: Free Press.

Jenkins, Roy. 1991. *A Life at the Center: Memoirs of a Radical Reformer*. London: Macmillan.

Jost, Hans-Ulrich. 1986. Critique historique du parti politique. *Annuaire suisse de science poltique* 26: 317-332.

Kalyvas, Stathis N. 1996. *The Rise of Christian Democracy in Europe*. Ithaca: Cornell University Press.

Katz, Richard S.; Mair, Peter. (eds.) 1992. *Party Organizations. A Data Handbook*. London: Sage.

Kershaw, Ian. 1999. *Hitler, 1926-1936: Hubris*. New York: W.W. Norton.

King, Anthony; Crewe, Ivor. 1991. *The Failure of the SDP to Bring About Realignment in Britain in the 1980s*. Washington: Presented at the Annual Meeting of the American Political Science Association.

King, Gary. 1988. Statistical Models for Political Science Event Counts: Bias in Conventional Procedures and Evidence for The Exponential Poisson Regression Model. *American Journal of Political Science* 32(3): 838-863.

King, Gary. 1989a. *Unifying Political Methodology: The Likelihood Theory of Statistical Inference*. Cambridge: Cambridge University Press.

King, Gary. 1989b. Variance Specification in Event Count Models: From Restrictive Assumptions to a Generalized Estimator. *American Journal of Political Science* 33(3): 762-784.

King, Gary; Keohane, Robert O.; Verba, Sidney. 1994. *Designing Social Inquiry. Scientific Inference in Qualitative Research*. Princeton: Princeton University Press.

Kitschelt, Herbert. 1988. Left-libertarian Parties. Explaining Innovation in Competitve Party Systems. *World Politics* 40(2): 194-234.

Kitschelt, Herbert. 1989. *The Logics of Party Formation. Ecological Politics in Belgium and West Germany.* Ithaca NY: Cornell University Press.

Kitschelt, Herbert. 1990. The Medium is the Message: Democracy and Oligarchy in Belgian Ecology Parties. In Rüdig, Wolfgang (ed.) *Green Politics One*, 82-114. Edinburgh: Edinburgh University Press.

Kitschelt, Herbert. 1991. The Formation of Party Systems in East Central Europe. *Politics & Society* 20(1): 7-50.

Kitschelt, Herbert. 1995. *The Radical Right in Western Europe.* Ann Arbor: University of Michigan Press.

Koelble, Thomas A. 1991. *The Left Unraveled. Social Democracy and the New Left Challenge in Britain and West Germany.* Durham: Duke University Press.

Koelble, Thomas A. 1992. Recasting Social Democracy in Europe: A Nested Games Explanation of Strategic Adjustment in Political Parties. *Politics & Society* 20(1): 51-70.

Koole, Ruud; Velde, Hella Van De. 1992. The Netherlands. In Katz, Richard S.; Mair, Peter (eds.) *Party Organizations. A Data Handbook.* London: Sage.

Krehbiel, Keith. 1988. Spatial Models of Legislative Choice. *Legislative Studies Quarterly* 3: 259-319.

Kriesi, Hanspeter. 1988. Local Mobilization for the People's Petition of the Dutch Peace Movement. In Klandermans, Bert; Kriesi, Hanspeter; Tarrow, Sidney (eds.) *International Social Movement Research.* Greenwich: JAI Press.

Kriesi, Hanspeter. 1993. *Political Mobilization and Social Change. The Dutch Case in Comparative Perspective.* Aldershot: Avebury.

Kriesi, Hanspeter. 1995. *Le système politique suisse.* Paris: Economica.

Kriesi, Hanspeter; Praag, Philip van. 1987. Old and New Politics: The Dutch Peace Movement and the Traditional Political Organizations. *European Journal of Political Research* 15(3): 319-346.

Lane, Jan-Erik; McKay, David; Newton, Kenneth. 1991. *Political Data Handbook OECD Countries.* Oxford: Oxford University Press.

LaPalombara, Joseph; Weiner, Myron. 1966. The Origin and Development of Political Parties. In Lapalombara, Joseph; Weiner, Myron (eds.) *Political Parties and Political Development.* Princeton: Princeton University Press.

Laver, Michael; Schofield, Norman. 1990. *Multiparty Government: The Politics of Coalition in Western Europe.* Oxford: Oxford University Press.

Lawson, Kay; Merkl, Peter H. (eds.) 1988. *When Parties Fail.* Princeton: Princeton University Press.

Lepzy, Norbert. 1989. Die Republikaner. Ideologie – Programm – Organisation. *Aus Politik und Zeitgeschichte* 41-42: 3-9.

Levi, Margaret; Hechter, Michael. 1985. A Rational Choice Approach to the Rise and Decline of Ethnoregional Political Parties. In Tiryakian, Edward A.; Rogowski, Ronald (eds.) *New Nationalism of the Developed West*, 128-146. Boston: Allen and Unwin.

Lijphart, Arend. 1983. Les Pays-Bas. In Cadart, Jacques (ed.) *Les modes de scrutin des dix-huit pays libres de l'Europe occidentale, leurs résultats et leurs effets comparés élections nationales et européennes*, 247-264. Paris: Presses Universitaires de France.

Lijphart, Arend. 1984. *Democracies. Patterns of Majoritarian and Consensus Government in Twenty-One Countries*. New Haven: Yale University Press.

Lijphart, Arend. 1994. *Electoral Systems and Party Systems. A Study of Twenty-Seven Democracies, 1945-1990*. Oxford: Oxford University Press.

Lijphart, Arend; Gibberd, R.W. 1977. Thresholds and Payoffs in List Systems of Proportional Representation. *European Journal of Political Research* 5: 219-244.

Lipset, Seymour M.; Rokkan, Stein. 1967. Cleavage Structures, Party Systems, and Voter Alignments: An Introduction. In Lipset, Seymour M.; Rokkan, Stein (eds.) *Party Systems and Voter Alignments*. New York: Free Press.

Little, Roderick J.A.; Rubin, Donald A. 1987. *Statistical Analysis with Missing Data*. New York: Wiley.

Lowe, Philip D.; Rüdig, Wolfgang. 1986. Review Article: Political Ecology and the Social Sciences – The State of the Art. *British Journal of Political Science* 16: 513-505.

Lucardie, Paul. 1980. *The New Left in the Netherlands. A Critical Study of New Political Ideas and Groups on the Left in the Netherlands with Comparative References to France and Germany*. Kingston: Queen's University, PhD thesis.

Lucardie, Paul. 1996. *'Prophets, Prolocutors and Pyromaniacs': New Parties in the Netherlands*. Oslo: Paper prepared for presentation at the ECPR Joint Sessions of Workshops.

Lucardie, Paul; Knoop, Jelle Van Der; Schuur, Wijbrandt van; Voerman, Gerrit. 1991. *Greening the Reds or Reddening the Greens: The Case of the Green Left Party in the Netherlands*. Washington: Presented at the Annual Meeting of the American Political Science Association.

Lucardie, Paul; Voerman, Gerrit; Schuur, Wijbrandt van 1993. Different Shades of Green: A Comparison between Members of Groen Links and De Groenen. *Environmental Politics* 2(1): 40-62.

Lustick, Ian S. 1996. History, Historiography, and Political Science: Multiple Historical Records and the Problem of Selection Bias. *American Political Science Review* 90(3): 605-618.

Mackie, Thomas T. 1991. General Elections in Western Nations During 1989. *European Journal of Political Research* 19(1): 157-162.

Mackie, Thomas T. 1992. General Elections in Western Nations During 1990. *European Journal of Political Research* 21: 317-332.

Mackie, Thomas T.; Rose, Richard. 1991. *The International Almanac of Electoral History*. Washington: Congressional Quarterly Inc.

Maddala, G.S. 1983. *Limited Dependent and Qualitative Variables in Econometrics*. Cambridge: Cambridge University Press.

Maguire, Maria. 1983. Is There Still Persistence? In Daalder, Hans; Mair, Peter (eds.) *Western European Party Systems*, 67-94. Beverly Hills: Sage.

Mair, Peter. 1983. Adaptation and Control: Towards an Understanding of Party System Change. In Daalder, Hans; Mair, Peter (eds.) *Western European Party Systems*, 405-429. Beverly Hills: Sage.

Mair, Peter. 1990. The Electoral Payoffs of Fission and Fusion. *British Journal of Political Science* 20(1): 131-142.

Mair, Peter; Koole, Ruud. 1992. Political Data Yearbook. *European Journal of Political Research* 23: 1.

Marsh, Michael. 1992. *Explaining the Rise of New Parties: Ireland in the 1980s*. Chicago: Paper prepared for presentation at the Annual Meeting of the American Political Science Association.

Maser, Werner. 1967. *Naissance du parti National-socialiste allemand*. Paris: Fayard.

Maser, Werner. 1981. *Der Sturm auf die Republik: Frühgeschichte der NSDAP*. Frankfurt/M : Ullstein.

Mayer, Nonna; Perrineau, Pascal. (eds.) 1989. *Le Front National à découvert*. Paris: Presses de la Fondation nationale des sciences politiques.

Mayer, Nonna; Perrineau, Pascal. 1992. Why Do They Vote for Le Pen? *European Journal of Political Research* 22(1): 123-141.

Mazmanian, Daniel A. 1991. Third Parties in American Elections. In Maisel, Louis Sandy (ed.) *Political Parties & and Elections in the United States: An Encyclopedia*, 1105-1116. New York: Garland.

McHale, Vincent; Skowronski, Sharon. (eds.) 1983. *Political Parties of Europe*. Westport: Greenwood Press.

Meadows, Donella H.; Club of Rome. 1974. *The Limits to Growth*. New York: Signet.

Müller, Wolfgang C. 1992. Austria (1845-1990). In Katz, Richard S.; Mair, Peter (eds.) *Party Organizations. A Data Handbook*. London: Sage.

Müller-Rommel, Ferdinand. (ed.) 1989. *New Politics in Western Europe. The Rise and Success of Green Parties and Alternative Lists*. Boulder: Westview Press.

Müller-Rommel, Ferdinand. 1990. *Political Success of Green Parties in Western Europe*. San Francisco: Paper presented at the 1990 Annual Meeting of the American Political Science Association.

Müller-Rommel, Ferdinand. 1991. Small Parties in Comparative Perspective: The State of the Art. In Müller-Rommel, Ferdinand; Pridham, Geoffrey (eds.) *Small Parties in Comparative Perspective*. London: Sage.

Müller-Rommel, Ferdinand. 1993. *Grüne Parteien in Westeuropa. Entwicklungsphasen und Erfolgsbedingungen*. Opladen: Westdeutscher Verlag.

Müller-Rommel, Ferdinand. 1995. Ethno-regionalist Parties in Western Europe: Ampirical Evidence and Theoretical Considerations. In De Winter, Lieven (ed.) *Non-State Wide Parties in Europe*, 179-196. Barcelone: Institut de Ciènces Politiques i Socials.

Müller-Rommel, Ferdinand. 1996. *The New Challengers: Explaining the Electoral Success of Green and Right-Wing Populist Parties in Western Europe*. Oslo: Paper prepared for presentation at the ECPR Joint Sessions of Workshops.

Muthen, Bengt; Jöreskog, Karl G. 1983. Selectivity Problems in Quasi-Experimental Studies. *Evaluation Review* 7(2): 139-174.

Neumann, Sigmund. 1965. *Die Parteien der Weimarer Republik*. Stuttgart.

Nohlen, Dieter. 1978. *Wahlsysteme der Welt. Daten und Analysen. Ein Handbuch*. München/Zürich.

Nohlen, Dieter. 1990. *Wahlrecht und Parteiensystem*. Opladen: Leske Verlag.

Ohlinger, Théo. 1983. L'Autriche. In Cadart, Jacques (ed.) *Les modes de scrutin des dix-huit pays libres de l'Europe occidentale, leurs résultats et leurs effets comparés élections nationales et européennes*, 109-144. Paris: Presses Universitaires de France.

Oppeln, Sabine von. 1989. *Die Linke im Kernenergie Konflikt: Deutschland und Frankreich im Vergleich*. Frankfurt: Campus.

Orlow, Dietrich. 1973. *The History of the Nazi Party*. Trowbridge: Redwood Press Limited.

Osborne, Martin J. 1993. Candidate Positioning and Entry in a Political Competition. *Games and Economic Behavior* 5(1): 133-151.

Osborne, Martin J. 1995. Spatial Models of Political Competition Under Plurality Rule: A Survey of Some Explanations of the Number of Candiates and the Positions They Take. *Canadian Journal of Economics* 28(2): 361-301.

Owen, David. 1991. *Time to Declare*. New York: Penguin. Viking.

Palfrey, Thomas R. 1984. Spatial Equilibrium with Entry. *Review of Economic Studies* 51(1): 139-156.

Palfrey, Thomas R. 1989. A Mathematical Proof of Duverger's Law. In Ordeshook, Peter C. (ed.) *Models of Strategic Choice in Politics*. Ann Arbor: University of Michigan Press.

Paltiel, Khayyam Zev. 1981. Campaign Finance: Contrasting Practices and Reforms. In Butler, David; Penniman, Howard R.; Ranney, Austin (eds.) *Democracy at the Polls*. Washington: American Enterprise Institute.

Parkin, Sara. 1989. *Green Parties: An International Guide*. London: Heretic.

Pierre, Jon; Widfeldt, Anders. 1992. Sweden. In Katz, Richard S.; Mair, Peter (eds.) *Party Organizations. A Data Handbook*. London: Sage.

Pinard, Maurice. 1967. One-Party Dominance and Third Parties. *Canadian Journal of Economics and Political Science* 33(August): 358-373.

Pinard, Maurice. 1973. Third Parties in Canada Revisited: A Rejoinder and Elaboration of the Theory of One-Party Dominance. *Canadian Journal of Political Science* 6: 439-460.

Pinard, Maurice. 1975. *The Rise of a Third Party: A Study in Crisis Politics (enlarged edition)*. Montreal: McGill-Queens University Press.

Poguntke, Thomas. 1987. The Organization of a Participatory Party – The German Greens. *European Journal of Political Research* 15(2): 609-633.

Poguntke, Thomas. 1989. The "New Politics Dimension" in European Green Parties. In Müller-Rommel, Ferdinand (ed.) *New Politics in Western Europe*, 175-194. Boulder: Westview Press.

Poguntke, Thomas. 1990. *The Politics of one Generation? The German Green Party and its Limits of Growth*. Paper presented at the Annual Meeting of the American Political Science Association, San Francisco.

Poguntke, Thomas. 1993. *Alternative Politics. The German Green Party*. Edinburgh: Edinburgh University Press.

Poguntke, Thomas; Boll, Bernhard. 1992. Germany. In Katz, Richard S.; Mair, Peter (eds.) *Party Organizations. A Data Handbook*. London: Sage.

Praag, Philip van Jr. 1991. The Netherlands: Action and Protest in a Depillarized Society. In Rucht, Dieter (ed.) *Research on Social Movements. The State of the Art in Western Europe and the USA*, 295-322. Frankfurt: Campus.

Pridham, Geoffrey. 1988. The Social Democratic Party in Britain: Protest or New Political Tendency? In Lawson, Kay; Merkl, Peter H. (eds.) *When Parties Fail: Emerging Alternative Organizations*, 229-256. Princeton: Princeton University Press.

Rae, Douglas W. 1967. *The Political Consequences of Electoral Laws*. New Haven: Yale University Press.

Rae, Douglas W.; Hanby, V.; Loosemore, J. 1971. Thresholds of Representation and Thresholds of Exclusion. *Comparative Political Studies* 1(3): 479-488.

Ragin, Charles. 1987. *The Comparative Method: Moving Beyond Qualitative and Quantative Strategies*. Berkeley: University of California Press.

Rebeaud, Laurent. 1987. *La Suisse verte*. Lausanne: L'âge d'homme.

Rohrschneider, Robert. 1990. *New Politics in Old Parties: Environmental Issues in Four West European Party Systems*. Paper presented at the Annual Meeting of the American Political Science Association, San Francisco.

Rosenstone, Steven J.; Behr, Roy L.; Lazarus, Edward H. 1984. *Third Parties in America*. Princeton: Princeton University Press.

Roth, Dieter. 1990a. Die Republikaner: Schneller Aufstieg und tiefer Fall einer Protestpartei am rechten Rand. *Aus Politik und Zeitgeschichte* 37/38: 27-39.

Roth, Dieter. 1990b. *"Die Republikaner": The Rise and Fall of a Far Right Protest Party*. Paper presented at the Annual Meeting of the American Political Science Association, San Francisco.

Rüdig, Wolfgang. 1990. *Explaining Green Party Development. Reflections on a Theoretical Framework*. Glasgow: Strathclyde Papers on Government and Politics.

Sainteny, Guillaume. 1991. *Les Verts*. Paris: Presses Universitaires de France.

Salvador Crespo, Mayte; Molina Alvarez De Cienfuegos, Ignacio. 1996. *A Supply-Side Explanation of the Formation and Success of Non-State Wide Parties in Spain*. Oslo: Paper prepared for presentation at the ECPR Joint Sessions of Workshops.

Sartori, Anne E. 1999. *Selection Bias in Probit Models When the Selection Stage and the Stage of Interest Have Idential Explanatory Variables*. Atlanta: Paper prepared for presentation at the American Political Science Association Annual Meeting, September 2-5.

Sartori, Giovanni. 1976. *Parties and Party Systems*. Cambridge: Cambridge University Press.

Schapsmeier, Edward L.; Schapsmeier, Frederick H. 1981. *Political Parties and Civic Action Groups*. Westport: Greenwood.

Schlesinger, Joseph A. 1991. *Political Parties and The Winning of Office*. Ann Arbor: University of Michigan Press.

Schmitt, Hermann. 1987. *Neue Politik in alten Parteien: Zum Verhältnis von Gesellschaft und Parteien in der Bundesrepublik*. Opladen: Westdeutscher Verlag.

Schoonmaker, Donald. 1988. The Challenge of the Greens to the West German Party System. In Lawson, Kay; Merkl, Peter H. (eds.) *When Parties*

Fail: Emerging Alternative Organizations, 41-75. Princeton: Princeton University Press.

Seiler, Daniel L. 1995. A Historical Overview on Non-state Wide Parties in Western Europe. In De Winter, Lieven (ed.) *Non-State Wide Parties in Europe*, 13-22. Barcelone: Institut de Ciènces Politiques i Socials.

Shamir, M. 1984. Are Western Party Systems "Frozen"? *Comparative Political Studies* 17(1): 35-79.

Shepsle, Kenneth A. 1991. *Models of Multiparty Competition*. Chur: Harwood Academic Publishers.

Shepsle, Kenneth A.; Cohen, Ronald N. 1990. Multiparty Competition, Entry, and Entry Deterrence in Spatial Models of Elections. In Enelow, James M.; Hinich, Melvin J. (eds.) *Advances in the Spatial Theory of Voting*. Cambridge: Cambridge University Press.

Shirer, William L. 1960. *The Rise and Fall of the Third Reich*. New York: Fawcett Crest.

Sjöblom, Gunnar. 1968. *Party Strategies in Multiparty Systems*. Lund: Studentlitteratur.

Sjöblom, Gunnar. 1983. Political Change and Political Accountability: A Propositional Inventory of Causes and Effects. In Daalder, Hans; Mair, Peter (eds.) *Western European Party Systems*. Beverly Hills: Sage.

Stachura, Peter D. 1983. *The Nazi Machtergreifung*. London: George Allen & Unwin.

Sternberger, Dolf; Vogel, Bernhard. (eds.) 1969. *Die Wahl der Parlamente und anderer Staatsorgane: ein Handbuch*. Berlin : W. de Gruyter.

Stevenson, John. 1993. *Third Party Politics Since 1945. Liberals Alliance and Liberal Democrats*. London: Blackwell.

Stimson, James A. 1985. Regression in Space and Time: A Statistical Essay. *American Journal of Political Science* 29: 914-947.

Stöss, Richard. 1975. Terra incognita der Parteienforschung: Splitterparteien in der Bundesrepublik. *Zeitschrift für Parlamentsfragen* VI(2): 254-266.

Stöss, Richard. 1990. *Die 'Republikaner'*. Köln: Bund-Verlag.

Sundberg, Jan; Gylling, Christel. 1992. Finland. In Katz, Richard S.; Mair, Peter (eds.) *Party Organizations. A Data Handbook*. London: Sage.

Sundquist, James L. 1983. *Dynamics of the Party System: Alignment and Dealignment of Political Parties in the United States*. Washington: Brookings Institution.

Svasand, Lars. 1992. Norway. In Katz, Richard S.; Mair, Peter (eds.) *Party Organizations. A Data Handbook*. London: Sage.

Taagepera, Rein; Shugart, Matthew Soberg. 1989. *Seats and Votes*. New Haven: Yale University Press.

Tellegen, Egbert. 1981. The Environmental Movement in the Netherlands. In O'Riordan, Timothy; D'Arge, Ralph C. (eds.) *Progress in Resource Management and Environmental Planning*. Chichester: J. Wiley and Sons.

Thomassen, Jacques; Deth, Jan van. 1989. How New is Dutch Politics? *West European Politics* 12(1): 61-78.

Union Interparlementaire. 1966. *Parlements: une étude comparative sur la structure et le fonctionnement des institutions représentatives dans quarante et un pays*. Paris: Presses Universitaires de France.

Urwin, Derek, W. 1983. Harbringer, Fossil or Fleabite? "Regionalism" and the West European Party Mosaic. In Daalder, Hans; Mair, Peter (eds.) *Western European Party Systems*, 221-256. Beverly Hills: Sage.

Vialatte, Jérome. 1996. *Les partis verts en Europe occidentale*. Paris: Economica.

Vogel, Bernhard; Schultze, Rainer-Olaf. 1969. Deutschland. In Sternberger, Dolf; Vogel, Bernhard (eds.) *Die Wahl der Parlamente und anderer Staatsorgane: ein Handbuch*, 189-411. Berlin : W. de Gruyter.

Webb, Paul D. 1992. The United Kingdom. In Katz, Richard S.; Mair, Peter (eds.) *Party Organizations. A Data Handbook*. London: Sage.

Woldendorp, Jaap; Keman, Hans; Budge, Ian. 1993. Political Data 1945-1990. Party Governments in 20 Democracies. *European Journal of Political Research* 24(1): 1-119.

Wright, William E. (ed.) 1971. *A Comparative Study of Party Organization*. Columbus: Charles E. Merrill Publishing Company.

Index